U0811026

热烈庆祝

中国科学院长春光学精密机械与物理研究所

建所 70 周年

Light: Science & Applications

创刊 10 周年

王卉 主编

光·觉

Light People

第2卷

時代文藝出版社

图书在版编目（CIP）数据

光·觉 = Light People. 第2卷 : 汉、英 / 王卉主编. -- 长春 : 时代文艺出版社, 2022.5
ISBN 978-7-5387-7005-6

Ⅰ. ①光… Ⅱ. ①王… Ⅲ. ①科学工作者－访问记－世界－现代－汉、英 Ⅳ. ①K816.1

中国版本图书馆CIP数据核字(2022)第070873号

光·觉：Light People 第2卷
GUANG·JUE DI－ER JUAN
王卉 主编

出 品 人：陈 琛
责任编辑：曾艳纯
装帧设计：张 帆
排版制作：任 奕

出版发行：时代文艺出版社
地　　址：长春市福祉大路5788号 龙腾国际大厦A座15层（130118）
电　　话：0431-81629751（总编办） 0431-81629758（发行部）
官方微博：weibo.com/tlapress
开　　本：880mm × 1230mm 1/32
字　　数：227千字
印　　张：17.125
印　　刷：吉林省创美堂印刷有限公司
版　　次：2022年5月第1版
印　　次：2022年5月第1次印刷
定　　价：179.00元

图书如有印装错误 请寄回印厂调换

Preface
前言

Going with the *Light*
与“光”同行

Hui Wang
王卉

Light is essential for human survival. As the study of light, optics is a long-standing discipline whose history can be traced back to more than 2,000 years ago. The earliest recorded knowledge of optics in the world can be found in the Chinese classic *Mohist Canon*, "Shadow: Light travels like arrows. When shooting through an aperture into a darkened chamber, the light from the lower part of a man travels to the upper part in the chamber, while the light from the upper part of a man travels to the lower part in the chamber."[1] This was the first scientific description of light traveling in straight lines. With the invention of convex lens and microscope, the discovery of the wave-particle duality of light, and the development of quantum optics, it can be said that every major optical discovery has brought about significant progress in social development. My encounter with people who study light and who go with light, began with an academic journal.

光对于人类生存有着非常重要的作用。而光学这门具有悠久历史的学科，其发展史可追溯到2000多年前。中国的《墨经》中记录了世界上最早的光学知识，如其中写道:“景，光之入照若射。下者之人也高，高者之人也下。”这是首次对光沿直线传播的科学描述。随着凸透镜、显微镜的发明，光的波粒二象性的发现，量子光学的发展，可以说光学史上每次重大成果的产生，都推动着人类历史里程碑式的进步。而能够让我有机会走近那些从事光学研究的“与光同行”的人们，认识并了解他们，就一定要提到一本学术期刊了。

In 2011, the Changchun Institute of Optics, Fine Mechanics and Physics (CIOMP), Chinese Academy of Sciences (CAS) and the Nature Publishing Group signed a cooperation agreement to jointly publish China's first open access academic journal, *Light: Science & Applications* (*Light*), which was launched online in March 2012. As the founding English editor of *Light*, I witnessed how the journal was started from scratch and quickly came to its own and dazzled all with brilliance. Even after I left the Editorial Department for the Department of International Cooperation of CIOMP, I continue to take a great interest in *Light* and my job with *Light* also turned out to be a valuable asset for me in my new role. One of my main tasks of my new position was to expand CIOMP's international exchange network and thus promote substantive international cooperation. I was able to reach out to contacts from my *Light* days and some of them indeed were interested in carrying out exchanges and cooperation with CIOMP and have now become dear colleagues and good friends. I think this is also the responsibility and mission that

Light has always undertaken, which is to go beyond being a mere academic journal, and serve scientific research and promote communication. At the same time, I also introduced *Light* to scientists I met at various international academic events. Along the way, more and more people joined hands with *Light*, including authors, readers, reviewers, editorial board members, and those who silently support and actively participate in the many and varied activities organized by *Light*. Without these people, *Light* would not be the success it is today.

2011年，中国科学院长春光学精密机械与物理研究所（简称“长春光机所”）与自然出版集团签署合作协议，共同创办中国第一本开放获取学术期刊——*Light: Science & Applications*（简称“*Light*”），并于2012年3月正式上线。作为*Light*的创刊英文编辑，我有幸参与并见证了*Light*从孕育、创刊、成长到如今光芒四射的全过程。即使后来因工作需要，从编辑部调入国际合作处，我也一直十分关注*Light*的发展并积极参与，从未走远。还记得刚刚调入国际合作处时，我的主要工作之一是扩大国际交流网络，从而促进实质性国际合作。而那些潜在的合作伙伴就是我之前担任*Light*期刊英文编辑时积累的人脉。我努力促进这些科学家们从认识*Light*期刊到与长春光机所开展交流与合作，双方的友谊逐步加深。我想这也是*Light*一直以来所承担的责任和使命，那就是超越期刊，服务科研，促进交流。同时，我也将*Light*介绍给那些在各类国际学术活动中认识的科学家们。一路走来，携手同行的人越来越多，他们中间有作者，有读者，有审稿人，有编委，还有默默支持和积极参与*Light*各种活动的人们。没有这些与*Light*同行的人们，就不会有今天 *Light* 的成功。

As *Light* celebrates its 10th anniversary, I would like to present it with a birthday gift, one that combines science and words. Through these in-depth interviews, we can feel the colorful life of each "Light People" and feel their brightness and warmth. As we strive to move forward, direction is of vital importance to our endeavor. Looking back on these ten years, I am filled with emotions.

Many guests interviewed for this book are inextricably connected with *Light*, including some who have worked hard to nurture *Light*'s growth and are considered as the journal's "parents". There are also those who have been resolute in their support for *Light* from when it was still relatively unknown. And then there are the people who have helped *Light* go from strength to strength in recent years. They are all "Light People" who have weathered storms and shared the delight at seeing rainbows with *Light*. My interviews with some of them allowed me to go through the past decade of *Light*'s development from another angle. Their spirit of scientific exploration and attitude towards life have refreshed my understanding of them and made me see them in a more "three-dimensional" perspective. I also hope that this book can give every reader spiritual enlightenment and resonance. If life is a journey on which constant adjustment of the direction is needed, may these "Light People" shine a light on the path that is right for you, illuminating your way forward.

今年是*Light*创刊十周年，我想送给它一份礼物，那就是文字。透过文字采访，我们能够感受每一位“Light People”的多彩人生，感受他们带给我们的光明和温暖。我们需要前行，但不能没有方向。回首这十年，我感慨万千。这本书中的很多嘉宾都与*Light*有着千丝万缕的联系，这些人中有“抚养”*Light*成长的“爸爸妈妈”们，他们一直细心呵护、辛勤耕耘；也有在*Light*籍籍无名时就毅然选择支持帮助它，为*Light*乘风破浪而保驾护航者；还有在*Light*初获佳绩而努力使之不断壮大的人。总之，他们都是与*Light*共经风雨，共见彩虹的“Light People”。我有幸采访了这当中的一些人，正好也是对过去种种的一种梳理。他们的科学探索精神和对人生的态度与感悟，不断地刷新我对他们的认知，让我看到了一个个更加“立体”的科学家，也希望本书能够给予每一位读者以心灵的启迪和共鸣。如果说人生是一场不断校正方向的旅行，愿他们成为你校正途中的光，照亮你前行的路。

Being an English major graduate (although I was a science major in high school and did well in mathematics, chemistry and physics in the college entrance examination), I am no scientist. However, as the French writer Flaubert said, "Science and art depart from the foothills and meet again at the top of the mountain." In this book, you will see the unique combination of science and art shining through the interviewees. The cognitive framework of science can and must be rigorous, which makes it seem cold, distant and aloof sometimes. But the beauty of art can only be appreciated through senses and will always be subjects of desire. The book aims to show readers that science doesn't have to be out of reach, it can be down to earth. In my opinion, the word "Light" represents the power that makes growth of all, bright things, and *Light* the journal. Meanwhile the difference between "insight" and "thinking" is that "thinking" is subjective contemplation, but "insight" is deep and intuitive understanding, which also appropriately shows the characteristics of this book. I believe this book will trigger new thoughts and understandings about science and life in the minds of its readers, and inspire them to embark on a journey of "Going with the *Light*".

从专业出发，我不读理工专业（虽然高中时我是名副其实的理科生，高考数理化成绩也还不错，却选择了英语作为我大学的专业），更不是科学家，但正如法国作家福楼拜所说：科学与艺术，从山麓分手，又在山顶汇合。在《光·觉》中你会看到被采访嘉宾所闪耀的那独特的科学与艺术相结合的光芒。在科学的认知框架中，它可以也必须是严谨的，所以有时它让我们感觉只可远观而不可亵玩焉；但是在艺术的感知框架中，它需要带有美学色彩，让我们感觉可欲也可求。这本书想要告诉读者，科学不仅是阳春白雪，也可以做到下里巴人。在我看来，“光”字代表着万物生长的力量，代表着一切光明的事物，代表着 *Light*；而“觉”字与“思”的区别在于，“思”是一种主观意识上的思考，但“觉”字更有灵光一现的顿悟之感，也正好恰如其分地展示了本书的特点，在阅读的过程中无意识地引发你对科学、对人生的新思考和新感悟，在思想的旅行中“与光同行”。

We live in a big world full of people with stories. These people have one thing in common — they have lives outside of their work. Though not a scientist, I have always worked in science-related fields and have come into contact with many celebrated scientists. Their scientific attainments are well known to the world, but in addition, they are also people with "lives". By "life" I do not mean just living, but really loving life, enjoying life, and giving it different meanings at different stages of life. In this book, you will meet James Wyant, the founding Dean of the College of Optical Sciences at the University of Arizona, who is deeply devoted to philanthropy and the advancement of optical engineering; and Chennupati Jagadish, president of the Australian Academy of Sciences, who has broken the barriers of races, transformed destiny

曹健林，原中华人民共和国科学技术部副部长，现任十三届全国政协教科卫体委员会副主任，兼任季华实验室理事长、应用光学国家重点实验室主任、国际半导体照明联盟理事长、集成电路产业技术创新战略联盟理事长。历任中国科学院长春光机所所长，中国科学院院长助理兼光电研究院院长，中国科学院副院长、党组成员，科学技术部副部长、党组成员，中国光学学会第五届第六届副理事长。

1982年毕业于复旦大学物理系，从事软X射线多层膜技术研究。两次获得国家科技进步二等奖（1995年、2001年）；荣获1995年度全国先进工作者，1996年度中国科学院第四届青年科学家一等奖，1996年国家杰出青年基金，1997年度中国光学学会科技奖。在国内外学术期刊发表论文百余篇。任*Light: Science & Applications*和*Light: Advanced Manufacturing*主编。

序二

光刻人生 觉者历程

——读《光·觉》心得

李军

光是什么?

辞书中说,“光”是一个物理学名词,其本质是一种处于特定频段的光子流。光源发出光,是因为光源中电子获得额外能量。如果能量不足以使其跃迁到更外层的轨道,电子就会进行加速运动,并以波的形式释放能量。如果跃迁之后刚好填补了所在轨道的空位,从激发态到达稳定态,电子就不动了。否则电子会再次跃迁回之前的轨道,并且以波的形式释放能量。光同时具备以下四个重要特征:光以直线传播、光以波的形式传播、不同波长的光呈现不同的颜色、光速在真空中为 299792458 $\approx 3\times10^{8}$ m/s。在量子光学中,光的能量是量子化的,称其为光量子,简称光子。

中国人对“光”的认识，更多的是一种文化认知，常用光阴、光辉、光明等表达。古人不用 m/s 度量光速，而是用“瞬”“刹”“刻”等等这种模糊的但又充满哲学意味的词形容。人文意义的“光”，王阳明有“此心光明”之句;《春江花月夜》有“此时相望不相闻，愿逐月华流照君。鸿雁长飞光不度，鱼龙潜跃水成文”之句;《红灯记》里有铁梅高举红灯“爹爹给我无价宝，光辉照儿永向前”的唱段……

我自幼喜欢读人物传记，也喜欢读科普的书。一口气读完《光·觉》，方知这是*Light: Science & Applications*发起的系列高端人物——“Light人物”的访谈录，也是关于光的科学的科普书。在我看来，《光·觉》更是一群光的觉者关于光与世界、与人类、与自然、与人生、与心灵的“谈思录”、“沉思录”和“随想曲”。

先打开的是第 2 卷第十六篇，是中国科学院长春光学精密机械与物理研究所王卉作为 *Light* 科学编辑，采访诺贝尔物理学奖获得者唐娜·斯特里克兰（Donna Strickland）的笔录。打开这篇文章，不只是因为唐娜是诺贝尔奖获得者，也不仅是因为她是为数不多的女性诺奖人，而是她的研究领域——啁啾脉冲放大研究。啁啾是汉语词语，形容鸟的鸣叫声，读作 zhōujiū，这是一个充满诗意的词。唐代白居易《燕诗示刘叟》曰："却入空巢里，啁啾终夜悲。燕燕尔勿悲，尔当返自思。"王维《黄雀痴》诗曰："到大啁啾解游飏，各自东西南北飞。"唐娜·斯特里克兰研究的"啁啾脉冲放大"是关于鸟的鸣叫声学的脉冲放大？不会，这是声学不是光学啊？啁啾脉冲放大究竟是什么？为什么用这么诗意的词命名这项研究呢？作为外行，借助万能的朋友圈和神通的"度娘"我才弄清楚，啁啾脉冲放大是关于激光放大的技术，用于超强超短脉冲激光系统，用放大前分散激光种子脉冲的能量放大后再集中的原理，使激光功率提高了一千倍到 TW 级，并得以从此稳步提高。这是唐娜·斯特里克兰就读博士期间在莫罗（Gérard Mourou）的指导下完成的。

我不是搞光学的，虽然不懂其原理，还是想知道为何用“啁啾”这个词。我们知道，过去有更多留学西方的中国人对陌生的世界，翻译出很多具有中国风格、中国意味的名字，例如，大家十分熟悉的 Champs-Elysées 被诗人徐志摩译作“香榭丽舍”，Fontainebleau 被作家朱自清译作“枫丹白露”。最绝的还是戴望舒翻译的法国诗人纪尧姆·阿波利奈尔 (Guillaume Apollinaire) 著名的《密拉波桥》*Le pont Mirabeau*。原文是：

Sous le pont Mirabeau coule la Seine
Et nos amours
Faut-il qu' il m' en souvienne
La joie venait toujours après la peine
Vienne la nuit sonne l' heure
Les jours s' en vont je demeure
Les mains dans les mains restons face à face
Tandis que sous
Le pont de nos bras passe
Des éternels regards l' onde si lasse

Vienne la nuit sonne l' heure

Les jours s' en vont je demeure

L' amour s' en va comme cette eau courante

L' amour s' en va

Comme la vie est lente

Et comme l' Espérance est violente

Vienne la nuit sonne l' heure

Les jours s' en vont je demeure

Passent les jours et passent les semaines

Ni temps passé

Ni les amours reviennent

Sous le pont Mirabeau coule la Seine

Vienne la nuit sonne l' heure

Les jours s' en vont je demeure

译文是：

密拉波桥下赛纳水长流

柔情蜜意

寸心还应忆否

多少欢乐事总在悲哀后

钟声其响夜其来

日月逝矣人长在

手携着手儿面面频相向

交臂如桥

却向桥头一望

逝去了无限凝眉底倦浪

钟声其响夜其来

日月逝矣人长在

恋情长逝去如流波浩荡

恋情长逝

何人世之悠长

何希望冀愿如斯之奔放

钟声其响夜其来

日月逝矣人长在

时日去悠悠岁月去悠悠

旧情往日

都一去不可留

through knowledge, and dedicated himself to help young researchers; Andreas Tünnermann, director of the Fraunhofer Institute for Applied Optics and Precision Engineering, who values close cooperation between research and industry and created the OptoNet cluster with a total turnover of 3.6 billion euros; and many more. You will find that these people are the light needed for younger generations who harbor the dream of science. This is the true meaning of "Light People".

世界很大，有故事的人很多，但有故事的人都有一个共性：他们有生活。不做科研的我一直从事的工作都是在服务科研。因为工作的关系，我接触到了很多不同领域的业界“大牛”，他们在科学上的造诣我想早已是世人皆知，然而后来我发现，尽管形式各有不同，但他们都是有“生活”的人，这里我所指的“生活”不是普通意义上的度日，而是真的热爱生活，享受生命，在人生的不同阶段，去赋予它不一样的意义。在《光·觉》中您将认识心怀感恩，热衷慈善事业，推动光学工程发展的美国亚利桑那大学光科学学院创始院长James Wyant，也会看到打破种族桎梏，靠知识改变命运，并致力于培养青年科研人才的澳大利亚科学院院长Chennupati Jagadish，还有重视科研与产业紧密合作，创建总营业额达36亿欧元的OptoNet集群的德国弗朗霍夫应用光学与精密工程研究所所长Andreas Tünnermann等等，你会发现对于那些怀揣科学之梦的青年来说，他们本身就是光，这也正是“Light People”的意义所在。

In recent years, *Light* has been constantly exploring how to make "Light" shine brighter and benefit more light chasers, and have more people learn of our story with "Light". From "Light Memory" to "Light People", from "Light Conference" to "Rising Stars of Light", we have never stopped our steps.

近几年，*Light*不断探索如何让“光”照耀并惠及更多的追光人，让更多的人知道我们与“光”的故事，从“Light拾光”到“Light People”，从“Light Conference”到“Rising Stars of Light”等等，我们从未停止脚步。

Time is the tide that sweeps away sand and leaving us with gold. We hope that Light can become a century-old brand of Chinese science and technology journals, and shine its own unique light in the world of academic journals.

光阴如潮，大浪淘沙，我们希望*Light*这个品牌能够成为中国科技期刊的百年老字号，在世界期刊总汇中，绽放出属于自己的独特光芒。

"Light people" together with you are always going with the light!

"Light people"永远与您一起与光同行！

参考文献

[1] 汪榕培，王宏译. 英译《墨经》：英汉对照. 上海：上海外语教育出版社，2010, P73.

序一

天工人巧日争新

曹健林

光阴似箭，转眼之间*Light*创刊已经十年。编辑部的同仁准备将始于2020年的“Light 人物”系列采访成果汇编成书出版，作为纪念创刊十周年的活动之一。我很赞成，也很高兴。

回首过去的十年，*Light*一路走来实属不易。我们为这本期刊殚精竭虑地工作的确换来了不少喜悦与自豪，然而更多的则是让我们体会到压力和危机感。从创刊时的能否生存下来到今天的如何百尺竿头更进一步，在与编辑部同仁的交流中，我能深切地体会到大家的担心，以及由此而产生的期盼。其中最期盼的是什么？答案很集中也很明确：期盼作者群的支持，包括那些帮我们与作者群建立联系的业界翘楚们。你们的认可和支持是*Light*的生命线。

因此，回首过去的十年，*Light*最要感谢的就是你们。请允许我代表编辑部全体同仁向你们表示衷心的感谢！感谢你们用优异的研究成果和培育幼苗、扶助新生力量的博大胸怀与深邃眼光支持了*Light*。现代科学技术的鲜明特点就是传播、普及与应用，作为一名同道，尤其是作为一名发展中国家的同道，我相信，你们的研究工作和你们的胸怀与眼光一定会在全球光学光电子学发展进程中留下浓墨重彩的一笔。

于是就有了“Light 人物”系列采访活动，有了这本书。读者们可以从中了解到光学光电子学这片繁茂科技丛林中若干活跃的研究领域和最新研究进展；了解到这些领域和进展的重要意义；特别是了解到其中的领军人物——他们的成长过程，选题方式，攻关思路，以及下一步的努力方向。事情都是人做的，书中的内容相信对于研究工作者和关心关注研究工作的同道们都是一份有学习、借鉴和参考价值的资料。

我在*Light*编辑部的主办单位中国科学院长春

光学精密机械与物理研究所（简称为长春光机所）学习工作了四十年。这个研究所被称为中国光学的摇篮，也是今天中国最大的光学光电子学研发机构之一。*Light*作者群中有许多人来过长春光机所，“Light人物”系列采访的对象中更有多人多次与长春光机所有过深入的交流合作，是我的老朋友。这种经历促使我学会了用历史的眼光来看*Light*，来思考光学光电子学的发展。的确，光学光电子学在今天的中国发展很快，一些产品和工程应用有很强的竞争力；在基础研究和应用探索的某些方面甚至走到了世界前列；基础教育和人才培养的规模也是世界最大。但是，中国同道们的短板也很明显，学科积累不够，少有开创性、突破性的创新成果，在鼓励和培植科学发展与技术进步的环境建设上也还要做大量长期艰苦的工作。从这点出发，我特别希望中国的同道们向书中的人物学习，让我们的“短板”尽快成长起来。

*Light*定位于高水平的国际科技期刊，其作者群中理所当然地有一大批非中国籍的科学家。绝大部

分科学家相信“科学无国界”，尽管今天的世界并不太平，而且坦白地说，与十年前比起来，包括科技交流在内的国际交流是退步了。原因不仅仅是全球大流行了两年多的新冠肺炎疫情。但我相信，就像新冠疫情大流行终究会过去一样，人类交流与合作中的障碍也终将会被逐渐克服和消解，而科学家应该成为克服和消解障碍的先锋。历史曾经证明过（我们中的许多人都曾是亲历者），也还将继续证明。

祝*Light*的下一个十年更加光明。

密拉波桥下赛纳水长流
钟声其响夜其来
日月逝矣人长在

（原载1944年11月25日香港《大众周报》4卷8期，选自《戴望舒诗全编》，浙江文艺出版社出版）

啁啾脉冲放大研究，是谁翻译的呢？使用“啁啾”这个词是不是也有戴望舒们的思维和意境呢？我想肯定是，或者我相信它是。读完对唐娜·斯特里克兰的专访，你会依稀懂得，唐娜女士一定有“啁啾”般的初心绽放，也有“脉冲”式的研究历程，更有“放大”的价值追求。给我印象很深的是，*Light* 科学编辑问道：“您在做 CPA 的过程中遇到哪些困难呢？您是如何克服它们的？”唐娜·斯特里克兰说：“我不记得有太多的困难。在做 CPA 的过程中我记得我们损坏了激光管，不得不等待更换。由于激光器老化陈旧，所以经常罢工。幸运的是，我们的团队里有一位非常优秀的电子学专家，他总是能够让这些老化陈旧的激光器工作。我印象最深的是，当我们第一次放大啁啾脉冲并观察它的光谱时，我们得到了意想不到的结果。基于增益光谱的信号中出现了本不应该出现的振荡，没过多久我们意识到这个振荡有可能是由一毫米的玻璃校准器引起的。我们用于控制脉冲进出再生放大器的普克尔盒一起使用的四分之一波片实际上是一块一毫米的玻璃。我们曾经在窄谱的再生放大器中使用了相同的波片和普克尔盒组合方法，并取得成功，因为其振荡周期比该光谱更宽。我们意识到解决 CPA 技术的方法是旋转普克尔盒，当其处于关闭位置时能充当四分之一波片，然后我们也能够移除这个波片。”

我所学的专业与化学有关，我当学员或做教员的时候，经常遇到实验做不下去或实验失败的时候，我们看《居里夫人传》，那里面记载了不少居里夫妇实验失败的事。唐娜·斯特里克兰不记得有什么困难？有清楚记忆的一次困难还是一名电工学专家解决的。读到这里，一般的读者都会说，这不太可能吧，就这么点儿困难？我要说的是这真可能。

我曾经与戚发轫院士有过交流，我也问到过类似的问题，我记得非常清楚，戚老说，遇到啥困难，不知道为什么，具体啥情况突然想不起来了，航天器飞上去的时候，喜悦占了脑子的一半，另一半想的是下一个航天器。人类历史上，正是因为有这样的科学家对困难的“云淡风轻”，才有对科学风景的“那边独好”。他们对困难的“忘痛”，是专心于事业的心理迹象，也是基于科学信心、饱经科学研究“压力测试”，无畏于一切艰难困苦的战略藐视，这难道不也是一种科学精神、科学态度吗？

最为打动我的是第1卷专访的首篇——专访中国计算电磁学和电磁超材料专家、中国科学院院士崔铁军。原因是，我认识崔铁军教授，还感叹于我俩名字里都有“军”字。还有一个原因是，访者——*Light*编辑郭宸孜我也非常熟悉，她是全国科技期刊青年编辑大赛一等奖获得者，作为评委，我为她颁过奖，感叹于这个孩子居然有这么好的讲述能力和一手漂亮的文字，还有良好的沟通能力和一名新闻记者特有的敏锐和胆魄。

我熟悉崔铁军院士是在一次论坛上，他对超材料进行了系统性研究，创造性地提出用数字编码表征超材料的新思想及控制电磁波的新方法，实现了数字编码和可编程超材料，能实时操控电磁波和编码信息，开创了信息超材料新方向。首次从微波传输线的角度研究表面等离激元（SPP）超材料，发明了一种超薄、柔性、条带式 SPP 传输线。与传统微带线相比，其传输特性可定制，并可显著降低传输线间的互耦和干扰。研制出一系列 SPP 无源器件和有源器件，开辟了基于 SPP 传输线的微波技术新方向。在传统超材料领域，实现了宽带、低损耗超材料的快速准确设计，在国际上率先用实验验证了“电磁黑洞”和三维宽带“隐身斗篷”等物理现象，解决了超材料在某些国防应用中的瓶颈问题，并应用于中国航天、航空、船舶等部门特种装备的研制。2014 年，崔铁军在 *Light: Science & Applications* 上首次提出用数字编码表征超材料的新思想，并研制出第一个现场可编程超材料，开辟了信息超材料新方向。之后，又在 *Light: Science & Applications* 发表了多篇文章。他作为*Light*人物首选，当之无愧。

郭宸孜问了崔铁军一个非常核心的问题：“能否为大家预测一下未来几年超材料相关的基础领域能否有重要的突破？此外，能否请您对超材料的未来进行下展望，因为您也有很多等离子体超材料的工作成果发表，您如何看待将来传统的超材料、等离子体超材料的研究会如何发展，以及编码超材料如何发展，除了数字编码超材料以外，其他的编码超材料的发展前景如何？”对国家尖端科技的领军者来说，这是一个宏大深远的话题，专访中，崔铁军大篇幅地回答了这个问题，如何回答的，我就不赘述了，只想谈谈自己的认识。

忠诚与归属，是一个人信仰的内化和使命的依归，尤其是家国栋梁。这应当是科学家一等一的最为重要的部分。崔铁军说：“对我来说，初中毕业时的抉择（读中专还是高中）对我的影响最重要。”

读到崔铁军这句话，使我想到了马克思曾写过的一篇文章《青年在选择职业时的考虑》。这篇文章，马克思写于1835年。文章写道：“我们应当认真考虑：所选择的职业是不是真正使我们受到鼓舞？我们的内心是不是同意？我们受到的鼓舞是不是一种迷误？我们认为是神的召唤的东西是不是一种自欺？但是，不找出鼓舞的来源本身，我们怎么能认清这些呢？伟大的东西是光辉的，光辉则引起虚荣心，而虚荣心容易给人以鼓舞或者一种我们觉得是鼓舞的东西；但是，被名利弄得鬼迷心窍的人，理智已无法支配他，于是他一头栽进那不可抗拒的欲念驱使他去的地方；他已经不再自己选择他在社会上的地位，而听任偶然机会和幻想去决定它。我们的使命绝不是求得一个最足以炫耀的职业，因为它不是那种使我们长期从事而始终不会感到厌倦、始终不会松劲、始终不会情绪低落的职业，相反，我们很快就会觉得，我们的愿望没有得到满足，我们的理想没有实现，我们就将怨天尤人。”马克思继续写道：“我们的父母，他们走过了漫长的生活道路，饱尝了人世的辛酸……”说到此处，马克思提到了文章主题——青年职业的选择。“如果我们把这一切都考虑过了，如果我们生活的条件容许我们选择任何一种职业，那么我们就可以选择一种使我们最有尊严的职业；选择一种建立在我们深信其正确的思想上的职业；选择一种能给我们提供广阔场所来为人类进行活动、接近共同目标（对于这个目标来说，一切职业只不过是手段）即完美境地的职业。”那么，什么是“完美境地的职业”呢？马克思说：“我们应该遵循的主要指针是人类的幸福和我们自身的完美……人类的天性本来就是这样的：人们只有为同时代人的完美、为他们的幸福而工作，才能使自己也达到完美。如果一个人只为自己劳动，他也许能够成为著名学者、大哲人、卓越诗人，然而他永远不能成为完美无瑕的伟大人物。”马克思最后写道：“历史承认那些为共同目标劳动因而自己变得高尚的人是伟大人物，经验赞美那些为大多数人带来幸福的人是最幸福的人。如果我们选择了最能为人类福利而劳动的职业，那么，重担就不能把我们压倒，因为这是为大家而献身。那时我们所感到的就不是可怜的、有限的、自私的乐趣，我们的幸福将属于千百万人，我们的事业将默默地、但是永恒发挥作用地存在下去，而面对我们的骨灰，高尚的人们将洒下热泪。”

“历史承认那些为共同目标劳动因而自己变得高尚的人是伟大人物，经验赞美那些为大多数人带来幸福的人是最幸福的人”，“面对我们的骨灰，高尚的人们将洒下热泪”。——写下这句子的人，是正在读初中的、风华正茂的十七周岁的马克思。

我相信，每本书专访的十二位科学家都有同样初心绽放的时刻，从而开启了一种对科学、对祖国、对实现人类梦想的追光之旅。十多个以至于千百个光刻人生、十多个以至于千百位觉者历程，影响着已走过十年的*Light*，影响着已经有着七十年历史的长光人的未来，也影响着读者，影响着被科学光芒普照的人们。

让我们打开这本书，跟着它追光。

写于2022年3月7日夜

李军，中国期刊协会副会长，中央宣传部传媒监管局原局长。曾任原国家新闻出版广电总局新闻报刊司司长。中华全国新闻工作者协会常务理事、特邀理事，建设世界一流科技期刊专家委员会专家委员，中国人文社科期刊评价咨询委员会委员。

长期从事新闻出版业务和行政管理工作，具有丰富的新闻出版工作经验。先后参与或组织起草《报纸管理规定》《新闻记者证管理办法》《新闻单位驻地方机构管理办法》《新闻从业人员职务行为信息管理办法》《报刊社会效益考核办法（试行）》《报刊出版质量管理规定》等多部重要法规。先后参与和组织实施治理党政部门利用职权摊派报刊、治理出版发行领域不正当竞争和商业贿赂、打击新闻敲诈和假新闻专项行动、中央新闻单位驻地方机构清理整顿、完善学术评价体系遏制论文发表不良倾向和繁荣发展学术期刊出版等专项工作。参与制订和组织实施中国科技学术期刊国际影响力提升计划，参与制订和组织实施《关于深化改革培育世界一流科技期刊的意见》及卓越行动计划等。

序三

十年踪迹十年心

白雨虹

作为*Light: Science & Applications*（以下简称*Light*）的主要发起人和创刊人之一，十年前，我本人、主编、创刊团队、主办单位、主管单位、中国期刊界、国际期刊界以及世界光学领域的专家学者们，没有人想到*Light*十年磨一剑，一朝天下知，会拥有今天这样的国际国内学术影响力。

创刊的十年间，算是我人生的惊喜时期，因为*Light*这本刊巩固了我与学界老朋友们的友情，又使我结交了很多新朋友。*Light*的十年，是我和许许多多新老朋友们为着一个梦想而共同耕耘的十年。

我接受的是标准的理工科教育，做的期刊*Light*又是一本纯学术的光学期刊，“编辑”这样一种幕后工作的性质和自身内向的性格，压抑着我骨子里对美好生活和人文科学的向往。人们常说文学即人学，爱文学的本质就是爱“人”，爱生命。我以为至高境界的科学与文学是融合的，我热爱科学，更爱那些为科学孜孜以求的科学“人”，一个爱“人”的认真生活的人，终会让梦想照进现实。

开设“Light People”专栏最初是由我提出来的。2020年初，随着*Light*声誉与日俱增，很多读者已经不仅仅满足于研判阅读*Light*发表的英文前沿原创学术论文，常常给编辑部写信希望我们能提供更多元的文章类型。学术期刊增加文章类型不是一拍脑袋就马上能办的事，需要时机和策划。彼时我们的“中国光学微信公众号”正想发力用中文全面推广*Light*，因为*Light*虽然在国际光学界已经得到广泛认可，但在中文的世界里所知者并不多。

“Light People”专栏我想达到三个目的：一、锻炼科学编辑。新时代的科学编辑完全突破了传统意义上单纯的“编、校、排”，他们深入一线调研学习科学前沿，他们走近一流科学家讨论交流学术难题，他们在浩如烟海的大量来稿中寻找创新点，这样有挑战性的工作使他们有机会了解更全面的科学家。二、传播科学文化。一切与*Light*有关的人都可以成为“Light People”。已经发表的二十几篇“Light People”，既有星光熠熠的诺贝尔奖获得者，也有小荷才露尖尖角的青年科学家；既有国际光学组织Optica的CEO管理者，也有联合国教科文组织“国际光年”和“国际光日”的倡议者和发起人，希望以“Light People”的形式将中国与世界联结。三、普及科学知识。与性格各异的科学家们打过交道之后，发现每一篇严肃的学术论文后面都潜藏着作者鲜活的个性和创造的精灵，因为这些科学人，我更加由衷地喜欢自己的工作，常常因为与这些智者的灵魂碰撞产生奇妙的思想火花。因此希望“Light People”在科学与大众之间架起一座桥梁，让公众特别是青少年通过了解科学家认识科学、热爱科学、尊重科学，使科学在人类社会生活中不神秘、不远离、不缺席。

2020 年“中国光学微信公众号”发表“Light People”第一期之后，反响热烈，广受读者好评，满足读者需求是我们办刊的最高宗旨，我们随即于2021年将这一专栏在*Light*英文刊正式启动。我们的愿景是将*Light*办成一本百年老刊，“Light People”也会与刊一起传承下去，因为“人”才是*Light*这本期刊的核心和灵魂。

“Light People”集结成书的起因非常偶然。2021年8月，在吉林省获得“第五届中国出版政府奖”获奖单位代表座谈会上，我与时代文艺出版社陈琛社长紧邻而坐，他作为出品人的获奖作品《山林笔记》从内容、设计、版式、色彩等各方面全方位引起我的兴趣，阅后《山林笔记》成为我特别欣赏的精品书，由此萌发了与时代文艺出版社合作系列出版“Light People”的想法。《光·觉》就是陈社长为“Light People”创意的中文书名，这书名点燃了我一颗热爱文艺的心。

这本书里的每一位人物，都与我有着或深或浅的交往，虽然没有一篇文章是我本人亲自采写，但他们每一位对光学研究的贡献和对生活的热爱我都可以如数家珍般一一道来。希望有缘阅读本书的你，成为下一位“Light People”。

做编辑是我的爱好而不仅仅是工作，当我发现自己不是为了生存而为人作嫁，而是为了某种召唤而为社会服务时，编辑工作就成为一种高尚和积极的体验。

白雨虹，博士，国家二级研究员，现任中国科学院长春光学精密机械与物理研究所Light学术出版中心主任，*Light：Science & Applications*执行主编。社会兼职：联合国教科文组织“国际光年”“国际光日”组织委员会委员，中国期刊协会常务理事，中国科技期刊编辑学会常务理事，中国科学院自然科学期刊研究会常务理事，吉林省政协委员。曾获：全国新闻出版领军人才，中国出版政府奖优秀出版人物奖，中国科学院“巾帼建功”先进个人等。

白雨虹负责的*Light：Science & Applications* 2021年获得第五届中国出版政府奖期刊奖；2019年获得中国科技期刊卓越行动计划领军期刊；2016年获得中国科协等六部委的中国科技期刊国际影响力

提升项目A类资助和中国科技期刊登峰行动计划资助；2014—2019年连续6年获中国科学院科学出版基金一等奖；2016—2021年连续6年获国家自然科学基金应急管理项目资助；2015年、2017年、2019年分别获中国“百强”科技期刊，连续6年入选中国最具国际影响力学术期刊。

目录

Contents

Professor Tünnermann

编者按

他是世界超快激光和激光加工领域的著名科学家，他的研究成果获得了诸多奖项，他是许多青年学者的领路人，他追求科研的实际应用，并与工业界保持紧密合作。他是弗朗霍夫应用光学与精密工程研究所所长，也是很多科研机构和科技公司的董事会成员或主席。在欧洲光学圈提起Andreas Tünnermann可谓无人不知，在世界激光领域也几乎是无人不晓。那么，他和*Light*有着怎样的渊源呢？

Trailblazer of Laser Industry
激光行业发展的引路人和推动者

Science Editor: Hui Wang 科学编辑 王卉

Editorial:

A world-renowned scientist in the field of ultrafast laser and laser processing, he has won many awards and mentored many young scholars. He pursues the practical application of scientific research and maintains close cooperation with the industry. He is Andreas Tünnermann, director of the Fraunhofer Institute of Applied Optics and Precision Engineering, and a board member or chairman of many scientific research institutions and technology companies. He is respected and celebrated by all in the European optical circle as well as the international laser field. So, what is his story with *Light: Science & Applications* (*Light*)?

Light People

Background: Professor Tünnermann and I, a newcomer to the field of optics then, met for the first time in 2011 thanks to the journal *Light*. In that year, Changchun Institute of Optics, Fine Mechanics and Physics (CIOMP), Chinese Academy of Sciences (CAS) and the Nature Publishing Group signed a cooperation agreement to jointly launch *Light*. I was fortunate enough to be appointed an English editor of *Light* which allowed me to witness the entire process of how the journal started from scratch and flourished into one of the top journals in the optics field. Back in 2011, we racked our brains in order to get high-quality papers to publish in *Light*. In order to achieve that goal, we launched the "International Conference on Laser Processing Frontiers" to promote the new publication and invited the speakers to publish their research papers on the budding journal *Light*. This conference is the predecessor of the now widely known "Light Conference". It was at this meeting that me, an obscure editor, was introduced to the legendary Professor Tünnermann. He is tall and burly, but the constant smile on his face makes everyone who comes in contact with him feel reassured and warm. So much so that I felt bold enough to invite him to be a judge for the "Best Student Poster Award", and to be one of the awards presenters at the awards ceremony. His paper[1], published after the launch of *Light* in 2012, was one of the top 10 papers of the year. When I was transferred from the Editorial Department to Department of International Cooperation at CIOMP, I immediately thought of getting in touch with Prof. Tünnermann because of his friendly and pragmatic attitude towards cooperation. He is based in Jena, Germany, where he is the director of the Fraunhofer Institute of Applied Optics and Precision Engineering, as well as professor and director of the Institute of

Applied Physics at the Friedrich Schiller University Jena. Jena is known as the center of Germany's optical precision instrument manufacturing, and home to famous companies such as Zeiss and Schott. More than 40% of the optical and laser products exported by Germany are produced in Jena. On the other hand, CIOMP is known as "the Cradle of China's Optics". If these two institutes can carry out international cooperation, they will complement each other and have far-reaching significance! With the support of the leaders of the two institutes, the two sides successfully signed a student joint training agreement. Later, when he visited the CAS Key Laboratory of Optical System Advanced Manufacturing at CIOMP, Prof. Tünnermann was so deeply impressed by its silicon carbide mirror technology that he invited Prof. Xuejun Zhang, deputy director of CIOMP, to present an invited talk at the world-famous "Freeform Surface Ultra-Precision Machining International Conference". Prof. Zhang was the only speaker from China at the conference at that time. Professor Tünnermann also proposed to change the conference from once every two years to once a year, with the odd-numbered years set in Changchun and the even-numbered years in Jena, proof of his endorsement of the scientific research strength of CIOMP. As time goes by, cooperation between the two parties has continuously deepened. At the beginning of 2020, Prof. Tünnermann accepted the invitation of *Light* to be its executive Editor-in-Chief, indicating that this collaboration, started with *Light* 10 years ago, will continue for many more glorious decades.

背景追溯：10年前作为光学小白的我与Tünnermann教授初识要感谢“*Light*”！2011年中科院长春光学精密机械与物理研究所（简称“长春光机所”）和自然出版集团签署合作协议，共同创办*Light：Science & Applications*（简称“*Light*”），时任英文编辑的我就有幸见证了*Light*从无到有并蓬勃发展的全过程。为给新刊*Light*约请高质量的稿件，我们可谓绞尽脑汁想出各种办法，发起并主办“激光加工前沿国际会议”来宣传新刊并向特邀报告人约稿就是其中之一，该会议也是现在大家所熟知的“Light Conference”的前身。就是这次会议让我这个默默无闻的小编辑认识了当时传说中的“大牛”Tünnermann 教授。他身材高大魁梧，脸上永远挂着微笑，给人以平和温暖的感觉，让我可以大胆地给他安排诸如担任“最佳学生海报奖”评委、在颁奖礼上颁奖等工作。他的邀请文章[1]在 2012 年 *Light* 创刊后发表并成为年度高质量论文 Top 10。基于他这种友好而务实的合作态度，我在因为工作需要调入国际合作处工作后，立刻想到要找他洽谈合作。他是德国弗朗霍夫应用光学与精密工程研究所所长，同时也是耶拿 · 弗里德里希 · 席勒大学应用物理系主任。他们的研究所坐落在素有德国光学精密仪器制造业中心的耶拿市，这里有著名的蔡司、肖特等公司，德国出口的光学和激光产品超过 40% 产自耶拿。长春光机所被称为“中国光学的摇篮”，如果能够使这两个研究所开展国际合作，将会相得益彰，意义深远！在两所领导的大力支持下双方成功签署了学生联合培养协议。随后他在访问长春光机所参观中科院光学系统先进制造技术重点实验室时，对我们的碳化硅反射镜技术印象深刻，因此在他们主办的世界知名“自由曲面超精密加工国际会议”上邀请长春光机所副所长张学军研究员做大会邀请报告，张学军是当时唯一来自中国的报告人。Tünnermann 教授还提议将该会由两年一次改成一年一次，单数年在长春，双数年在耶拿举办，这是他对长春光机所科研实力的认可，双方的合作不断加深。时光流转，10 年仿佛弹指一挥间，2020 年伊始，Tünnermann 教授接受 *Light* 邀请担任期刊执行主编，使得这场始于 *Light* 的合作必将继续进入下一个更加辉煌的 10 年，甚至更久。

Biography: Prof. Andreas Tünnermann, Director of the Fraunhofer Institute for Applied Optics and Precision Engineering and Chair for Applied Physics at Friedrich-Schiller-University Jena, enjoys an excellent reputation in the laser physics community. He leads one of the most creative and productive laser research groups in the world. His research interests include fundamental principles as well as sophisticated technical aspects and applications associated with the tailoring of Light. Prof. Tünnermann's work yielded a variety of developments in laser technology and has found many advanced applications in basic science and industry. He is a sought-after expert in the optics and photonics industry, member of the supervisory boards of many listed companies and founder and member of the board of directors of the industry driven cluster OptoNet

Jena, one of the most dynamic regional optics clusters in Europe. Today, OptoNet represents companies with more than 14,000 employees and a total turnover of 3.6 billion euros around the city of Jena – prominent partners include companies such as Zeiss, Jenoptik and Schott. Major laser companies have adopted his concepts to develop advanced solid-state lasers. He is also known for his pioneering work in utilizing high power femtosecond lasers for material processing. This blend of experience and knowledge has attracted considerable attention and manifests itself in more than 650 peer-reviewed publications in reputable journals, in addition to more than 250 invited talks including plenary talks and tutorials at prestigious national and international conferences (h-index: 78).

专家简介：Andreas Tünnermann 教授是弗朗霍夫应用光学与精密工程研究所所长兼耶拿·弗里德里希·席勒大学应用物理系主任。Tünnermann 教授在激光物理界享誉盛名，领导着世界上最具创造力和生产力的激光研究小组。他的工作促进了激光技术的发展，并且他的多项成果在基础科学和工业中都得到了应用。此外，他还是多家上市公司的监事会成员，环耶拿工业驱动光学网络集群（OptoNet Jena）的创始人和董事会成员，该集群是欧洲最具活力的区域光学集群之一。如今，OptoNet Jena 拥有超过 14,000 名员工，总营业额高达 36 亿欧元，合作伙伴包括蔡司、耶拿光学和肖特等。作为世界著名的超快激光和激光加工科学家，他在多个国际知名学术期刊上发表文章，H 指数高达 78。

1: You have published 7 papers in the journal *Light* with a total of 410 citations. The top cited article[1] is the one you published in the *Light* in its launching year of 2012, which was cited 207 times. It's very impressive. Could you please tell us what is your reason for choosing *Light* to publish your papers? And particularly in 2012, when it was just launched and practically unknown.

1. 到目前为止您已经在*Light*期刊上发表了7篇论文，总共被引用了410次。令人印象深刻的是您于2012年*Light*创刊时投稿的文章，单篇引用了207次。您能否告诉我们您选择在*Light*上发表论文的原因是什么？特别是在2012年它刚刚创刊时，在光学领域还鲜为人知的情况下。

Prof. Tünnermann: The photonics community realized in the beginning of the new century that there was a lack of a journal that summarizes applied research results from their specialist area. From my point of view, the launching of the new journal *Light: Science & Applications* was a consistent approach to overcome this deficit. For me personally it was therefore important to support the initiative to establish a new journal by submitting high-quality articles from the start.

Tünnermann教授：在本世纪初，光学界意识到在专业领域里缺乏一本高影响的期刊来总结应用研究的成果。在我看来，新期刊*Light*的发行恰好是弥补了这一不足。因此对我个人而言，在创刊伊始通过投递高质量的文章来支持新期刊的这种首创精神是非常重要的。

CIOMP Vice President Prof. Xuejun Zhang awarding Prof. Tünnermann the *Light: Science & Applications* Certificate for Outstanding Paper

长春光机所副所长张学军研究员向获得*Light*优秀文章作者的Prof. Tünnermann颁发奖状

2. You are a world-famous scientist in ultrafast laser and laser processing who have received many awards for your research achievements. Could you please tell us what do you think of the current situation as well as the future development of this field? Germany is a world leader of laser technology and Laser World of Photonics in Munich and is a good brand for the global laser community. In your opinion, why is Germany so

advanced in laser technology?

2. 您是世界著名的超快激光和激光加工科学家，您的研究成果获得了许多奖项。您能告诉我们您如何看待激光领域的现状和未来发展吗？德国是激光技术的世界领导者，并且目前慕尼黑光电展已经成为全球激光甚至是光学领域的知名品牌。在您看来德国为何在激光技术方面如此先进？

Prof. Tünnermann: Ultrashort pulse lasers are an indispensable tool in industrial production today. The laser industry in Germany in particular has laid important foundations for this. On the one hand, basic research programs created a fundamental understanding of the interaction between laser and matter, while new laser geometries, such as the disk laser or the fiber laser, were developed at the same time. The key to the success of the German laser industry, however, lies in the close strategic cooperation between business and science along the entire value chain.

Tünnerman教授：超短脉冲激光器是当今工业生产中必不可少的工具，而德国的激光行业为此奠定了尤为重要的基础。一方面，基础研究计划使人们对激光与物质之间的相互作用有了基本的了解，同时又开发了新的激光体制，例如碟片激光器或光纤激光器。然而，在整个产业价值链中工业与科学之间紧密的战略合作是德国激光产业成功的关键。

3. You are the founder of the industry-driven cluster OptoNet Jena around the city of Jena. It is one of the most dynamic regional optics clusters in Europe with more than 14,000 employees and a total turn-over of 3.6 billion Euros. With prominent partners including Zeiss, Jenoptik and Schott, it's really a good example of how research can be combined with industry successfully. I wonder what motivated you to set up this cluster and how are you able to run it so successfully?

3. 您是环耶拿工业驱动光学网络集群（OptoNet Jena）的创始人。它是欧洲最具活力的区域性光学集群之一，拥有超过14,000名员工，总营业额达36亿欧元。能够联合包括蔡司（Zeiss）、耶拿光学（Jenoptik）和肖特（Schott）在内的著名合作伙伴，它是科研与产业成功结合的示范。我想知道是什么促使您想要建立这样的一个集群，您又是如何成功运行它的？

Prof. Tünnermann: More than twenty years ago, colleagues from business and science observed with great concern that the transfer of knowledge from universities and non-university institutions to business was increasingly deteriorating. There was also a lack of qualified specialists. This jeopardized the industry's ability to innovate.

A group of experts –of which I was a member -

founded the OptoNet cluster with the following aims:

- Developing a comprehensive roadmap for the photonics industry in Jena

- Securing the training of skilled workers

-And promoting the networking of business and science.

In the years that followed, we succeeded in increasing the innovative strength of the member companies and thus promoting growth through numerous coordinated individual measures.

Tünnermann教授：20多年前，来自工业和科学领域的同事关注到，从大学和非大学科研机构向工业的科研成果转移转化情况正在日益恶化，同时也缺少有资质的专业人士。这危及到了工业领域的创新能力。

基于以下目标，有一组专家（我是其中一员）创建了OptoNet集群：

——在耶拿创建光电子行业的综合路线图

——确保对专业技术工人的培训

——促进科学和工业的交流与转化

在随后的几年中，我们成功地提高了会员公司的创新实力，通过众多量身定制的协调方法促进了公司的成长。

4. As a mentor to young scientists, you have established an exemplary system to promote independent scientific personal development. What would be your advice for young scientists in their early research career?

4. 作为年轻科学家的良师益友，您建立了一种模范体系，通过独立的科研活动促进个人发展。您对年轻科学家的早期研究工作有何建议？

Prof. Tünnermann: Excellence in science is based on original research and on the one hand on cooperation, on the other hand on competition. It is therefore important for young scientists to cooperate and to compete with others to develop and implement their own original ideas.

Tünnermann教授：科学的卓越性基于原创研究，一方面基于合作，另一方面基于竞争。因此，对于年轻的科学工作者来说，通过与他人合作以及开展良性竞争来发展和实现自己的原创想法是非常重要的。

5. To do research sometimes means you have to work with other researchers, and take part in team work. As a director of such a famous institute as the IOF and a member of the board of many organizations, you are a proven leader. So what do you think makes a good leader?

5. 进行科学研究意味着您有时必须要与其他研究人员一起工作，参与团队合作。作为IOF如此著名的研究所的负责人和许多组织的董事会成员，您是公认的杰出领导者。那么您认为怎样才能成为一个好的领导者?

Prof. Tünnermann: My personal guiding principle in leadership is: "challenge and encourage". However, basic requirement for building up a successful institute is the establishment of a suitable culture - a mission - that promotes inventions and collaborations. We have defined the following mission statements for our research:

Excellence in science!

Cross border!

Create, not follow!

Change the game!

Make mistakes!

Culture trumps strategy!

Tünnermann教授：我个人的指导原则是“挑战与鼓励”。然而，建立一个成功的研究所的基本要求是建设一种合适的文化——一种使命——从而促进发明与合作。我们为自身的研究定义了以下几种使命：

科学卓越！

跨越界限！

创造，而不是跟随！

改变游戏规则！

犯错误！

文化胜过战略！

IOF-CIOMP-University of Toronto Joint Summer School held successfully in Jena
由Prof. Tünnermann提议的中德加暑期夏令营在耶拿成功举办

6. You have cooperated with CIOMP in many ways, including a joint education program, the Ultra Precision Manufacturing Workshop (UPM), joint research projects and you are now also an Executive Editor-in-Chief of the journal *Light*. Could you tell us why did you decide to work with the CIOMP? And what do you think of this cooperation?

6. 您已经与长春光机所在许多方面进行了合作，包括开展研究生联合培养计划，共同主办自由曲面超精密加工国际会议，从事科学研究合作项目等，并且您2021年还出任*Light*期刊执行主编。您能

International Workshop on Ultra Precision Manufacturing of Aspheres and Freeforms, co-organized by IOF and CIOMP, was held successfully in Changchun in 2017
由IOF和CIOMP联合组织的自由曲面超精密加工国际会议2017年在长春光机所成功举行

否告诉我们您为什么决定与长春光机所合作？您如何看待这种合作？

Prof. Tünnermann: Cooperation is an essential building block for establishing and maintaining excellence in research - this creates new knowledge and ultimately forms the basis for innovation. CIOMP has original competencies that complement our own competencies. Our cooperation creates added value for both partners.

Prof. Tünnermann visiting the CIOMP pavilion at the LASER-World of Photonics in Munich

Prof. Tünnermann参观长春光机所在德国慕尼黑光电展的展厅

Tünnermann教授：合作是建立和保持科研卓越性的重要组成部分——这既能创造新知识，也能最终为创新打下基础。长春光机所的原始创新能力与我们的能力相互补充。我们的合作使彼此相互促进，相得益彰。

Reference

参考文献

[1] LIMPERT J, STUTZKI F, TUNNERMANN A, et al. Yb-doped large-pitch fibres: effective single-mode operation based on higher-order mode delocalisation. Light: Science & Applications, 2012,1:8.

Professor Dieter Bimberg

编者按

很荣幸能够邀请到半导体激光领域的领军科学家，德国科学院院士、美国国家工程院外籍院士、俄罗斯科学院外籍院士，Light Conference 2018大会主席和*eLight*编委，年近80岁还在做滑雪、潜水等极限运动的人生赢家——Dieter Bimberg接受我的采访。一直以来，Dieter Bimberg院士给我的印象是：

一、大佬风范，并不限于他多国院士和学术泰斗的身份，更多的是他海纳百川有容乃大的处事风格。

二、永远年轻、富有探索精神，在工作和生活中，都保持着充沛的精力和对新鲜事物的渴望。

三、品位高，对研究和食物以及音乐等有着极高的品位。

在这次采访中，Dieter Bimberg院士就量子点激光器和半导体激光器中的关键问题，做出了讨论和回答；并分享了其学术生活的见解和有趣体验。

Light People: Professor Dieter Bimberg Spoke about Quantum Dot Laser

学海无涯乐作舟 名满天下遍知己

Science Editor: Chenzi Guo 科学编辑 郭宸孜

Editorial:

It's my great pleasure to interview Prof. Dieter Bimberg, a leading scientist in semiconductor lasers, member of the German Academy of Sciences, foreign member of the US National Academy of Engineering and Russian Academy of Sciences, Chair of the Light Conference 2018 and editorial board member of journal *eLight*. Though nearly 80 years old, he is still a fan of extreme sports such as skiing and diving. Through the years we knew each other, I have learned several things about Dieter:

First, he is not only famed for his research, but also for being generous, patient and supportive.

Second, he is forever young and energetic in spirit, and always interested in new things.

Third, he loves research, food and music.

In this interview, Prof. Dieter Bimberg answered key questions on quantum dot lasers and semiconductor lasers. He also shared insight and experiences about his academic life.

Light People

Biography: Dieter Bimberg, member of the German National Academy of Sciences, the Russian Academy of Sciences, and the National Academy of Engineering and the National Academy of Inventors in the United States. He is the founding director of the Center of NanoPhotonics and the Department of Applied Physics at Technische Universität Berlin in Germany, and Distinguished Adjunct Professor at King Abdul-Aziz University in Saudi Arabia. Currently he is a Distinguished Professor at CIOMP, CAS. Prof. Bimberg is among the first inventors of quantum dot lasers, and a leading scientist in semiconductor lasers. His scientific work has led to 1,600 publications, 61 patent families, and 6 books with more than 64,000 citations and >111 H-index. He is a recipient of the Russian State Prize in Science and Technology, the Max-Born, William Streifer and Heinrich-Welker Awards, Nick Holonyak, Jr. Award, and the UNESCO Nanoscience Medal.

专家简介：Dieter Bimberg，德国科学院院士、俄罗斯科学院院士、美国国家工程院院士、美国发明院院士。他是柏林工业大学纳米光子学中心的创始人，曾担任阿卜杜勒阿齐兹国王大学杰出兼职特聘教授，现任中科院长春光机所中德绿色光子学研究中心主任。Dieter Bimberg是量子点激光器的发明人之一，纵向光子晶体激光器概念的提出者，高速面发射激光器低功耗纪录创造者，是半导体激光领域的顶尖科学家。Dieter Bimberg院士发表了超过1600篇论文，61个专利，6本书，总引用量6.4万次，H因子高达111，为ISI web of knowledge高引作者，曾获俄罗斯国家科学技术奖，马克斯·玻恩奖, William Streifer奖，Heinrich-Welker奖，Nick Holonyak, Jr.奖，以及联合国教科文组织纳米科学奖章等。

1. With Quantum dots (QDs) being discovered with high gain in 1990s, you were among the first to lead the research of QDs and invented QD lasers in the early 1990s. In the past decades, QD lasers have attracted enormous attention, what were the major difficulties when you worked on QD lasers. Do you have any intended ideas for QD lasers which have not been explored or realized yet?

1. 高增益量子点（QD）于上世纪90年代被发现，您是最早引领量子点研究的人之一，并于90年代初发明了量子点激光器。在过去的几十年里，量子点激光器引起了极大的关注，您能否谈谈在研究量子点激光器时遇到的主要困难是什么？您当初对量子点激光器有哪些设想还有哪些尚未探索或实现的呢？

Dieter Bimberg: The material gain of QDs is sensationally large, as discovered by us in 1993 and much larger than theoretically predicted by a team from Tokyo Institute of Technology in the 80s. The waveguide of a laser, where the light travels, shows absorption and scattering losses, which partly counterbalance the gain. The difficulty was to achieve a positive balance. We managed by stacking QD layers on top of each other without introducing crystal defects, up to ten for practical lasers. Secondly, we discovered how to grow low loss waveguides and avoid scattering of light in the waveguide, meaning minimize the losses. We are working at CIOMP on QD lasers for automotive applications like LIDAR or sensing in a wavelength window predicted to show largest eye safety and largest range in foggy air. This window is not accessible to classical double heterostructure lasers based on GaAs or InP.

Dieter Bimberg：我们团队在1993年发现，量子点材料的增益高得惊人，这比80年代东京工业大学研究组的理论预测值要大得多。激光波导的吸收和散射损耗，在一定程度上抵消了增益，因此获取高增益的主要困难正在于此。首先，我们通过将量子点层叠在一起（可以实现多达10层的量子点层叠）而不引入晶体缺陷。其次，我们发现了如何生长低损耗的波导，避免光在波导中的散射，这意味着可以将损耗最小化。现在，我们在长春光机所的团队正在研究用于汽车应用的量子点激光器，如激光雷达或是在人眼最安全的波长范围内、在有雾天

Prof. Bimberg and Prof. Ping Jia, President of CIOMP, co-signing the agreement on establishing the Chinese-German Green Photonics Center

Dieter Bimberg院士与中科院长春光机所所长贾平签署中德绿色光子学研究中心合约

气实现最大射程的传感，而这样的波段，通常是无法用基于GaAs或InP的经典双异质结激光器来实现的。

2. QD lasers have shown great promise in silicon photonics and are among the game changers in integrated optics. In the communication bands, QD lasers have stood out in practical use. Could you share some opinions about the trend of QD lasers and semiconductor lasers, in both researches and industries? What are the major obstacles in QD lasers applied in silicon photonics, and what cross-disciplines should be involved but were not paid enough attention?

2. 量子点激光器在硅基光子学领域展示出了巨大的发展前景，是影响集成光学领域规则的技术之一。在通信波段，量子点激光器已经在实际应用中大展身手。您能谈一谈量子点激光器和半导体激光器在研究和工业上的发展趋势吗？量子点激光器应

用于硅基光子学的主要障碍是什么？有没有哪些研究和学科有可能对量子点激光器在硅基光子学的应用产生重要影响但却没有引起足够重视的呢？

Dieter Bimberg: The term "silicon photonics" refers to integrating passive optical or still active devices like lasers based on III-V-compounds monolithically on Si and thus enabling an integrated technology, which would be advantageous from many different points of view. A lot of research in the last 10 years focused on growing QD layers on large Si substrates, thus enabling to fabricate lasers on Si substrates. After surmounting many difficulties presently, a number of groups all over the world have achieved good performance data for edge emitting lasers. Extended lifetime tests, which are finally decisive, are still missing.

Green photonics is presently thought to be a major sunrise direction of R+D with huge impact in particular on communication systems, like workstation clusters or supercomputers. Their energy consumption is now approaching or already surmounting 500 MW for new installations. Most of their energy is spent for interconnects in different distance ranges from module to module to workstation to workstation. Integration of surface emitting lasers on low energy but high-speed drivers based on CMOS technologies would bring at the same time cost and power consumption down. The VCSELs could be either based on QWs or QDs, depending on the expected emission wavelength. We are working on this integration in national and international teams.

Dieter Bimberg："硅基光子学"指的是将基于 III–V 族化合物的无源光学器件或静态有源器件（如激光器）整体地集成在硅上，从而实现集成技术，这从多方面来看都是有利的。近 10 年来，大量的研究集中于在大尺寸的硅衬底上生长量子点层，从而在硅衬底上制造激光器。在克服了许多困难之后，世界各地的一些研究小组已经取得了良好性能的边缘发射激光器。但是，最终具有决定性意义的延长寿命试验仍然处于困境。

Prof. Bimberg was awarded an honorary doctorate by Lancaster University in July, 2015
在2015年7月英国兰卡斯特大学的毕业典礼上，Dieter Bimberg院士被授予名誉科学博士

此外，值得一提的是，绿色光子学被认为是相关科学研究和开发的一个主要趋势，它将对通信系统，如工作站集群或超级计算机等产生重要影响。

这些新装置的能源消耗现在接近甚至可能超过500兆瓦，这其中，大部分的能耗发生在从模块到模块，从工作站到工作站的互连上。如果将面发射激光器与CMOS技术集成，可以降低成本和功耗，且VCSEL（垂直腔面发射激光器）可以根据预期的发射波长，采取量子阱或量子点结构。我们正和多个国家的团队合作，开展这方面的研究。

3. As I know, you are a member of US National Academy of Engineering (NAE) board for appointing foreign fellows from countries like China, chair of the IEEE Photonics Society fellow appointment board and many other important institutions; I think our audience would love to know how they can get involved, could you please share some insight into what board members value most?

3. 因为我知道，您是美国国家工程院（NAE）院士，同时是NAE选拔中国等国外籍院士的董事会成员，也是IEEE光子学会选拔会士的委员会主席，并担任了许多重要机构的委员。我想我们的读者应该很想知道，他们如何能更好地参与到这些国际顶尖的科学协会，能否请您分享一下这些科学协会的董事会成员最看重的是什么？

Prof. Bimberg's IEEE Jun-ichi Nishizawa award
Dieter Bimberg院士荣获IEEE Jun-ichi Nishizawa奖及奖章

Dieter Bimberg: We stimulate nominations by identifying outstanding researchers and their potential nominators and supporters. In each case it is helpful for a successful nomination to demonstrate a large international impact of the work given e.g. by large citation rates and the Hirsch factor. Previous national recognition of the work is also contributing to the success of a proposal. Writing a nomination is very time consuming and those who believe, they can do it in an afternoon typically fail, but not because of the low quality of the researcher. The success rate is only in the few 10% level, but a submission is valid for several years. At the end a carefully written nomination of an outstanding researcher will pass through. Presently nominations of females are additionally supported by additional slots.

Dieter Bimberg：关于会士（院士）选拔，我们通常会关注这些研究人员本身是否杰出，并关注其潜在的提名者和支持者。首先，无论在什么情况下，如果能够证明这些研究人员在国际上有巨大影响力，比如工作的被引很高，或是H指数很高，都将有助于提名成功。此外，国家对研究人员工作的认可也有助于提名的成功。其次，撰写提名这个过程，本身就非常耗时，那些相信他们可以在一个下午写完的人通常都会失败，即使提名的研究人员本身素质并不低。通常，这些国际顶尖学术组织的申请成功率只有10%左右，但是申请有效期可以长达

Prof. Dieter Bimberg was invited by Prof. Z.I.Alferov to his Nobel Prize ceremony in Stockholm at 2000

Dieter Bimberg教授受到2000年诺贝尔物理学奖得主Z.I.Alferov教授的邀请，参加其诺贝尔奖颁奖典礼

几年。最后，那些本身就十分杰出的研究人员，加上精心撰写的提名和申请书，一般会通过。此外，我们格外支持对女性科学家的提名。

4. I've seen it by myself, you are a very skilled skier, and rumor says you are very proficient at diving, climbing, and some other extreme sports. I think everyone who knows you would feel the youth and strength from the bottom of your heart. How do you balance your life and entertainments? Do you keep adventurous spirits in both life and work?

4. 我亲眼见证，您的滑雪技巧非常高超，而且据说您也非常精通潜水、攀岩等其他极限运动。我想每个认识您的人都会感受到来自您心底的青春和力量。您是如何平衡生活和娱乐的呢？您在生活和工作中都有冒险精神吗？

Dieter Bimberg: You are right, but yourself have also

a lot of courage racing down the snowy hills in the vicinity. An old proverb from the Latin period of time says "mens sana in corpore sano" in rough translation "a healthy mind resides in a healthy body" and I follow this proverb. Doing sports makes fun and helps a lot to resist the stress from my daily work. At CIOMP I am playing

Prof. Bimberg on the skiing slope
Dieter Bimberg院士在雪道上

badminton and here in Europe at the end of summer, when you have middle autumn days, I am sailing a catamaran for a few days in the Mediterranean.

Dieter Bimberg：对，你也非常勇敢，我们一起去雪山滑雪的时候，你能够从山顶上直接滑下去。有一句来自拉丁语时期的古老谚语：mens sana in corpore sano，可以粗略翻译为“健康的心灵寓于健康的身体中”，我个人遵循这句谚语。做运动很有趣，对我的日常工作很有帮助。在长春光机所我打羽毛球，在欧洲夏末或是中秋的时候，我会开着双体船在地中海航行几天。

5. You have been deeply involved in "Light Conference", bearing many responsibilities such as Chair and plenary speaker. In this challenging time of COVID-19 pandemic, scientists from all around the world are trying to move things online to keep the business around. Do you appreciate this less face-to-face

way? How long do you think this online conference trend will last? Also due to the COVID-19, many universities worldwide are facing a cut down in research funding, and millions of researchers, especially junior researchers would be affected, do you have any advice in helping young researchers get by this challenging time?

5. 在过去几年，我们的“Light Conference”也有幸能得到您的深度关注，包括您曾经担任我们的大会主席和大会报告发言人。当下，在这个艰难的疫情时期，来自世界各地的科学家们都在尝试将学术会议和报告转移到网上，从而保证科研与交流的正常运转。您喜欢这种非面对面的方式吗？您认为这种网上会议的趋势会持续多久？同样由于COVID-19，世界上很多大学都面临着科研经费削减的问题，数百万科研人员，尤其是年轻的科研人员都受到了影响，您能否提一些建议帮助我们的年轻科研人员度过这个时期？

Dieter Bimberg: Specialized conferences, where you meet your colleagues and peers of the field deliver much more than just listening to a presentation: You meet people, who have a social relevance, and can spontaneously interact and further develop your thoughts during intense discussions. I benefitted a lot from face to face meetings and discussions in the past by jointly developing and testing new ideas. Remote conferences are also important: One avoids costly and time-consuming travelling and listens only to those talks, which are interesting for you. In the future we will have both. Right now, I see however an inflation of dubious on-line events, which are not primarily organized by experts of a given field, but by money making groups having just a computer and which are easy to organize.

Cut downs of research funding and phasing out young researchers is no good idea. In research one needs continuity in transferring ideas and technical skills.

Having e.g. in my field a high end test lab for photonic devices it will take you several years to catch up again, if you cut the education of young people, where one layer of experience builds up on the previous one. Also, industry needs a continuous supply of freshly educated scientists.

Dieter Bimberg: 在专业的线下会议上，你会遇到你的同事和同行，而不仅仅只是听一个报告：你会认识一些人，我们可以在热烈的讨论中自发地互动并进一步发展我们的想法。过去，我就从面对面的会议和讨论中受益匪浅，共同开展和测试了很多新想法。远程会议也很重要：你可以避免昂贵和耗时的旅行，只听那些你感兴趣的东西。我认为，未来我们将两者兼而有之。但是需要注意的是，现在有一些不怎么样的线上活动正在扩张，这些活动的发起人不是某一领域的专家，而是一些只要有一台计算机就只顾赚钱的人。

Prof. Bimberg at "Light Conference" 2018
Dieter Bimberg院士在2018年*Light*会议

削减研究经费和逐步淘汰年轻的研究人员不是一个好主意。在研究中，研究人员在转化思想和技术的时候，需要连续性的支持。举例而言，如果是在我的领域里的一个高端光子器件测试实验室，知识和经验是累积的，是建立在之前基础上的，所以如果减少对年轻人的教育和支持，回头就需要几年的时间才能重新赶上。此外，工业界也需要不断输入新鲜的科学家血液。

6. Your authored book, *Quantum Dot Heterostructures*,

is called the Bible in quantum dots, as I quoted from a peer. I personally enjoyed reading this book a lot. It was very careful, enlightening, informative and practical. Could you share some ideas what elements a good book should include and recommend some books for students who major in semiconductor lasing, nanophotonic devices, nanomaterials and nanostructures?

6. 您的著作之一《量子点异质结构》，被称为量子点领域的圣经（这里我是引用了一位同行的话）。我个人也从这本书中受益匪浅，它很准确，有启发性，信息量大且实用性强。您能否分享一下您认为一本好书应该包括哪些要素吗？同时，能否向我们主修半导体激光、纳米光子器件、纳米材料和纳米结构等专业的学生推荐一些书籍？

Dieter Bimberg: A good book should put its subject in a frame of what has been done by others before – we are always standing on the shoulders of titans and we are never walking alone – and should show where we might go, a little speculation is always good for the phantasy of the reader. Good books on lasing and devices exist a lot, so the authors of books seeing what I recommend shall forgive me, not mentioning their work:

1. my students like to read as an introduction the book by S.L. Chuang *Physics of Optoelectronic Devices*, New York: Wiley, 1995.

2. Recent work on semiconductor lasing, nanophotonic devices, nanomaterials and nanostructures was edited or authored by me and my students:

a) nanomaterials: V. A. Shchukin, N. N. Ledentsov and D. Bimberg, *Epitaxy of Nanostructures*, Springer 2004. D. Bimberg ed. , *Semiconductor Nanostructures*, Springer 2008.

b) Devices: G. Eisenstein and D. Bimberg eds., "Green Photonics and Electronics", Springer 2017.

Dieter Bimberg：一本好书应该把它的主题放在

别人已经做过的事情的框架中——我们总是站在巨人的肩膀上，我们从不孤独行走——并且应该显示出将来可能会怎么发展，小小的猜测总是有助于读者的想象。关于激光及其器件的好书很多，所以我这里列举几本，不能一应而全，希望那些好书的作者不要因为我没有提及他们的著作而怪我。

1.我的学生喜欢读S.L. Chuang的*Physics of Optoelectronic Devices*。

2.我个人或是我的学生近期一些关于半导体激光、纳米光子学器件、纳米材料和纳米结构方面的著作：

(1) V. A. Shchukin, N. N. Ledentsov and D. Bimberg, *Epitaxy of Nanostructures*, Springer 2004。

D. Bimberg ed. , *Semiconductor Nanostructures*, Springer 2008。

(2) Devices: G. Eisenstein and D. Bimberg eds., *Green Photonics and Electronics*, Springer 2017。

Professor Luc Thévenaz

编者按

时光荏苒，倏忽一年。本期我们荣幸地邀请到*Light*期刊共执行主编、光纤传感领域的泰斗——瑞士联邦理工学院（洛桑）Luc Thévenaz教授。

Luc Thévenaz教授为人亲和友善、率真洒脱，治学严谨审慎、追求卓越。30余年的科研生涯中，包括布里渊分布式光纤传感技术、光纤中快光和慢光、空芯光纤光放大等在内，Thévenaz教授先后取得了多项引领行业发展的重要研究成果。

在本期采访中，Thévenaz教授针对空芯光纤光放大技术等问题与科学编辑进行深入交流，并对低损耗空芯光纤未来的机遇与挑战进行了展望。同时，Thévenaz教授也分享了对如何保持学术创造力，如何培养学生等问题的独到见解，并回顾了其与*Light*期刊“相识、携手”的故事，表达了对期刊发展的建议与期待。

Optical Fiber:
Chasing the Light, Building a Dream
追光而行 以纤筑梦

Science Editor: Jingze Yuan 科学编辑 袁境泽

Editorial:

Time flies, swiftly the years. In this issue, we are honored to invite Prof. Luc Thévenaz, the co-executive editor of *Light: Science and Applications* (*Light*) and a leading scientist in the field of optical fiber sensing, from the École Polytechnique Fédérale de Lausanne (EPFL), Switzerland.

Prof. Luc Thévenaz, a rigorous and prudent scholar in pursuit of excellence, is friendly and forthright. In his more than 30 years of research, Prof. Thévenaz has produced a lot of important research achievements and contributions that have led the industry, including Brillouin distributed fiber sensing, fast & slow light in optical fibers, and optical amplification in hollow-core fibers.

In this interview, Prof. Thévenaz discusses with the scientific editor about optical amplification in hollow-core fibers and the opportunities and challenges of low-loss hollow-core fibers in the future. Prof. Thévenaz also shares his insights on how to maintain academic creativity and how to train students. Furthermore, he recalls his story of "Meeting and Working together" with the *Light*, and expressed his suggestions and expectations for the development of *Light*.

Light People

Biography: Luc Thévenaz received the M.Sc. and Ph.D. degrees in physics from the University of Geneva, Switzerland. In 1988, he joined the École Polytechnique Fédérale de Lausanne (EPFL), Switzerland, where he currently leads a research group (Group for Fiber Optics) involved in photonics, namely fiber optics and optical sensing. Research topics include Brillouin-scattering fiber sensors, slow and fast light, nonlinear fiber optics and laser applications in gases. He achieved with his collaborators the first experimental demonstration of optically controlled slow and fast light in optical fibers, realized at ambient temperature and operating at any wavelength since based on stimulated Brillouin scattering. He also contributed to the development of Brillouin distributed fiber sensing by proposing innovative concepts pushing beyond barriers. During his career, he stayed at Stanford University, at the Korea Advanced Institute of Science and Technology, at Tel Aviv University, at Shanghai Jiao Tong University, at the University of Sydney, and at the Polytechnic University of Valencia. In 2000, he cofounded the company Omnisens that is developing and commercializing advanced photonic instrumentation based on distributed fiber sensing.

He was member of the Consortium in the FP7 European Project GOSPEL "Governing the speed of light", was Chairman of the European COST Action 299 "FIDES: Optical Fibers for New Challenges Facing the Information Society" and Coordinator of the H2020

Marie Skłodowska-Curie Innovative Training Networks FINESSE (FIberNErve Systems for Sensing). He is member of the Steering Committee of the International Conference on Optical Fiber Sensors and General Chairman of this conference that he hosted in 2018. He has served in the Technical Committee of several conferences, such as ECOC, CLEO-Europe, APC, etc and has been Associate Editor of *Photonics Technology Letters* and the *Journal of Lightwave Technology*. He is now co-Executive Editor-in-Chief of the journal *Light: Science & Applications* and is Fellow of the IEEE and the Optical Society.

专家简介：Luc Thévenaz在瑞士日内瓦大学获得物理学硕士和博士学位。1988年，他加入瑞士洛桑联邦理工学院（EPFL），目前领导一个研究小组（光纤组），从事光子学，即光纤和光学传感的研究。研究课题包括布里渊散射光纤传感器、慢光和快光、非线性光纤和气体中的激光应用等。他及他的团队首次通过实验验证了光纤中慢光和快光的光学控制，基于受激布里渊散射效应，在环境温度下实现了任何波长的光学控制。Luc Thévenaz教授还提出了超越障碍的创新概念，为布里渊分布式光纤传感的发展做出了贡献。在他的职业生涯中，他曾在斯坦福大学、韩国高级科学技术研究所、特拉维夫大学、上海交通大学、悉尼大学以及瓦伦西亚理工大学工作。2000年，他共同创立了Omnisens公司，该公司致力于开发和商业化基于分布式光纤传感的先进光子仪器。

Luc Thévenaz 教授是 FP7 European Project "Governing the speed of light"（GOSPEL）的基金会成员，也是European COST Action 299 "FIDES: Optical Fibres for New Challenges Facing the Information Society" 的主席，是H2020 Marie Skłodowska-Curie Innovative Training Networks FINESSE（FIbreNErve Systems for Sensing）的负责人。他是国际光纤传感器会议的指导委员会成员，也是他在2018年主持这个会议并担任总主席。Luc Thévenaz教授曾在多个学术

会议的技术委员会任职，如ECOC、CLEO-Europe、APC等，并担任*Photonics Technology Letters*和*Journal of Lightwave Technology*的副编辑。Luc Thévenaz教授现在担任*Light: Science & Applications*杂志的联合执行主编，同时也是IEEE和光学学会的会员。

1. First of all, congratulations! In 2020, you have a number of outstanding research results have been published in top journals such as *Nature Photonics*, *Physical Review Letters*, and so on. Your latest work with the title of "Giant Brillouin Amplification in Gases"[1] was also selected by OSA as one exciting breakthrough of "Optics in 2020". In this work, your team has developed a technology based on the Brillouin Scattering in gas that can amplify light in hollow-core optical fibers. The signal is amplified up to 200,000 times and the gain coefficient is at least improved by up to 6 orders of magnitude. How did you come up with such a creative idea? Did you encounter any difficulties during

the research process? How did you deal with it?

1. 首先要祝贺您2020年有多项杰出研究成果在*Nature Photonics*, *Physical Review Letters*等顶级期刊发表，最新工作更是以“Giant Brillouin Amplification in Gases”[1]为题入选2020年度OSA光学进展“Optics in 2020”。在这项工作中您的团队通过利用气体布里渊效应实现了空芯光纤里的光放大，信号放大200,000倍，增益系数比之前的工作至少提高了6个数量级。您是如何想到这样具有创造性的研究方案？研究过程中是否遇到了困难？您又是如何突破的？

Prof. Thévenaz: Actually, this was an idea floating in my mind for some 15 years, but we could not realize it before for a quite trivial combination of reasons: absence of support for this research (it remains a hopeless objective to make a visionary idea funded), unavailability of hollow-core fibers and no motivated collaborators to develop this idea. This last point was maybe the most crucial: yes, you need people in your team who believe in this idea and show enough faith in this research! Of course, we never find what we are not curious to seek.

My original thinking was that stimulated Brillouin scattering can be quite important in gas, since it can be strongly compressed, resulting in a higher chance of density and thus refractive index – than in a solid. The secret wish was that this effect could overcompensate the penalty due to a lower material density in a gas. It is actually far from being the case at atmospheric pressure, which was fairly disappointing when we collected the first results.

However, there is a quadratic dependence on the pressure that we did not initially expect and was theoretically confirmed later, and this leads to a massive increase of the gain by raising the gas pressure to some tens of bars, even overcoming what can be obtained in the most efficient solid materials! This turns out to be simply the higher nonlinear gain ever obtained in a transparent dielectric material.

Thévenaz教授：实际上，这个想法一直在我的脑海中萦绕了将近15年，只是因为许多原因致使这个想法一直没有得以实现：首先这个项目缺乏资助（愿景似的构想总是很难得到资助），其次没有空芯光纤，而且也没有积极的合作者来开发这个想法。最后一点也许是最关键的一点：团队中需要有人相信这个想法并且也非常有信心来完成这项研究！当然我们只会去研究我们所感兴趣的方向。

我最初的想法是，气体中受激布里渊散射效应非常重要，因为气体可以被极大地压缩，从而导致密度和折射率的变化相比于固体中更高。我们其实很希望这种效应可以补偿由于气体的低材料密度所造成的损失，但实际上，在大气压下的情况并非如此，我们测到的第一个结果让我们大失所望。

气体的布里渊增益是和气压成二次方关系的，我们最初并没有预料到这一点，但后来在理论上得到了证实。这就意味着，当气压升高至几十bar时，布里渊增益也会极大增强，甚至远超最有效的固体材料石英光纤。我们的分析还表明，气体的布里渊增益甚至可以超过所有的透明电介质中的非线性效应。

From left to right: Prof. Luc Thévenaz, Dr. Flavien Gyger, and Dr. Fan Yang
©Alain Herzog, EPFL
从左至右分别为：Luc Thévenaz教授、Flavien Gyger博士与杨帆博士
©Alain Herzog, EPFL

2. In the special issue of OSA "Optics in 2021 & Beyond", you mentioned that "2021 will likely witness

the advent of low-loss hollow-core fiber outperforming classical solid-core fibers. This will be a revolutionary breakthrough". Would you please say something about the areas where this technology will have a profound impact in the future? What are the opportunities and challenges?

2. 在OSA栏目“Optics in 2021 & Beyond”中，您提到“2021年，性能优于经典实心光纤的低损耗空芯光纤即将问世，这将是革命性的突破”。可否请您谈一谈该技术将在未来哪些领域中产生深远影响？存在什么样的机遇与挑战呢？

Prof. Thévenaz: The idea of guiding light in a vacuum or in a tenuous gas is simply luminous: the interaction with matter is reduced to a minimum value while keeping all advantages related to waveguiding such as light confinement. This means a potentially lower loss, less dispersion, and less impact of nonlinear effects that all impair the capacity of an optical transmission line. The consequences will be simply optical transmission lines with higher capacities and over a longer repeater less distance.

But several other advantages are not yet entirely perceived: these fibers can transmit light over a much broader spectral range, from UV to mid-IR, upscaling the capabilities for wavelength multiplexing. They are also very immune to radiation, so perfectly suitable for space applications and highly radioactive environments. This may only be the emerged tip of the iceberg: I also see another crucial advantage in the sense that these fibers can be customized, by filling them with different fluids (gas or liquid). This opens avenues for new classes of fiber devices, for lasing, optical processing, and sensing.

The new antiresonant hollow-core fibers show now losses slightly above the attenuation of silica under single mode propagation and 2021 will hopefully see the breaking of another glass ceiling present for some 40 years, which is the 0.15 dB/km loss observed in silica. This will be a fantastic breakthrough and I am really optimistic it will happen soon thanks to the talented teams hardly working to reach this objective.

Thévenaz教授：在真空或稀薄气体中传导光的想法很亮眼：最大程度地降低光与物质的相互作用，同时保留所有与波导（如光约束）相关的优势。这也就意味着我们可以获得更低的损耗，更少的色散和更小的非线性效应影响，以降低对光传输线容量的损害。其结果将是简单的光传输线具有更高的容量和更长的无中继距离。

但是还有一些其他优势尚待发掘：这些光纤可以在更宽的光谱范围内（从紫外到中红外）进行光传输，从而提高了光纤波长复用的能力。此外，它们有良好的抗辐射性能，因此非常适用于太空和高放射性环境。这可能只是冰山一角：我还看到了另一个重要的优势，通过填充不同的流体（气体或液体），这类光纤可以按需求定制。这就为新型光纤器件、激光器、光学信号处理和传感开辟了道路。

现在，反谐振空芯光纤现有的损耗仅仅比石英光纤略高，而且能保证单模传输。2021年将有望实现一个近40年来前所未有的突破，比二氧化硅中0.15 dB/km的损耗极限还要低。这将是一个了不起的突破，我非常相信通过卓越团队的共同努力将会很快实现这一目标。

3. As a leading scientist in the field of optical fiber sensing, you have achieved the first experimental demonstration of optically-controlled slow & fast light in optical fibers, and also contributed to the development of Brillouin distributed fiber sensing by proposing innovative concepts. You have been working in this research field for more than 30 years, and achieved a lot

of breakthroughs and contributions. What is your magic to stay creative in researches? So far, which research result makes you feel most satisfied? Or what's the most memorable one to you? Why is it?

3. 作为光纤传感领域的学术泰斗，您不但首次通过实验验证了光纤中慢光和快光的光学控制，还提出创新性研究理念，为布里渊分布式光纤传感技术的发展奠定基础。在您从事该领域研究工作30多年中，有许多突破性的成就和贡献。您是如何保持学术创造力的？截止目前，最令您满意、难忘的工作又是什么？为什么？

Prof. Thévenaz: The process of how creative ideas come up to your mind remains mysterious for me and this is a quality that cannot be substituted by "hard working". For sure the societal environment matters and stimulates creativity if it leaves enough space for free thinking and the search for truth. Natural curiosity and the pleasure to challenge limits are certainly of prime importance and the creative person questions all issues, even those hurting. I am quite convinced that creative persons have somehow a rebel and iconoclastic personality, and are often subject to some degree of laziness...

It is difficult to judge what my most memorable achievement is, it is like to decide which your favorite one among your children is, and you love them all! I would say that it may be the invention of the modulation technique in 1992 to synthesize all optical waves for the Brillouin interaction from a single laser. So far it was only performed using several frequency-locked lasers and the concept of synthesizing new optical waves by modulation was totally disruptive at that moment. It is now universally used for all Brillouin-based systems and certainly many current actors are totally unaware today that the technique did not come out naturally. It remains my most cited research and I am particularly proud of it since I was fairly young at that moment and I had a deep feeling that it will be certainly impactful.

Of course, the first realization of slow & fast light in optical fibers was also an exceptional strong moment in 2004. This was also a fantastic playground for research, nearly all newly collected results brought a major breakthrough. We really thought that slow & fast light may enter the field of real applications through this achievement. However, we quickly built the conviction that slow & fast light is a bad good idea and there is no striking good application for it.

Finally, our very recent discovery that massive amplification can be realized in hollow core waveguides using stimulated Brillouin scattering in gases occupies a special place in my heart. This is one of the rare achievements – or maybe the only one in my career for which the results were much better than our anticipations! In addition, it is so easy to implement and I am deeply convinced that it may have a strong impact in the field and even society. The open question is to know how long it will take until the community will adopt it if ever it does.

Thévenaz教授：对我而言，如何能提出创造性想法仍然是未知且神秘的，这是一种“努力工作”所不能取代的品质。当然，如果社会环境给自由思考留有足够的空间，那么它在激发创造力方面也会起到一定的作用。保持追求真理的好奇心和挑战极限的乐趣无疑是最重要的，富有创造力的人往往会质疑所有的问题，即使是那些伤人的问题。我十分相信具有创造力的人一定程度上都具有叛逆和打破传统的个性，而且往往在某种程度上“有些懒”……

很难说我最难忘的成就是哪项，这就好比要在你的孩子们中选哪一个是你最喜欢的一样！我觉得可能是1992年发明的调制技术，可以通过单个激光器合成布里渊相互作用的所有光波。到目前为止，它只需使用几种锁频激光器就可以实现，而通过调制合成新光波的概念在当时是完全颠覆性的。现在已被广泛应用于所有基于布里渊的体系中，当然现在的许多相关科研工作者完全没有意识到这项技术并不是自然产生的。这项工作一直是我最高引用的研究，我对此特别自豪，因为那时我还很年轻，但我却坚信它在未来肯定会产生深远的影响。

当然，第一次在光纤中实现快慢光也算是在2004年的一个高光时刻。这也是一项极好的研究，几乎所有新获得的结果都带来了重大突破。通过这一成果，我们一度认为快慢光可以进入实际应用领域。然而，我们很快又意识到：快慢光不是一个好想法，也没有什么特别好的应用。

我们最新的研究发现在我的心中也已占有举

足轻重的位置：通过利用气体布里渊散射效应，我们在空芯光纤中实现了极强的光放大。这是我职业生涯中为数不多的——或者可能是唯一的——结果远超乎预期的成就！而且它很容易实现，因而我深信它可能会在该领域甚至于整个社会产生巨大的影响。但有待解决的问题是：科研界需要多长时间来接受它。

Prof. Luc Thévenaz ©Alain Herzog, EPFL
Luc Thévenaz教授© Alain Herzog, EPFL

4. We know Omnisens is a world leader in high performance fiber optic monitoring. Omnisens produces

instrumentation and systems based on optical metrology and photonics. Using fiber optic-based sensing, Omnisens offers continuous, reliable monitoring solutions for users in key fields such as oil, natural gas, and electric power and civil engineering facilities. As the co-founder of this company, could you please share with us about your original intention of "starting a business", as well as your impressive stories and insights?

4. 瑞士Omnisens公司是分布式光纤传感领域的世界领导者。Omnisens先进的分布式光纤监测系统可为石油、天然气、电力和土木工程设施等关键领域的用户提供实时有效的资产完整性监测解决方案。作为公司的联合创始人，您可以和我们分享一下您“创业”的初衷，以及您认为印象深刻的故事和感悟吗?

Prof. Thévenaz: I would say this is just a question of opportunity since it was never in my plans to start a business. The idea never made me particularly excited. I was just bored that all my research results were so poorly exploited by the companies supporting my research, mostly by lack of resources and vision. So it was just the opportunist encounter of an interesting research product in my lab, some entrepreneur friends with financial resources and potential customers that decided to launch the business by founding the company.

I basically dislike to mix roles and I think that I am a pure academic person, so I never took an executive position in the company and l always kept 100% active in my University position. I reckoned that I could much better give my contribution to the general society as an academic person. Logically I let the company be run by more talented persons in business, this was for me a sane sharing of competencies.

I am still convinced that I made the right choice and

it was more beneficial for both the company and my University research group. Eventually, the company is still independently running after 20 years of operation, which is quite a success.

Thévenaz教授：这其实只是个机遇问题，因为创业从来都不是我的计划，这个想法也并没有让我觉得很兴奋。我只是厌倦了我的所有研究结果无法被支持我研究的公司充分利用与开发（主要是因为缺乏资源和远见）。当一些有资金和潜在客户的朋友们在我的实验室里发现了他们感兴趣的研究时，他们决定通过创立公司来开展业务。这就是Omnisens创立的过程。

我其实不喜欢有多重身份，我认为我是一个纯粹的学者，所以我从没在公司担任行政职务，只是全力以赴地做好我在大学里的研究工作。我认为我作为一名学术人员能更好地为社会做贡献。我让更多的商业人才经营公司，这对我来说是一种更为理智的能力分配。

我始终坚信我做出了正确的选择，这对公司和我在大学的研究团队都更加有利。历经20年后，Omnisens公司仍然可以独立运营，这无疑是相当成功的。

5. In January 2016, you published your research work[2] in *Light* for the first time. In July 2018, we were honored to successfully invite you to serve as the co-executive editor of *Light*. From the author to the EIC, you have contributed to the development of *Light* for almost 5 years, and we have also developed a close and a deeper friendship. Could you still recall the story about your first contact with *Light*? How do you appraise this Journal? What is your expectation to *Light*?

5. 2016年1月，您首次在*Light*期刊上发表研究成果[2]。2018年7月，我们非常荣幸地邀请到您担任

***Light*期刊共执行主编。从作者到主编，近5年的时间里，您为*Light*的发展献力献策，我们也建立了更紧密的联系和更深厚的情谊。您是否还能回忆起最初与*Light*结缘的故事？您对*Light*期刊如何评价？又有哪些期待呢？**

Prof. Thévenaz: I was actually informed at an early stage about the *Light* project, maybe in 2009 or 2010, during a casual conversation with my old friend Rachel Won, Editor for *Nature Photonics*. I found it a brilliant idea since there was no real space for the publication of top quality applied photonics research. I thought at that moment that my next experimental breakthrough would be for that journal, and it turned out to be the case.

Later, I had strong cases of disagreement with editorial decisions (as author and reviewer!) and, instead of taking a break-up attitude, I found it more constructive to bring my support by joining the editorial team, because

I deeply believe in the potentiality of the journal and a little help may make the difference to reach excellence.

This can be maintained by never compromising on some principles: consider only breaking novelties with respect to the state-of-the-art, introducing entirely novel concepts, and a careful choice of independent and experienced reviewers.

Thévenaz教授：早在2009年（或2010年）与老朋友Rachel Won（*Nature Photonics*编辑）的一次闲聊中我就了解到了*Light*的创刊计划。我觉得这是一个非常棒的想法，因为当时的确还没有一本真正以发表光学领域重大应用研究为目标的高水平期刊。那个时候我就想，我的下一个突破性实验成果要发表在*Light*上，事实上我们也确实是这样做的。

之后，我作为作者和审稿人，都曾与编辑部在稿件决策问题上产生较大的分歧。与其抱着与*Light*

决裂的态度，我发现加入编辑团队来支持期刊的发展应该是更有建设性的解决方式。因为我深信*Light*的潜力，我的一些帮助也许有助于期刊成就卓越。

当然想要保持卓越就不能在一些原则问题上做丝毫的妥协与让步：只发表与最先进技术相关的研究工作或展现全新概念的创新突破，同时谨慎选择公正且经验丰富的审稿人。

Prof. Luc Thévenaz, President of the 26th International Conference on Optical Fiber Sensing (OFS, EPFL), visited the Journal booth of *Light: Science & Applications* (*Light*) and promoted the journal © Alain Herzog, EPFL

第26届光纤传感国际会议(OFS, EPFL)，大会主席Luc Thévenaz教授到访*Light*期刊展位，并宣传期刊© Alain Herzog, EPFL

6. As the leader of an outstanding scientific research team, how do you allocate time to your students and collaborators? You have cultivated many excellent scientific researchers in the optical fiber field. What do you think is the most important thing a mentor should offer to his/her students?

6. 作为一名杰出科研团队的领导者，您平时是怎样分配时间给您的学生和合作者的呢？您已经在光纤领域内培养了许多优秀的科研人才，您觉得好的指导老师最应给予学生的是什么？

Prof. Thévenaz: First you have to know that, according to the EPFL organizational scheme, my team is small: maximum of 5 students and 2 postdocs. It means I have time to meet and to have personal contact with all members of my team. My office room is next to the lab and the door is always opened, so my people can always come and I let them know they are my priority. We have no formal group meetings (or very occasionally), but we have the tradition to share the lunch together all sitting around the same table. It is the time to have informal discussions, related to our activities of course, but also to address all topics of discussion, even on social and political themes. This is a very enriching moment since the members of my teams come from very different origins in 4 continents. We debate about everything! I learned a lot about the different ways of thinking and of handling situations in different cultures.

I am convinced that a stimulating attitude is constitutive of a good mentor: you must help them when they face difficulty, suggesting a solution when needed and giving complementary knowledge. And never be too directive and give useless pressure, and always have a constructive and rewarding attitude. A stressed and depressed researcher never makes a good job and the absence of human warmth is definitely a killer for creativity.

Thévenaz教授：根据EPFL的组织架构要求，我的研究团队很小：最多5名学生和2名博士后。这意味着我有较为充分的时间和团队的每位成员接触。我的办公室就在实验室旁边，办公室的门也总是开着的，我的团队成员随时可以进来，而且我会以他们为先。我们没有正式的（或者极偶尔有）组会，但我们有同桌共进午餐的习惯。我们会利用这个时间进行一些非正式的讨论，当然会与我们的工

Prof. Luc Thévenaz and his team on a hiking excursion
Luc Thévenaz教授与团队成员登山郊游

作有关，但是也会讨论到其他各种话题，甚至涉及一些社会和政治议题。每当这时我都感到非常充实，因为我的团队成员来自4个大洲的不同地区，我们什么事都会讨论！在不同的文化中，我学到了很多不同的思维方式和解决问题的方法。

我相信，善于激励是一位好导师必要的素养。导师应该在学生面临困难时给予帮助，在必要时为学生提出解决方案，并教授他们所需要的知识。不要总是命令学生，也不要给学生施加无谓的压力，应该始终以积极和鼓励的态度来对待学生。要知道，一位压力大、情绪低落的研究人员永远做不出好的研究成果，关怀与温暖的缺失绝对是创造力的杀手。

7. We know you are used to visit China and also have cooperated with some Chinese Institutes, such as Shanghai Jiao Tong University, Beijing University for Post and Telecommunications, University of Electronic

Science and Technology of China, Huazhong University of Science and Technology, Jinan University, etc. Could you please talk something about your cooperative projects? What are your criteria and requirements for choosing overseas collaborations? If it's possible, would you like to consider to establish cooperation with our CIOMP?

7. 您经常到访中国，并与国内多所高校，包括上海交通大学、北京邮电大学、电子科技大学、华中科技大学及暨南大学等有学术合作。可否请您谈一谈这些合作项目？您基于什么样的原则标准来选择合作伙伴？如果有合适的机会，您是否愿意和中科院长春光机所合作？

Prof. Thévenaz: My team is involved in a certain number of projects with Chinese partners, some formal, some informal, but with a great variety of objectives and frameworks. Some are very prestigious such as the 111 projects with UESTC in Chengdu. Above all I appreciated hosting junior and even senior researchers through the CSC support: it was a very fertile way to collaborate and certainly an intensive experience for the visitors.

By principle, I am practicing science and sharing experiments indifferently with any human beings and my motivations are fully philanthropic, implicitly setting a limit to my collaborations: it must contribute to the universal welfare, and not only for local benefits or promotions, and even less for military purposes. So I have fundamentally no issue about setting a collaboration with CIOMP (I recently participated in a workshop during the visit of a delegation from CIOMP at EPFL) if this is something profitable for the entire mankind!

From a more general point of view, I find it quite fascinating to experience and to challenge our mutual cultural visions, which are more similar than expected at first glance. I always felt that our senses of friendship and commitment are quite comparable. And of course, I have a big admiration for the millennial culture of China, for the quick technical development of the country due to the exceptional qualities of hard-working among Chinese people, taking their personal development into their own hands. On the other hand, the limits set to curiosity do not favor a fertile ground for creativity. In general, knowing others having a different cultural background humbly puts a light on your own limits, but also on your qualities, this is an extremely enriching personal experience.

Thévenaz教授：我的团队参与了一定数量的中方项目，有正式的，也有非正式的，合作的目标和框架各不相同。其中包括一些知名的项目，如成都电子科技大学的111项目。而最为重要的，我很感谢能有机会接收由中国国家留学基金委等支持的访问学者，并与之合作，在我看来这是一种非常有益的合作方式，当然对访问者来说也是一次充实、有益的经历。

原则上，我从事科学研究并愿与所有人一起分享我的实验成果，但我的初衷一定是公益性的，这在无形中也为我的合作设置了一个条件：合作的目的须为普世性福祉做出贡献，而不仅仅是为了当地的发展利益，对军事目的的考量则更少。所以，如果是在对人类社会发展有益的事情上合作，我很乐意与中科院长春光机所携手（而且我最近也参加了CIOMP代表团在EPFL访问期间的一个研讨会）。

我发现体验和挑战不同国家与地区的文化视野非常有趣，其实我们的文化背景比最初预期的更为相似。我坚信我们对友谊和责任感有着同样的认知。我也非常钦佩中国悠久的历史文化，钦佩中国科技的快速发展，这些都是基于中国人民勤勉的卓越品质，紧紧掌握着自己的命运。从另一方面来

Prof. Luc Thévenaz visited CIOMP for "Light Conference" in 2019
Luc Thévenaz教授到访长春光机所参加2019年“Light Conference”

说，限制好奇心将不利于创造力的培养。总的来说，通过了解有着不同文化背景的人，能使人谦逊地明白自己的局限与优势，这是一种大有裨益的个人经历。

References

参考文献

[1] YANG F, GYGER F, THEVENAZ L, Intense Brillouin amplification in gas using hollow-core waveguides. Nature Photon,2020,14:700-708.

[2] DENISOV A, THEVENAZ L, SOTO M A1, Going beyond 1000000 resolved points in a Brillouin distributed fiber sensor: theoretical analysis and experimental demonstration. Light: Science & Applications, 2016,5:16074.

特别鸣谢

在此，对专访筹备过程中杨帆博士（EPFL）所给予的建议与帮助，蕉海菁、张冬娜［南方海洋科学与工程广东省实验室（珠海）］在材料整合等方面的工作致以衷心的感谢。

Professor Donna Strickland

编者按

一位副教授获得诺贝尔奖的情况实属罕见，更何况她还是历史上第三位获得诺贝尔物理学奖的女性科学家，但是唐娜·斯特里克兰博士却做到了。她的脸上永远挂着笑容，让人觉得亲切友善；她说话语速飞快，这是她思维敏捷的表现。唐娜·斯特里克兰不仅是学生眼中动手能力强、工作效率高的导师，而且在同行眼中也是一位积极向上的学者。她致力于参加各种学术组织和科学科普工作，她将科学视为“乐趣”。本期，著名的加拿大物理学家唐娜·斯特里克兰将做客“Light People”，与我们分享她的故事。

Challenging the Critical Power
激光“临界功率”的挑战者

Science Editor: Hui Wang 科学编辑 王卉

Editorial:

It is rare for an associate professor to win the Nobel Prize for Physics, even more so when she was only the third woman in history to do so, but Dr. Donna Strickland did just that. A permanent smile on her face expressing her friendliness, the fast–speaking speed showing her quick thinking, Dr. Strickland is not only a good tutor with strong hands–on ability and high working efficiency in the eyes of her students, but also an optimistic and diligent scholar in the eyes of her peers. Taking an active part in academic societies and the popularization of science, she regards scientific research as "fun". The famous Canadian physicist Donna Strickland talks exclusively to *Light: Science & Applications* (*Light*).

Light People

Biography: Donna Strickland is a professor in the Department of Physics and Astronomy at the University of Waterloo and one of the recipients of the Nobel Prize in Physics 2018 for developing chirped pulse amplification with Gérard Mourou, her PhD supervisor. Together they paved the way toward the most intense laser pulses ever created. Their research has several applications today in industry and medicine—including the cutting of a patient's cornea in laser eye surgery and the machining of small glass parts for use in cell phones.

Strickland was a research associate at the National Research Council Canada, a physicist at Lawrence Livermore National Laboratory, and a member of technical staff at Princeton University. She is a recipient of a Sloan Research Fellowship, a Premier's Research Excellence Award, and a Cottrell Scholar Award. She served as the president of the Optical Society (OSA) in 2013 and is a fellow of OSA, the Royal Society of Canada, and SPIE (International Society for Optics and Photonics). Strickland is an honorary fellow of the Canadian Academy of Engineering as well as the Institute of Physics. She received the Golden Plate Award from the Academy of Achievement and holds numerous honorary doctorates.

专家简介：唐娜 · 斯特里克兰，现任加拿大滑铁卢大学物理与天文学系教授，2018 年她和导师热拉尔 · 穆鲁因提出啁啾脉冲放大技术而获得 2018 年诺贝尔物理学奖。两个人共同为激光脉冲的发展铺平了道路，其研究成果广泛应用在工业和医学等领域，包括在激光眼科手术中切割患者的角膜以及为手机加工小玻璃部件等。唐娜·斯特里克兰曾是加拿大国家研究委员会的研究助理，劳伦斯利弗莫尔国家实验室物理学家，普林斯顿大学技术委员会委员。她曾荣获斯隆研究奖、总理研究卓越奖和科特雷尔学者奖。她曾担任2013年美国光学学会的主席，是美国光学学会、加拿大皇家学会和国际光学工程学会的会士。唐娜·斯特里克兰还是加拿大工程院和物理学院的荣誉院士，曾获得美国成就学院颁发的“金盘奖”，并拥有众多荣誉博士学位。

1. The Chirped Pulse Amplification (CPA) technology has revolutionized the development of laser intensity, which has increased by 6–7 orders of magnitude in less than 10 years. In your opinion, is there anything that might restrict the further rapid development of CPA?

1. 啁啾脉冲放大（CPA）技术的发明可以说彻

底改变了激光强度的发展，使其在不到10年的时间里增加了6–7个数量级。制约CPA进一步快速发展的瓶颈技术是什么？

Donna Strickland: The first few orders of magnitude were the easy ones as kilojoule level lasers already existed, but they could only amplify nanosecond long pulses. With the development of CPA along with the development of large gratings with a high damage threshold, kJ lasers could amplify picosecond pulses. Terawatt level lasers became petawatt level lasers. It has taken another 25 years to go one more magnitude and reach the 10 PW level. The power can still be increased but the progress might not be rapid. Raising the energy is costly as it requires larger-scale lasers. Using OPCPA, the pulse duration has been reduced to only a few periods of oscillation, so it won't be easy to reduce the pulse duration further at the same wavelengths. We should be able to increase the power of CPA or OPCPA systems by another order of magnitude. China already has plans to develop a 100 PW system. Increasing the intensity by orders of magnitude will probably require reducing the wavelength. The minimum focused beam diameter is limited to wavelength dimensions as is the shortest pulse duration. For each order of magnitude reduction in wavelength, the focused intensity can then be increased by three orders of magnitude. For this to happen, we need to either develop broadband laser amplifiers that can handle the shorter wavelengths or we have to be able to convert the near infrared pulses from conventional CPA systems to the ultraviolet with very good efficiency.

唐娜·斯特里克兰：由于千焦耳级激光器已经存在，所以最初的数量级比较容易达到，但它们仅能放大纳秒级脉冲。随着 CPA 技术以及具有高损伤阈值的大型光栅的发展，千焦耳级激光器开始能够放大皮秒脉冲。太瓦级激光器变成了拍瓦级激光器，在此基础上，它又经过了 25 年才增加一个数量级，达到 10 PW 级别。功率虽然能够增加，但进展可能不会很快。由于它需要更大规模的激光器，所以提高能量的成本会很高。使用 OPCPA 技术，将脉冲持续时间减少到只有几个振荡周期，这样在相同波长的条件下，进一步减小脉冲的持续时间会更难。我们应该能够将 CPA 和 OPCPA 系统的强度再提升一个数量级。中国已经计划开展研制 100 PW 系统。以数量级为尺度提升强度的关键是减小波长，并将最小聚焦光束直径和最短脉冲持续时间控制在波长范围内。波长每减少一个数量级，聚焦强度便增加 3 个数量级。因此为了实现该目标，我们需要开发能够处理更短波长的宽带激光放大器或者将传统 CPA 系统的近红外脉冲转换为更高效率的紫外脉冲。

2. I have learned that your group is also focusing on the research of fiber CPA of mid-infrared generation, what are the future potential applications of fiber CPA?

2. 据我所知，贵小组也在研究中红外波段的光纤CPA，能否介绍一下光纤CPA未来的潜在应用？

Donna Strickland: The role of fiber CPA is in applications requiring high average power as well as high peak power. This would apply to laser machining applications as well as sensing applications where the higher average power would lead to better signal to noise.

唐娜·斯特里克兰：光纤CPA的作用体现在需要高平均功率和高峰值功率的应用中，比如激光加工以及传感，在这些应用中，高平均功率能够实现更好的信噪比。

3. Would high power attosecond laser be another important topic for CPA? If yes, what might be the main challenge?

3. 高功率阿秒激光将是CPA的另一个重要课题

吗？如果是，主要的挑战是什么？

Donna Strickland: Attosecond pulses are necessarily out in the EUV region of the spectrum, where the period of oscillation is in the attosecond regime. As I have already answered this will most likely be what is needed to gain orders of magnitude higher intensity. We would need to combine attosecond technology with EUV and X-ray laser amplification technology. The gain medium will have to have an extremely wide gain bandwidth to maintain the attosecond duration after amplification and as far as I know, this has not yet been achieved. It is not clear whether stretching the pulse would be necessary as the gain media will most likely be a plasma and to achieve significant gain could require guiding in a plasma channel and so self-focusing may not be an issue. It could be similar to fiber CPA where the beam is confined in a channel, but nonlinearities would help increase the bandwidth and cancel gain narrowing.

唐娜·斯特里克兰：阿秒脉冲必定在光谱的极紫外（EUV）区域外，而此区域的振荡周期在阿秒范围内。正如我在前几个问题中所说，这可能是获得更高强度的数量级所需要的条件。我们需要将阿秒技术与EUV、X射线激光放大技术相结合。增益介质必须具有极宽的增益带宽，以此来保持放大后阿秒的持续时间，而据我所知，这还尚未实现。目前，我们还无法明确是否需要扩展脉冲，因为增益介质很可能是等离子体，而获得显著的增益可能需要在等离子体通道中进行引导，因此自聚焦可能不是问题。它类似于光纤CPA，光束被限制在一个通道中，但非线性会帮助增加带宽并消除增益变窄。

4. How do you think the femtosecond laser fabrication, perhaps one of the most important applications of the CPA technology, has led to the advancement of fabrication, especially for micro/nano fabrication of special materials?

4. 飞秒激光加工是CPA最重要的应用之一，您如何看待飞秒激光先进加工技术的发展，特别是用于特殊材料的微纳米加工？

Donna Strickland: Long pulse or continuous wave high power laser machining is a result of a thermal process through absorption of the light. This has two consequences, first, the spot diameter is affected by thermal migration, and secondly, the machining must start at the surface where the light is initially absorbed. With CPA, the machining is initiated by nonlinear ionization which occurs only in the focal region. The light does not need to be absorbed so it can machine transparent objects such as glass and the cornea of an eye. Also, the beam focus can occur inside the medium rather than on the surface allowing micro-modifications to the interior of the material. As an example, the refractive index can be changed and so waveguides can be written inside the glass.

唐娜·斯特里克兰：长脉冲或连续波大功率激光加工是通过吸收光进行热处理。它能够产生两个结果，首先是光斑的直径会受到热迁移的影响，其次，加工必须从最初吸收光的表面开始。使用CPA时，加工是在焦点区域发生的非线性电离时开始。在此过程中，它不需要吸收光，因此可以加工透明物体，例如玻璃和眼角膜。此外，光束聚焦可以发生在介质内部而不是表面，从而能够对材料内部进行微修改。例如，通过更改折射率，可以在玻璃内部制作波导。

5. What difficulties did you encounter in your research on CPA? How did you overcome them?

5. 您在研究CPA的过程中遇到哪些困难呢？您是如何克服它们的?

Donna Strickland: I don't remember too many difficulties. We damaged laser rods and had to wait for replacements. The lasers were old and so they quit working often. Luckily, we had a very good electronics person working with us and he was able to keep the lasers working. It was not my responsibility. The one time I remember getting unexpected results was when we first amplified the chirped pulse and looked at its spectrum. There was an oscillation in the signal that should not have been there based simply on the gain spectrum. It didn't take us too long to realize that the oscillation looked like it was caused by a 1 mm glass etalon. The quarter waveplate that was used along with a Pockel cell for switching the pulses in and out of the regenerative amplifier was indeed a 1 mm piece of glass. We had used the same combination of waveplate and Pockel cell in regenerative amplifiers for narrow spectra and had no problems because the oscillation period was broader than that spectrum. We realized the solution for CPA was to rotate the Pockel cell so that in its off position, it would act as a quarter waveplate and we

光·觉 100/101

could then remove the 1 mm quarter waveplate.

唐娜·斯特里克兰：我不记得有太多的困难。我记得我们损坏过激光管，不得不等待更换。由于激光器老化陈旧，所以经常罢工。幸运的是，我们的团队里有一位非常优秀的电子学专家，他总是能够让这些老化陈旧的激光器工作。我印象最深的是，当我们第一次放大啁啾脉冲并观察它的光谱时，我们得到了意想不到的结果。基于增益光谱的信号中出现了本不应该出现的振荡，没过多久我们意识到这个振荡有可能是由1毫米的玻璃校准器引起的。我们用于控制脉冲进出再生放大器的普克尔盒一起使用的四分之一波片实际上是一块1毫米的玻璃。我们曾经在窄谱的再生放大器中使用了相同的波片和普克尔盒组合方法，并取得成功，因为其振荡周期比该光谱更宽。我们意识到解决CPA技术的方法是旋转普克尔盒，当其处于关闭位置时能充当四分之一波片，然后我们也能够移除这个波片。

6. You have mentioned that when your Ph.D. supervisor, Dr. Gerard Mourou, said the CPA technique would make petawatt lasers possible, you thought that his remark was audacious, but he was correct. You also once said that the idea (CPA) was Mourou's, but you got to make it work. Do you think it is the ideal student-teacher relationship that the senior scientists should guide the young researchers by coming up with original ideas and showing them the research prospects, and the young should have the capability of understanding and turning the ideas into reality? How do you mentor your students?

6. 您曾提到当您的博士导师Gerard Mourou教授说CPA技术将使拍瓦激光成为可能时，您当时认为这种说法很大胆，但事实证明他是正确的。您也曾经说过做CPA是导师的想法，但您让想法变成现实？从这两个例子来看，我们可否这样理解您和导师的关系：导师提出原创思想并展示给您研究前景，而您有足够的悟性领会导师的想法并通过努力把理想变成现实？您认为这是理想的导师与学生的关系吗？您又是如何来指导学生的呢？

Donna Strickland: There are probably many ways for a supervisor and student to work together. New science is a result usually of an exchange of ideas. When students consider joining my group, we have a discussion of the ongoing projects. Since it is an experimental group, initially the new student's project will be limited to working with existing equipment. It is through many discussions together that we agree on what would be best to study for their thesis to work toward overall goals in the group.

唐娜·斯特里克兰：导师和学生可以通过多种方式在一起工作。新科学的产生往往是思想碰撞的成果。当学生考虑加入我的小组时，我们会讨论正在进行的项目。由于这是一个实验小组，所以学生的项目仅限于使用现有设备。通过多次讨论，我们确定最有益于其毕业论文的研究内容，并朝着小组的总体目标而努力。

7. You were not a "full" professor when you won the Nobel Prize in Physics because you had never applied for that rank, even though you were already an excellent and celebrated scientist, for instance, you are a former president of The Optical Society (OSA) and director of Academic Affairs for the Canadian Association of Physicists. So what's the reason that you did not apply for full professorship?

7. 当您获得诺贝尔物理学奖的时候，您还不是一名“正教授”，尽管您在学术生涯中表现很出色，如您曾担任美国光学学会主席和加拿大物理学家协会学术事务主任，但您此前并未申请过教授这个职称。您没有申请的原因是什么呢？

Donna Strickland: The title Full Professor means different things at different institutions. In my case, I simply didn't see sufficient benefit to being a Full Professor. As an Assistant Professor, you must apply for tenure and application to Associate Professor. It is your own decision to apply to become a Full Professor. I want to be clear that it was not because I was a woman. Except for me, all the female faculty in the department, with sufficient experience were Full Professors at the time. I had male colleagues suggest to me that I apply to become a Full Professor.

唐娜·斯特里克兰：在不同的机构，正教授的头衔有不同的含义。于我而言，我只是没有看到足够益处要成为一名正教授。作为助理教授，你必须申请终身教职并申请成为副教授。而正教授的申请则取决于个人意愿。我想说明一点，这并不是因为我是女性，因为除我之外，当时系里有经验的女教师都是正教授。正因如此，我的男同事们便建议我也申请成为正教授。

8. As the OSA's Vice President you visited the Changchun Institute of Optics, Fine Mechanics and Physics (CIOMP), Chinese Academy of Sciences, with an OSA delegation in 2012 when CIOMP celebrated its 60th birthday. What's your impression of CIOMP?

8. 2012 年是中国科学院长春光学精密机械与物理研究所（简称“长春光机所”）建所 60 周年，您作为美国光学学会（OSA）副主席随代表团访问长春光机所，您对长春光机所的印象如何?

Donna Strickland: I was very happy to be included as part of the OSA delegation at the 60th birthday of CIOMP. CIOMP is known as the "cradle of China's optics" and the celebration showcased the wonderful advancements that the institute has made over the 60 years. We were shown state-of-the-art research facilities and the tours

Group photo of CIOMP executives and the OSA delegation at CIOMP in 2012
2012年长春光机所领导与美国光学学会代表团合影

were given by very knowledgeable and professional students. OSA's partnership with this well-known institute has provided opportunities for members of our global community to interact and foster collaboration. In fact, OSA hosted IONS-Asia 3/Changchun at CIOMP, just ahead of CIOMP's 60th-anniversary celebration. OSA was then proud to partner with the Institute to host the second CIOMP-OSA Summer Session in 2013. OSA was honored to invite CIOMP to participate in OSA's 100th-anniversary celebration which took place in 2016.

唐娜·斯特里克兰：我很高兴能作为OSA代表团的一员在长春光机所建所60周年时进行访问交流。众所周知，长春光机所被誉为“中国光学的摇篮”，在庆祝的学术会议上，长春光机所展示了建所60年来的各项先进成果。我们参观了所内最先进的科研设施，与训练有素的学生交流。OSA与众所周知的长春光机所进行合作，为全球的业内同行们提供了交流与合作的机会。事实上，在此前夕，OSA与长春光机所联合举办的亚洲第三届IONS（International OSA Network of Students）会议在长春刚刚落幕。此外，OSA也非常荣幸于2013年与

Dr. Strickland with some founding members of the journal *Light: Science & Applications* and her OSA colleagues

唐娜·斯特里克兰博士及OSA代表与几位*Light*创刊成员的合影

长春光机所联合举办了暑期夏令营活动，并在2016年邀请了长春光机所的领导参加OSA成立100周年的庆祝活动。

The OSA delegation visited the Changchun New Industries Optoelectronics Technology Co., Ltd. based at CIOMP
OSA代表团访问长春新产业光电技术有限公司

9. What kind of mentality and quality should scientific researchers have? Should we stick with a research topic if its results continuously fall short of our expectations? (This question is chosen from a selection of questions from the CIOMP graduate students.)

9. 科研工作者应该具备怎样的心态和素质？若从事的课题成果长期达不到心理预期，还应该坚持吗？（该问题由长春光机所研究生提问）

Donna Strickland: I believe researchers need creativity to come up with new ways to investigate a scientific question. They certainly need patience because the answers to most scientific questions do not come easily. It can be difficult to know when to stop pursuing an idea. You have to stop when you cannot think of another avenue to find the solution to the problem. You will stick with problems longer if you think the answer is truly worth investigating.

唐娜·斯特里克兰：我认为科研工作者需要创造性地提出研究科学问题的新方法。作为科研工作者需要有耐心，因为大多数科学问题的答案都来之不易。何时停止对某一科学问题的追逐是一个未知命题。当你想不出其他方法来解决问题时，你不妨停下来重新思考。如果你依旧认为这个答案值得研究，那么你可以花费更多的时间来寻找答案。

10. The COVID-19 Pandemic has delayed or interrupted the research work of many academics. Most hard hit are young scholars who are at the start of their careers. What suggestions or advice would you give to these young people concerning their future careers? (This question is chosen from a selection of questions from the CIOMP graduate students.)

10. 受疫情影响，许多学者的研究工作都被迫推迟或中断，这对科研事业刚起步的年轻学者的影响非常大。在这样的特殊背景下，您对他们未来的职业发展有什么建议？（该问题由长春光机所研究生提问）

Donna Strickland: I agree that COVID-19 has put added stress on young researchers who need to show strong research output to get the next position. It is probably harder on the experimentalists than theorists because they not only have lost time in the lab doing the needed experiments, but there have been delays getting new equipment and servicing of equipment is being slowed because of travel restrictions. For all scientists, networking has become more difficult as conferences cannot be held in person. I am sure that senior researchers and managers are very aware of the situation and will take COVID-19 into account when reviewing the output of scientists. My advice would be to work on what you can accomplish during these times. Look for new ways to network with colleagues in your field. Most importantly try your best to stay positive.

唐娜·斯特里克兰：毫无疑问，新冠肺炎疫情给年轻的科研人员带来更多的压力，因为他们需要有重量级的科研成果来获得成长的机会。相较于理论人员，对实验人员的挑战难度可能更大，因为他们不仅失去了大量在实验室做实验的时间，而且由于目前物流行业暂停，导致购买新设备以及旧设备的维修也无法进行。对于科学家而言，由于无法亲临现场参加会议，建立合作网络变得更加困难。我相信，科学家和管理者对目前所面临的困境已经非常了解，在审查科研成果时也会考虑新冠疫情对此造成的影响。我的建议是在这段时间做力所能及的事情，寻找新方式在自己所属的科研领域与同行交流。最重要的是尽量保持积极的心态。

11. How do you choose your research topic? According to your interest or for its future application? Why?

11. 您如何选择您的研究课题？根据您的兴趣还是考虑其应用前景？为什么？

Donna Strickland: I choose based on interest mostly. Sometimes it is an opportunity. Sometimes the topic is brought to me. My group developed a two-color CPA laser system because I inherited a two-color, short-pulse laser. I wondered what I would do with this laser and of course, I would CPA it. That led me to look into what nonlinear optics experiments needed two colors. When the group had built the system, Dr. Leonid Losev who was working in Russia asked if he could come to Waterloo to use the laser to try out his idea to increase the efficiency of a nonlinear optical effect known as multi-frequency Raman generation. That is how I started studying multi-frequency Raman generation. Then my graduate student noticed that there were extra peaks between the multiple Raman peaks and together we wondered what they were so the group started investigating these extra peaks just because we wanted to know the answer. I am also championing the Global Environmental Measurement and Monitoring initiative with OSA. Since I also work on mid-infrared generation I will look to see if it can be applied to environmental sensing. I am open to new avenues of research from a number of different sources.

唐娜·斯特里克兰：我是根据自己的兴趣来选择研究课题。当然也不排除某种机缘巧合会让我与某个研究课题相遇。比如我知道研究非线性光学实验需要两种颜色，而我此前也一直研究双色短脉冲激光器，所以我想尝试一下看看，用这种双色短脉冲激光与CPA技术如何结合，后来我的研究小组成功研制开发了一个双色CPA激光系统。我的研究小组建成这个系统后，在俄罗斯工作的Leonid Losev博士问我，他是否可以尝试一下他的想法，使用MRG来提高非线性光学效应的效率。正因如此，我开始研究MRG。我的学生发现在多个拉曼峰之间还存在其他的峰。出于好奇，我们团队开始研究产生这些额外峰的原因。此外，我们与美国光学学会一起开展全球环境测量与监测的倡议行动。由于我也从事中红外的研究工作，因此，我想尝试是否可以将它用于环境传感。我对来自各个渠道的新研究方法均持开放态度。

12. You are reputed to be a great teacher. I heard once your student accidentally broke an infrared mirror but you only said "don't worry! It's common in the laboratory". Then you spent $2,000 on a new one. Another story was also from a former student of yours who said that he received feedback within three days of submitting his graduation thesis to you, so his graduation was very smooth. What qualities do you think a good mentor should have?

12. 您平时对学生很宽容，有一次您的学生不小心摔坏了组里的红外镜，没想到您只说了句“没事，实验室里常有的事”，然后花了$2,000买了个新的。您对学生的研究非常认真，曾经有您的学生说他提交给您的毕业论文，3天就收到了反馈意见，所以毕业的时候很顺利。请问您认为一位好的导师应该具备哪些素质呢？

Donna Strickland: Well, I don't know who you have

been talking to. Thank you for finding the students who had nice things to say. I would think most experimental supervisors would understand equipment being broken as long as the student doesn't make a habit of it. I certainly broke things along the way and my supervisors were not angry with me, so I would have no business being angry with my students. I do think it is the duty of the supervisor to provide feedback in a timely manner. I think the supervisor is there to be encouraging for the student and mostly to help the student to learn the field and help solve the scientific and technical problems and teach them how to ask the correct questions.

唐娜·斯特里克兰：我不知道您是从哪里听说的，但是非常感谢您找到对我有如此高评价的学生。只要学生不是出于本意破坏设备，而是由于意外，我想大多数的导师都能够理解。当然同样的事情也曾经发生在我的身上，当时我的导师也没有生气，所以我也不会因此动怒去责备学生。我认为对学生的论文做到及时反馈是身为一名导师的责任。同时，我也认为作为导师就应该鼓励学生并且尽可能地帮助学生解决科学和技术问题，教他们如何去提出正确的问题。

13. You are a senior member or chairman of many national and international academic organizations. How has this affected your academic work?

13. 您在许多国内、国际学术组织工作并担任要职，这对您的学术工作有何影响？

Donna Strickland: First, I would say that the organizations benefit researchers and so that it is in our interest to support the organizations. I have also found that volunteering with organizations gives you a much broader understanding of your field. It also helps you make connections not only with scientists outside your research field, but also with government and society in general. This broad networking opens avenues that you might not have otherwise considered.

唐娜·斯特里克兰：首先，我想说，参与各类学术组织对科研人员是大有裨益的。所以我们要支持这些学术组织的工作。从我的亲身经历来说，我发现在这些学术组织中做志愿者让我对自己从事的研究领域有了更广泛、更深层次的了解。它不仅帮助我与其他领域的科学家建立联系，而且也帮助我与政府、社会建立联系。如此广泛的社交网络会带给你意想不到的结果。

14. You said you have great faith in lasers, but no one's putting one near your eye. Why is that? Is it a kind of occupational psychology?

14. 您说您对激光很有信心，但没人能把它放在您眼睛附近。为什么？我们是否可以认为这是一种职业心理？

Donna Strickland: I am a very squeamish person. I would not have surgery unless absolutely necessary. I would simply rather wear glasses than have surgery. If I had to have surgery, then I think a laser is an excellent surgical tool.

唐娜·斯特里克兰：我是一个非常敏感的人。除非绝对需要，否则我是不会做激光手术的。我宁愿戴眼镜也不愿意做手术。但是如果非要做手术，我觉得激光会是一个非常好的手术工具。

15. Both you and your daughter are engaged in scientific research. Do you think it is a natural love of science or family influence?

15. 您和您的女儿都从事科研工作，您觉得她是天生对科学充满热爱还是受家庭影响呢？

Donna Strickland: I suppose it is some of both.

Both my husband and I are scientists in the same field so our children would have grown up listening to us discuss our work. She would be more aware of science as a career. She was also a good math and science student and inherently inquisitive, so it was also a natural choice for her.

唐娜·斯特里克兰：我想这两种因素或多或少都会有吧。我和我的丈夫是同一领域的科学家。所以我们的孩子在成长的过程中经常会听到我们谈论工作，从而使她更加了解科学家这一职业。她在理工科方面成绩突出，天生好奇心强，因此对于她选择科研作为自己的事业，可能也是水到渠成的事。

16. You once said in an interview that you were raised by a strong woman who would follow her heart not listening to anybody else. How do you rate this quality?

16. 您曾经在一次采访中说过，您是由一个内心强大的女人抚养长大的，她只会跟随自己的心而不会听从任何人。您如何看待这种性格?

Donna Strickland: I think we need confidence in ourselves and I think my mother helped instill confidence in me. I don't mean that you should not listen to other people's points of view, but when it comes to making decisions about your own life, you know better than anyone what you want to do.

唐娜·斯特里克兰：人是需要自信的。我认为我的母亲帮助我树立了自信心。自信并不意味着完全不听取别人的意见，它仅表示当你需要对自己的生活作出决定时，你比任何人都清楚什么是你自己想要的。

17. Have you heard of the journal *Light: Science & Applications* ? What do you think of it?

17. 您听说过*Light：Science & Applications*期刊吗？您如何评价？

Donna Strickland: Yes, of course. I have heard of *Light: Science & Applications*. The journal's contributions to the dissemination of advancements in this field of research support the scientific community.

唐娜·斯特里克兰：我当然听说过《光：科学与应用》。这是一本服务科研，专注于发表光学科研领域最新成就和进展的期刊。

18. How do you choose which journals to submit your articles to?

18. 您是如何选择投稿何种期刊的？

Donna Strickland: As you have noted, I have been the president of OSA: The Optical Society, which publishes

19 high-quality, peer-reviewed journals in its publishing portfolio, which also serve the full breadth of the optics and photonics community. I will always be partial to OSA journals, however, I usually let the students decide where they want to submit their papers.

Prof. Strickland, then OSA President with Ms. Hui Wang, Science Editor for this interview and one of the journal's founding members, at an international conference at the University of Rochester in 2013
2013年时任OSA主席的唐娜·斯特里克兰教授与*Light*创刊成员、科学编辑王卉在美国罗切斯特大学举办的国际会议上合影

唐娜·斯特里克兰：正如您所知，我曾担任过OSA的主席，OSA出版19种具有高质量且同行评议

的期刊，它服务于整个光学和光电子领域。我非常喜欢向OSA投稿，但是我也会让我的学生自行选择向哪个期刊投稿。

Chennupati Jagadish

编者按

2018年一部印度电影《起跑线》将大众的视线聚焦到了印度的教育问题上，它在反映父母竭力为子女争取教育资源，不想让孩子输在起跑线的同时，也侧面反映了底层人民争取平等教育资源的艰辛。回归现实，Chennupati Jagadish教授在南半球的一端也在努力为包括印度在内的发展中国家的优秀青年人才打开通向世界的窗口。他是澳大利亚国立大学电子材料工程系杰出教授和澳大利亚桂冠学者（Laureate Fellow），澳大利亚科学院院长和澳大利亚工程院院士。2018年因他对纳米科学与纳米技术发展所做的贡献，被授予联合国教科文组织奖。他身兼多职、获奖无数，却追求不忘初心，坚守科研之路，一切始于心，终于心。Jagadish教授是如何取得今天的成绩？他成立基金的初心是什么？他对年轻学者有什么建议？带着一系列问题，今天我们将探寻Jagadish教授一路成长的故事。

Breaking Boundaries, Opening Windows

冲破“种族”“材料”桎梏，开启“人才”“创新”窗口

Science Editor: Hui Wang 科学编辑 王卉

Editorial:

In 2018, the Indian film *Starting Line* focused the public's attention on the issue of education in India. It depicted the length some Indian parents were willing to go to secure educational resources for their children, as well as the difficulties faced by those disadvantaged in society in their fight for equal educational opportunities. In reality, many brilliant young Indian talents have been able to study in Australia through a fund set up by Prof. Chennupati Jagadish, a Distinguished Professor of the Australian National University. Prof. Jagadish is a Fellow of the Australian Academy of Science and the Australian Academy of Technological Sciences and Engineering. In 2018 he was awarded a UNESCO Prize for his contribution to the development of nanoscience and nanotechnology. He holds many positions, and has won numerous awards. What started Prof. Jagadish on his scientific research career? How did he become the respected scientist he is today? What was his intention in setting up the educational fund for students from developing countries? What advice does he have for young researchers? Here are the answers from Prof. Jagadish.

Light People

Biography: Prof. Jagadish is a Distinguished Professor of the Australian National University. He is serving as Editor-in-Chief (EIC) of *Applied Physics Reviews* and also served as EIC of *Progress in Quantum Electronics*. His research interests include compound semiconductor, optoelectronics, nanotechnology, photovoltaics and neurotechnology. He is a Fellow of the Australian Academy of Science and the Australian Academy of Technological Sciences and Engineering, a Fellow of IEEE, APS, OSA, SPIE, AAAS, TWAS, etc., a Foreign Member of the US National Academy of Engineering, a Foreign Fellow of the Indian National

Science Academy and Indian National Academy of Engineering.

He has been awarded the Australian Federation Fellowship (2004-2009) and the Australian Laureate Fellowship (2009-2014) by the Australian Research Council. He has received many awards, including The Quantum Device Award (ISCS, 2010), IEEE Pioneer in Nanotechnology Award (2015), IEEE Photonics Society Engineering Achievement Award (2015), Distinguished Fellow of the Chinese Academy of Sciences President's International Fellowship Initiative (2016), Welker Award from ISCS (2017) and Lyle Medal from the Australian Academy of Science (2019).

专家简介：Chennupati Jagadish教授是澳大利亚国立大学杰出教授。目前担任《应用物理评论》以及《量子电子学进展》期刊主编。研究方向包括化合物半导体、光电子器件、纳米技术、光伏、神经科学和神经技术。Chennupati Jagadish教授是澳大利亚科学院和澳大利亚工程院院士，IEEE（国际电子电气工程师学会），APS（美国物理学会），OSA（美国光学学会），SPIE（国际光学工程学会），AAAS（美国科学促进会），TWAS（发展中国家科学院）等学会的会士（Fellow），美国国家发明家科学院（NAI）会士（Fellow）以及印度科学院、印度国家工程院名誉院士。

Chennupati Jagadish教授于2004年—2009年荣获澳大利亚联邦奖学金并被澳大利亚研究理事会授予澳大利亚桂冠学者（Laureate Fellow）的荣誉称号。他获奖无数，包括2010年量子器件奖、2015年IEEE纳米技术先锋奖和光子学社会工程成就奖、2016年中科院国际人才计划—国际杰出学者奖、2017年ISCS的Welker 奖以及2019年AVS的纳米技术奖等。

1. You have cooperated with the University of Oxford and others to develop a new miniature device, which

can provide safe and high-definition medical imaging technology through the use of terahertz radiation to help doctors identify and treat deadly cancers as early as possible. Can you tell us the advantages of this device? What other issues need to be resolved? How far is it from clinical application?

1. 您与英国牛津大学等机构合作研发了一款新式微型设备，通过使用太赫兹辐射可进一步应用于安全且高清的医疗影像技术，从而帮助医生尽早识别致命癌症，并采取治疗。您能介绍一下这个设备的优势吗？目前还有哪些问题需要解决？离临床应用还有多远？

Prof. Jagadish: Our development of semiconductor nanowire based THz detectors which are sensitive to polarization, phase and amplitude has the potential to make a significant impact in the field. Many of the detectors are amplitude sensitive but not phase sensitive.

We have developed both phase and amplitude sensitive broad bandwidth THz detectors with Oxford colleagues as part of Ms. Kun Peng's PhD project. With these detectors, you have to do at least two measurements to get the polarization information while rotating the detector by 90 degrees. This is time consuming and complex to do realignment etc. Our new device, allows us to measure both x-and y-polarization state due to orthogonal arrangement of nanowires. This work is a collaborative effort involving Oxford, Strathclyde and Australian National University (ANU). The compact nature of these detectors will allow us to be able to pack multiple detectors within the THz beam spot providing high resolution THz images. In order to use these detectors in biomedical imaging applications, arrays of detectors need to be fabricated with appropriate electronics which is the next step. Hopefully industry will be interested in these detectors.

Jagadish教授：我们开发的基于半导体纳米线的太赫兹检测器可能在不久的将来在该领域产生重大影响。相比大多数检测器只对振幅敏感，而对相位不敏感的情况，太赫兹检测器实现了对偏振、相位和振幅均敏感。作为彭坤女士博士项目的一部分，我们与牛津大学的同事一起研发了同时对相位和振幅均敏感的宽带太赫兹检测器。在使用过程中，需要将检测器旋转90度，至少要进行两次测量才能获得偏振信息。这非常耗时，而且重新对准等操作步骤也非常复杂。它使我们能够测量因纳米线正交排列而产生的x和y偏振状态。这项工作是在牛津大学、斯特拉斯克莱德大学和澳大利亚国立大学（ANU）科研人员的共同努力之下完成的。宽带太赫兹检测器的紧凑性使我们能够在太赫兹束斑内封装多个探测器，从而提供高分辨率太赫兹图像。为了使宽带太赫兹检测器在生物医学成像领域得到更加广泛的应用，下一步我们计划使用适当的电子设备制造探测器阵列。希望未来这项成果能够引起工业界的关注。

2. As a leading expert on III-V nanomaterials and devices, what do you think are the most significant scientific and technological challenges in this field? What will be the most promising emerging or future technologies based on the III-Vs?

2. 作为III–V纳米材料和器件领域的权威专家，您认为在该领域最大的科技挑战是什么？在此基础上最有前途的新兴技术或未来技术是什么？

Prof. Jagadish: III-V semiconductor based devices are widely used in electronics, optoelectronics and communication systems, CD/DVD players, LED lighting, high efficiency solar cells etc. In terms of the future, opportunities are there to develop single photon sources and detectors for quantum communications applications, flexible electronic and optoelectronic devices including flexible solar cells, nonlinear optics and meta-optical systems, nanolasers and detectors for miniaturized optical systems for holography, augmented reality, LiFi, LIDAR etc.

Jagadish教授：基于III–V半导体的器件已经被广泛地应用于电子、光电子和通信系统、CD/DVD播放器、LED照明和高效太阳能电池等。未来有突破性的方向将会出现在用于量子通信的单光子光源和探测器，包括柔性太阳能电池，非线性光学和超光学系统的柔性电子和光电设备，用于全息小型光学系统的纳米激光和探测器、可见光通信和激光雷达等。

3. You have been engaged for years in the research of III-V compound semiconductor materials and devices, and have made many achievements and won many important international academic awards, including the IEEE Third Millennium Medal in 2000, the Quantum Device Award in 2010, Electronics and Photonics Division Award of the Electrochemical Society in 2012

and UNESCO Medal in 2018. Would you like to tell us the key to good scientific research according to your own experience?

3. 您长期从事 III–V 族化合物半导体材料与器件的研究，并取得了许多国际领先的卓越学术成就，获得了多项国际重要学术奖，包括 2000 年的 IEEE 千禧年奖章（Third Millennium Medal），2010 年的量子器件奖（Quantum Device Award），2012 年电化学学会的电子与光子学奖（Electronics and Photonics Division Award）和 2018 年联合国教科文组织奖等，请您结合自身的经历，谈谈做好科研的关键是什么？

Prof. Jagadish: The important thing is to choose something you are passionate about. Once you are enjoying what you are doing, good things happen. Choosing difficult scientific problems of global interest is important. Once we solve the problem, it will have a global impact. Good students and post-docs are critical to any research. I have been fortunate that I had many wonderful students and post-docs during my past 30+ years at the ANU and many of them are from China. Collaborations are also absolutely critical. We cannot be expert in everything. By focusing on our expertise and by collaborating with other experts who can bring complementary expertise can allow us solve scientific problems in a multi-pronged approach. I have also had wonderful collaborators from 30+ countries during my career including many from China. As I first visited China in 1996 and I have seen phenomenal developments in science and technology and the society during the past 25+ years in China. Good team makes great science happen. My job is to inspire them, motivate them and recognize their contributions.

Jagadish教授：我认为最重要的是一定要选择自己真正热爱的事业。一旦你很享受自己所做的工作，那么好运便会不期而至。选择引起全球广泛关注的科学难题具有重要的意义，因为一旦你解决了这项难题，那么它将产生全球性的影响。无论做什么性质的研究工作，优秀的学生和博士后都是至关重要的。令我感到欣慰的是，过去30多年来，我在澳大利亚国立大学拥有许多优秀的学生和博士后，他们中有许多来自中国。此外，我认为懂得相互合作也同样重要。我们不可能在所有事情上都是专家。专注于我们的工作并与其他能够带来专业互补的专家进行合作，将使我们多渠道地解决科学问题。回顾我的职业生涯，我曾与来自30多个国家和地区的专家合作过，其中包括许多优秀的中方专家。1996年我第一次赴中国访问，当我看到过去25年来中国在科学技术与社会发展上取得的成就，我备感震惊。优秀的团队可以成就伟大的科学。我的工作就是激励他们，鼓励他们并认可他们对科学所做的贡献。

4. You have been elected fellow of 12 professional

societies and the scientific communities, for instance the Institute of Electrical and Electronics Engineers (IEEE), the American Physical Society (APS), the Materials Research Society (MRS), and the Optical Society (OSA). You have been involved in the work and activities, and have made great contributions. I wonder if you could tell us the benefits of these experiences to your scientific research career?

4. 作为国际电子电气工程师学会（IEEE）、美国物理学会（APS）、美国材料学会（MRS）、美国光学学会（OSA）等 12 个国际重要专业学会和科学团体的会士（Fellow），您参与了这些学会和科学团体的工作和活动并为其做出了巨大贡献，请问这些经历对您的科研事业有哪些助益？

Prof. Jagadish: Being involved in professional societies has allowed me to be able to work with colleagues from various parts of the world in promoting science and technology, mentoring young scientists and serving the community. I found many of my collaborators through interactions in the professional societies. Many of the friends I made through being involved in serving professional societies have been great supporters of our research. The pleasure of giving is much more immense than receiving. I have enjoyed giving something back to the community by being involved in various roles in professional societies. Professional societies bring people together to exchange ideas, knowledge and develop networks and nurture the discipline and people working in the field.

Jagadish教授：参与这些专业学会给我提供了一个与世界各地同行一起工作的机会，能够促进科学技术的发展，指导年轻科学家并服务社会。在参与的过程中，我不仅找到了合作伙伴，也结交了许多新朋友，他们一直是我学术道路上的支持者。给予远比得到更快乐。我很乐意在专业学会中扮演各种角色来回馈社会。专业学会能够将人们聚集在一起，彼此相互沟通，交流想法和专业知识，扩大社交网络，培养专业人士，促进学科发展。

5. You have initiated a fund to help Indian students to study in Australia. What prompted you to set up this fund? How does it work? How many students have been supported so far?

5. 您发起成立了一个基金会，主要是帮助来澳大利亚留学的印度学生，请问是什么让您想到要成立这个基金会呢？该基金会是如何运转的？到目前为止一共资助了多少名学生呢？

Prof. Jagadish: First of all, I want you to know that the fund is open to students and young scientists from developing countries, not just from India, though many of the students come from India. Whenever we get requests from students from Europe to visit us for

3-6 months, we are happy to host them as they come with their financial support. However, whenever we get requests from developing countries, we say no to them as they need financial support and we do not have funding to support them. China is an exception as it has lots of programs to support students to visit international laboratories through scholarships such as the Visiting Student Scholarship by China Scholarships Council and also Chinese Academy of Sciences (CAS) and other universities have funding to support these visits. I have been feeling guilty as having started my life in a small village in India, without others giving me the opportunity I wouldn't be where I am today. Two of my high school teachers and my parents have supported me to complete my high school and further studies. My wife Vidya and I have decided to create an Endowment at the ANU to support students and young scientists from developing countries. ANU has kindly agreed to provide matching funding to support our donations. The fund was launched in 2015 with our own donations and ANU's support. We started by giving 4 scholarships to Bachelor degree or Master degree students to visit ANU to spend their summer (10-12 weeks) to gain research experience, showcase their abilities and develop their networks. We also give 1 young scientist fellowship per year. So far students and young scientists have come from India, Indonesia and Malaysia. Based on the success of our Endowment, ANU also started future research talents program to support students from India and Indonesia to visit ANU and work with my colleagues in various parts of the University. Our aim is to create an Endowment of AU$ 1 Million so that this will support up to 6 students and 1 young scientist every year in perpetuity. Every year we donate some funds to ANU and ANU matches our donation. Again this is all part of giving something back to the community and supporting the younger generation.

Jagadish教授：首先，我向您解释一下，我发起的这个基金会对所有发展中国家的学生和青年科学家都是开放的，而不仅针对印度，尽管这其中有很多学生来自印度。每当我们收到欧洲学生申请来澳访问3~6个月时，我们都会非常高兴，因为他们有经费支持。但是，当我们收到发展中国家学生的来访申请时，我们不得不对他们说“不”，因为他们需要经费支持，但我们却无法提供资助。中国是一个例外，因为中国有许多奖学金项目来资助学生赴国外访问国际实验室，例如中国国家留学基金委员会奖学金、中国科学院和其他大学的奖学金资助项目等。我从小在印度的农村生活，这让我感到很自卑，如果不是我的父母和两位高中老师资助我完成学业，我不可能有今天这样的成绩。正因如此，我和我的妻子Vidya决定在澳大利亚国立大学成立捐赠基金会，以资助发展中国家的学生和青年科学家。澳大利亚国立大学非常赞成我们的提议，并主动提出提供匹配资金来支持我们的基金会。在我们的捐赠和澳大利亚国立大学的共同努力下，基金会于

2015年正式启动。开始时，基金会资助了4名本科生和研究生在暑假（10~12周）期间访问澳大利亚国立大学来获取研究经验，展示其科研能力并建立社交网络。此外，我们每年还有一个青年科学家奖学金的名额。成立至今基金会已经资助了来自印度、印度尼西亚和马来西亚众多学生和青年学者。基于此基金会的成功，澳大利亚国立大学还启动了未来科研人才项目，用以资助印度和印度尼西亚的学生来访并与校内各部门人员一起工作。我们的目标是让基金会的资产总额达到100万澳元，如此一来我们便能够每年资助6个学生和1名青年科学家赴澳深造学习。每年我们都会向澳大利亚国立大学捐赠资金，而大学也会向我们匹配资金支持。当然，我们所做的这些都是为了回馈社会，支持年轻一代的发展。

6. As a distinguished scientist of the CAS President's International Fellowship Initiative (PIFI), you have visited Changchun Institute of Optics, Fine Mechanics and Physics (CIOMP) and later received a visiting

scholar from CIOMP to work with your team in ANU. What is your impression of CIOMP?

6. 您作为中科院杰出访问学者访问中科院长春光学精密机械与物理研究所（简称“长春光机所”），并接受长春光机所的访问学者到您的团队交流工作，请问您对长春光机所及其科研人员的印象如何？

Prof. Jagadish visited CIOMP as a CAS PIFI Distinguished Scientist in 2016
2016年Jagadish教授作为中科院PIFI国际杰出学者到长春光机所访问交流

Prof. Jagadish's group with Dr. Lijie Wang from CIOMP as a Visiting Scholar in ANU in 2019
2019年长春光机所汪丽杰博士在澳大利亚国立大学Jagadish教授研究组作访问学者

Prof. Jagadish: I have enjoyed my visit to CIOMP. I was very impressed with CIOMP and its research activities. The scales of optics activities are very impressive. From nanoscale optics to huge optics for telescopes and other applications, it is truly admirable. The ability of CIOMP to cover from fundamental science and industry applications to creating industries is excellent and I wish continued success to CIOMP in its endeavors.

Jagadish教授：我非常享受访问长春光机所的整个过程。长春光机所在光学领域的研究成果让我印象非常深刻。从纳米光学到用于望远镜和其他大型设备应用的光学研究，着实令人钦佩。此外，长春光机所在基础研究、工程应用以及产业创新的能力也同样非常出色，我希望长春光机所能够不断突破自身，取得更多优异的成绩。

7. You served as an editor of *Light: Science & Applications* (*Light*) until the beginning of 2020. Could you please talk about your reasons for joining and quitting?

7. 您曾接受邀请担任*Light: Science & Applications*（*Light*）期刊编委且于2020年初卸任，能谈谈您加入和退出的原因么?

The Science and Technology Counselor Mr. Qiang Wang (third from right) of the Chinese Embassy in Australia met with Prof. Jagadish and two founding members of *Light*

中国驻澳大利亚科技参赞王强等会见Jagadish教授及两名*Light*创刊成员

Prof. Jagadish: It was a pleasure and honor for me to serve as an Editor of *Light* and I enjoyed working with the *Light* team. In January 2020 I took up the role of Editor-in-Chief of *Applied Physics Reviews*. My contract for this position will not allow me to be an Editor of other journals. In view of this, I had to step down from my role as an Editor of *Light*. I wish continued success to *Light*.

Jagadish教授：对我来说担任*Light*期刊编委是一种荣幸，我很高兴与期刊团队一起工作。2020年1月我开始担任《应用物理评论》的主编。由于这个岗位不允许我担任其他期刊的编委。鉴于此，我不得不辞去*Light*编委的职务。在这里衷心祝愿*Light*未来能够成功永驻。

8. Do you have any advice for young researchers about how to do research well?

8. 对于如何做好科研工作，您能给年轻的学者们提些建议吗？

Prof. Jagadish: The most important thing in life is self-belief and developing a can-do, positive attitude. Choosing something they are passionate about and working hard and smart to achieve their goals. Perseverance and persistence are important in life. We fail many times, but determination to succeed will allow one to keep going and to get over the failures. Be kind and generous to others and develop good communication skills (both oral and written) and ability to work as part of a team is important in life. Work-life balance is important and also one needs to look after their health. Health is the most important thing in life, but we ignore it and only realize its importance once we lose it. Everything is possible in life. One sets a goal, works smart and hard and persists with the goal despite the hurdles. Sky is the limit! Keep trying and never give up! Good luck!

Jagadish教授：最重要的是养成自信和“我能做”的积极态度。选择自己热爱的事情，努力工作并运用智慧来实现目标。毅力和坚持在生活中也很重要。我们也许会失败很多次，但成功的决心将会激励我们不断前进并克服困难。要记住，对他人友善和慷慨，要培养良好的沟通技巧（包括口头和书面），要培养团队能力。工作与生活之间的平衡也很重要。健康是人生命中最重要的事情，但是我们却经常忽略它，只有在失去时才意识到它的重要性，所以要时刻关注自身的健康情况。生活中一切皆有可能，只要设定了目标，你只管努力，用智慧克服重重阻碍，用汗水去实现目标。你们前途无量！请不断努力，永不放弃！祝你们好运！

Prof. Jagadish with Ms. Hui Wang, Science Editor for this interview, in his office when Ms. Wang visited his laboratory in 2016

2016年科学编辑王卉女士参观Jagadish教授实验室时合影

（摄于Jagadish教授办公室）

Professor Lin Li

编者按

如何应对气候变化以及如何减缓甚至扭转气候变化可能是21世纪最热门的科学领域。你是否知道一名华人科学家成功实现了柴油汽车 PM2.5 减排 35%—40%，为控制气候变化做出了贡献？这位专家就是英国皇家工程院院士、英国曼彻斯特大学激光加工中心创始人——李琳。当然这仅仅是李琳教授科研成就中的冰山一角，作为超分辨率微球放大镜的先驱，他的团队与新加坡同事合作，突破了光学显微成像中的光学衍射极限，实现了对生物病毒的无干扰实时观测，他用激光合成新纳米材料，可以在杀死耐药菌的同时对多种人体细胞无害，从而推动了相关研究领域的发展与突破。本期，我们非常荣幸邀请到了李琳教授接受采访。他将从自身经历出发，回忆多年科研从业经历，畅谈未来激光材料加工发展的趋势。

Creating Future Materials through Laser Processing
深耕激光加工，笃行智库赋能

Special Guest: Heng Gu Science Editor: Hui Wang
特邀嘉宾 顾衡 科学编辑 王卉

Editorial:

How to deal with climate change, how to mitigate or even reverse it, maybe the hottest scientific topic of the 21st century. Do you know that a Chinese scientist and his team contributed to climate change control by reducing PM2.5 in diesel car exhaust by 35–40%? That scientist is Prof. Lin Li, a Fellow of the Royal Academy of Engineering and founder of the Laser Processing Research Centre at The University of Manchester, United Kingdom. Of course, this is only one example of Prof. Li's scientific achievements. As a pioneer of microsphere super–resolution lens, his team, in collaboration with Singapore colleagues, broke the optical diffraction limit in optical microscopic imaging, making real–time observation of biological viruses without interference possible. He also used lasers to synthesize new nanomaterials which kill drug–resistant bacteria while remaining harmless to healthy human cells, which led to the development and breakthrough of related research fields. We are much honored to have Prof. Lin Li for an exclusive interview in which he recalls his years of scientific research experience and talks about the future development trend of laser material processing.

Light People

Biography: Professor Lin Li is Director of Laser Processing Research Centre at The University of Manchester, UK. He served as President of Laser Institute of America (2016), President of International Academy of Photonics and Laser Engineering (2013-2015), and President of Association of Industrial Laser Users (AILU-2017-2019).

He is an elected Fellow of Royal Academy of Engineering (FREng), Fellow of Laser Institute of America (LIA), Fellow of International Academy of Production Engineering (CIRP), Fellow of International

Academy of Photonics and Laser Engineering (IAPLE), and Fellow of Institute of Engineering and Technology (IET). He is an author and co-author of over 400 publications in peer-reviewed journals related to laser-based manufacturing and an inventor or co-inventor of more than 60 patents. He received Sir Frank Whittle Medal from the Royal Academy of Engineering in 2013 for innovative manufacturing that has generated significant economic impacts. In 2014 he received Wolfson Research Merit Award from the Royal Society for his research on laser nano-fabrication and nano-imaging and received the Researcher of the Year medal from The University of Manchester in 2014. He received the Arthur Schawlow award from Laser Institute of America in 2019 for distinguished achievements in laser-based manufacturing, and the Donald Julius Groen Prize, and the Arthur Charles Main Award from the Institution of Mechanical Engineers for leadership in additive manufacturing.

He obtained a BSc degree in Control Engineering from Dalian University of Technology (China) in 1982 and a Ph.D. degree in Laser Engineering from Imperial College London (UK) in 1989. He worked at The University of Liverpool (UK) between 1988 and 1994 as a Research Associate and Research Fellow in laser material processing and became a Lecturer in Manufacturing at The University of Manchester Institute of Science and Technology (UMIST), UK, and was promoted to a Full Professor in Laser Engineering in 2000. He served as the Deputy Head of School of Mechanical, Aerospace and Civil Engineering at The University of Manchester during 2009-2013 and served as the Associate Dean of Faculty of Science and Engineering at The University of Manchester during 2015-2020.

专家简介：李琳教授是英国曼彻斯特大学激光加工研究中心主任，曾任美国激光学会主席（2016 年）、国际光电子与激光工程学会主席（2013—2015 年）、英国工业激光用户协会主席（2017—2019年）。

李琳是英国皇家工程院院士，美国激光学会会士，国际生产工程学会会士，国际光电子与激光工程学会会士以及英国工程与技术学会会士。作为作者或共同作者发表同行评审论文400余篇，申请专利60余项。2013年，凭借在激光工程领域的创新与成就他被皇家工程院授予弗兰克·维特爵士勋章。2014年他凭借在激光纳米制造和纳米成像上的研究成果获得英国皇家协会沃尔富森优秀科研奖，同年当选为曼彻斯特大学最佳科研工作者。2019年，他因在激光制造方面的杰出成就而获得美国激光学会颁发的肖洛奖，此外，因在增材制造方面的成就他被英国机械工程师学会授予Donald Julius Groen奖和Arthur Charles Main奖。

李琳教授于1982年在大连理工大学获得控制工程学士学位。1989年获得伦敦帝国理工学院激光工程博士学位。1988年至1994年他在利物浦大学（英国）担任激光材料加工研究助理和研究员，后成为英国曼彻斯特理工大学讲师，并于2000年晋升为正教授。2009—2013年担任英国曼彻斯特大学机械、航空航天和土木工程学院副院长，2015—2020年担任英国曼彻斯特大学科学与工程学院院长。

1. You are a pioneer in laser material processing who has been active in the field of laser drilling, laser welding, laser cutting, laser surface treatment, laser additive manufacturing, laser cleaning, and laser micro-nano manufacturing. Your work has been widely applied in manufacturing, medical, biological, new energy, and many other fields. What do you think are the key challenges facing laser material processing today? And what is its future development trend?

1. 作为激光材料加工的先驱者，您一直活跃在激光打孔、激光焊接、激光切割、激光表面处理、激光增材制造、激光清洗以及激光微纳制造等领域，应用范围涉及制造、医疗、生物、新能源等多个领域。您认为目前激光材料加工面临的挑战是什么？它未来的发展趋势是什么？

Lin Li: I started laser processing research in 1985 at Imperial College London in the UK with Professor Bill Steen who is widely recognized as the father of laser material processing. From him, I learned that no matter what you do, curiosity and society's needs are always the key drivers for research. At that time in the 1980s, lasers were considered as a solution looking for problems. Over the past 40 years, significant advances have been made including ultrafast (picosecond and femtosecond pulsed) lasers and the use of these lasers for micro and nanofabrication. The availability of high-powered fiber lasers has revolutionized laser cutting and welding processes and systems with much higher energy efficiency, processing precision, and flexibility than the previously used CO_2 and Nd:YAG lasers. Additive manufacturing of metallic components using high-power lasers has evolved from a laboratory rapid prototyping tool to a widely recognized and applied rapid manufacturing tool, saving energy, cost, materials, and time. Today, we are still facing many scientific and technological challenges in laser processing. One challenge is the application and integration of artificial intelligence and in-process sensors in laser processing systems and research to allow better process control and innovation. Another challenge is to overcome the micro/nano and macro processing barrier to enable micro/nano processing precision to be realized in macro processes and the efficiency of macro-processing to be realized in micro/nano processes. I gave a keynote presentation at the 31st ICALEO conference held in the USA in 2012 on "The Interface and Crossover between Laser Micro/Nano Fabrication and Macro Processing". This challenge is still facing us today. The third challenge is to further improve the energy efficiency of laser processing to aim at net zero-emission in laser processes and to enable zero energy waste in laser processing through reflection, and thermal conduction to the bulk energy losses.

李琳：1985年，我在英国伦敦帝国理工学院开始从事激光加工研究，师从业界公认的激光材料加工之父Bill Steen教授。从他那里我学到，无论做什么，求知欲和社会需求永远是科研的关键驱动力。在20世纪80年代，激光被认为将会在许多应用中大展身手。激光领域在过去40年已经取得了重大进步，包括超快（皮秒和飞秒脉冲）激光器的研发以及基于这些激光器的微/纳米制造技术应用。除此之外，大功率光纤激光器的研发和应用使激光切割和激光焊接领域发生了翻天覆地的变化。与以往的二氧化碳激光器和Nd: YAG激光器相比，光纤激光器具有更高的能源效率，更好的加工精度以及灵活性。使用大功率激光来实现金属零件的增材制造已从快速产品雏形制作发展成被业界广泛认可和应用的快速制造工具，它节省了大量的能源、成本、材料和时间。今天，我们在激光加工领域仍面临着许多科学和技术上的挑战。挑战之一是人工智能和实时传感器在激光加工系统和科学研究中的应用与集成，以此实现更好的过程控制和创新。另一个挑战是攻克微/纳米加工和宏观加工之间的屏障，让宏观加工可以达到微/纳米加工的精度，同时又能使微/纳米加工具有宏观加工的效率。2012年在美国召开的第31届ICALEO会议上，我作了题为“激光微/纳米制造

Prof. Lin Li received Sir Frank Whittle Medal from the Royal Academy of Engineering in 2013

2013年李琳教授荣获英国皇家工程院颁发的弗兰克·维特爵士勋章

与宏观加工的衔接与交叉”主题报告。可以说，直到今天，我们仍然面临着这一挑战。第三个挑战是要进一步提高激光加工的能源效率，争取在激光加工中实现零排放，并通过控制和减少激光的反射和非加工热传导能量损失，来实现激光加工中的零能

量浪费。

2. Multi-material laser additive manufacturing is a current research hotspot. Recently, your team has developed a laser powder bed fusion (LPBF) additive manufacturing system which utilizes ultrasonic vibration to achieve precise powder delivery during the deposition of different powder materials. Multi-material and functionally graded components made of metal, ceramic, glass, and polymer were successfully fabricated, providing a new solution to achieving multi-material laser additive manufacturing. As a pioneer of this technology, what do you think are the main applications for this technology? What kind of challenges might it face?

2. 多材料一体激光增材制造是当前的研究热点，近年来您的团队研发了基于超声波振动来实现多材料精准送粉的激光粉床增材系统，打印出了金属–陶瓷–玻璃–塑料相结合的多功能零件，为实现多材料增材制造提供了一种全新的设计思路。作为多材料增材技术的开拓者，您认为此项技术将来主要有哪些方面的应用？又有哪些挑战？

Lin Li: In our lives, hardly any products and tools we use are made of a single material. This is because different materials have different properties and play different roles. In conventional manufacturing, different parts of materials made of different materials are manufactured separately and then they are assembled together using various joining techniques. This requires different machines and operators with multiple steps, thus would consume more energy. Although additive manufacturing or 3D printing has been around for nearly 40 years, today it is still dominated by the use of a single type of materials in each component. In laser-based additive manufacturing, the challenge in combining different types of materials in a single component is that the laser processing will need to tailor for different material properties including melting point, thermal expansion coefficient, thermal conductivity, laser light absorption, and material compatibility to each other. For example, metal and ceramics are completely different types of materials. Joining them together is very challenging. The functional grading approach is used to vary gradually from one material to another in additive manufacturing. This requires multiple material 3D printing technologies. Potential applications of multiple material additive manufacturing include next-generation medical implants with combined high strength, corrosion resistance, light-weight, biocompatibility, controlled biodegradability, and self-monitoring. Another application would be in an aero-engine where high temperature and light-weight are required. A third area would be in impact-resistant personal protection products where lightweight and high-impact resistance are required. Multiple material additive manufacturing is a new field of study. Many material science issues also need to be understood including the control of intermetallic phases.

李琳：在我们日常生活中，我们使用的产品和工具往往都不是由单一材料制成的。这是因为不同的材料具有不同的性能，能够发挥不同的作用。在传统制造过程中，不同材料的零部件通常会被分开

Prof. Lin Li received the Arthur Schawlow award from the Laser Institute of America in 2019.
2019年李琳教授荣获美国激光学会肖洛奖

来制造，然后使用各种连接技术将它们再组合到一起。这需要不同的机器和操作员进行多个步骤，因此会消耗很多物力和人力资源。虽然增材制造（3D打印）已经发展了近40年，但是目前打印一个零件仍然是以使用单一材料为主。在激光增材制造中，将不同类型的材料组合加工成一个零件的主要挑战在于，激光加工需要考虑不同材料在性能上的区别，包括熔点、热膨胀系数、热导率、激光吸收率和不同材料间的兼容性。例如，金属和陶瓷是两种完全不同类型的材料，因此将它们连接在一起非常具有挑战性。在增材制造中使用功能梯度的加工方法可以实现从一种材料到另一种材料的平缓过渡，这就需要多材料3D打印技术。多材料增材制造的潜在应用包括下一代医疗植入体，它可以综合高强度、耐腐蚀、轻量化、生物相容性、可控生物降解性和自我监测等特点。另一种应用是在需要高温和轻量化的航空发动机中。此外，它还能够用于轻质和高抗冲击性能的个人防护产品。多材料一体增材制造是一个新的研究领域，因此许多材料科学上的问题，比如金属间化合物的控制仍然需要去探讨并解决。

3. We all know that graphene was first separated at The University of Manchester. In recent years, your team has published many academic papers on laser direct writing of graphene. You have also applied for a patent using this new method of producing graphene. What are the advantages of using lasers to prepare graphene? Did you encounter any difficulties when carrying out this research?

3. 我们都知道石墨烯诞生于曼彻斯特大学，近年来您的团队发表了多篇关于激光直接制备石墨烯的学术论文，还申请了专利。您能谈一下用激光制备石墨烯有哪些优点？在研究这项技术时您遇到的主要困难是什么？

Lin Li: The common method for producing high-quality graphene is by chemical vapor deposition. It requires a metallic catalyst substrate such as Cu or Ni and carbon-containing gases such as methane to react at high temperatures of over 1000 ℃. Then for practical applications, graphene formed in such a way needs to be lifted from the metallic substrate and transferred to the real substrate. To improve the adhesion, a binding material is applied which would affect the performance of the graphene. The production cost is high and the transfer process is difficult to ensure good bonding. Also, it is difficult to apply graphene to a large area over a substrate rather than Cu and Ni. We have developed a special organic ink material that can be printed on any substrate such as polymer and glass. Then we used a laser at UV wavelength to transfer the material to graphene without affecting the substrate. Another process we have developed is the production of large-area graphene using olive oil on glass. We applied laser direct writing of graphene for the production of the electrode in Li-S battery that showed two times the higher electrical capacity with rapid charging (3C) than that of current commercial Li-ion batteries with graphite electrode and retained almost 100% charge capacity even after 500 cycles. Another application of laser direct writing of graphene that we have shown is to produce strain sensors directly on textile material. Both have been published. The difficulties that we came across were the understanding of chemical processes and atomic level reactions involved. It is multiple disciplinary research requiring not only engineering, physics, material science but also chemistry.

李琳：制备高质量石墨烯最常用的方法是化学气相沉积。在制备过程中需要将甲烷等含碳气体在1000 摄氏度以上的高温环境下与铜或镍等金属薄膜催化剂基底进行反应。在实际应用中，通常需要将石墨烯从这些金属薄膜基底上揭出来，转移到其他材料基底上。为了提高石墨烯在其他材料上的附着力，需要添加一些结合材料，但这样做会影响石墨烯的性能。这种制备石墨烯的方法生产成本高，并且在转移过程中很难保证能有良好的结合。此外，相比于铜和镍，石墨烯难以在其他基底上进行大面积应用。对此，我们开发了一种特殊的有机油墨材料，可以打印在任何基底上，比如聚合物和玻璃。然后使用紫外波段的激光在不影响基底的情况下可以将这些油墨材料转变成石墨烯。我们开发的另一项工艺是在玻璃上用橄榄油来大面积制备石墨烯。我们将石墨烯激光直接制备技术应用在锂硫电池的电极制作中，该电池在快速充电（3C）下的电容量是目前使用石墨电极的商用锂离子电池的两倍，并且即使在500次充放电循环后依然能够保持几乎

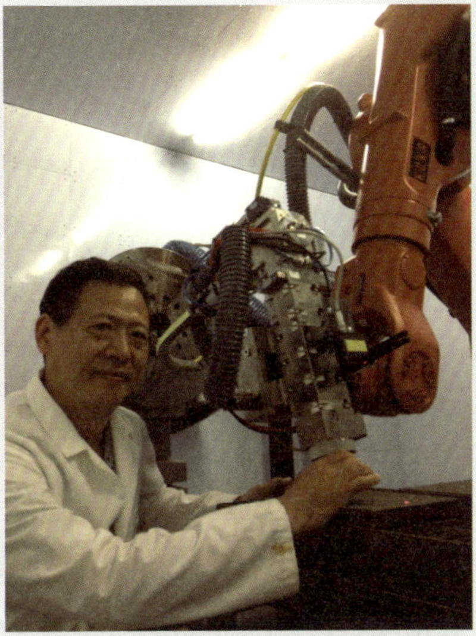

Prof. Lin Li in the laboratory
李琳教授在实验室

100%的电容量。同时，我们也将这项技术应用在纺织材料上制备应变传感器。这些成果都已经发表。在研究过程中我们遇到的困难主要是对化学过程和原子级反应的理解。这是一个多学科交叉的研究，不仅需要了解工程、物理和材料科学，还需要化学方面的知识。

4. From your research paper published in *Light: Science & Applications* (*Light*) in 2013[1], a method for direct white-light optical observation of 75-nm adenoviruses was demonstrated for the first time by coupling a standard optical microscope with a $BaTiO_3$ microsphere in water without fluorescent labeling. This work opens new opportunities for the study of virus/cell/bacteria/drug interactions to better understand the causes of various diseases. Against the backdrop of the current COVID-19 Pandemic, this technology seems to carry extra significance. Has this technology been put into the application?

4. 您于2013年在*Light: Science & Applications*（*Light*）上发表的研究成果中[1]，通过使用普通光学显微镜和$BaTiO_3$微球，在白光和没有荧光颗粒标记的条件下，首次在水中直接观察到了75 nm的腺病毒，这项工作为深入了解病毒/细胞/细菌/药物之间的相互作用提供了新的方法。目前在新冠疫情的影响下，这项技术似乎会具有非凡的意义，得到实际应用了吗?

Lin Li: Our team has commercialized this technology in a spinout company: LIG Nanowise Ltd, in Manchester, UK, to have developed the world's first commercial optical nanoscope (Nanoro-M model) with super-resolution microsphere amplifying lens (SMAL) that has been sold worldwide including USA, Japan, China, Russia, and South Korea. We have realized super-resolution and high-resolution imaging with large areas at the same time. This is often difficult to achieve. Often a higher resolution microscopic imaging is associated with smaller imaging areas. Examples of real commercial applications of our optical nanoscope include semiconductor inspection by Samsung and credit card examination by Beijing Credit Card Testing Centre. The technology overcomes the theoretical optical diffraction limit of 200 nm in visible light and has realized a 50 nm direct optical resolution with white light and 25 nm with a single wavelength. We are currently collaborating with medical scientists and material scientists to study the interaction of coronaviruses with their detectors and personal protection materials at The University of Manchester. Recently, Nikon, the world's top microscope company, has announced that they will collaborate with LIG Nanowise Ltd to integrate our SMAL lens technology with Nikon optical microscopes to enable super-resolution imaging for the mainstream market.

李琳：我们团队在英国曼彻斯特的LIG Nanowise公司将此项成果进行了商业化，开发出了世界上第一台带有超分辨率微球放大透镜（SMAL）的商用光学纳米显微镜（Nanoro-M型号），并将其销往美国、日本、中国、俄罗斯和韩国等世界各地。此外，我们实现了大面积成像与超分辨率成像结合。这通常是很难实现的，一般情况下，高分辨率显微成像只能在较小的成像区域上实现。我们的光学纳米显微镜的实际商业应用包括三星的半导体检测和北京信用卡测试中心的信用卡检查。这项技术克服了可见光200纳米的理论光学衍射极限，实现了白光50纳米的直接光学分辨率和单一波长25纳米的光学分辨率。目前，我们正与医学和材料领域的科学家合作，在曼彻斯特大学研究冠状病毒与病毒检测传感器和个人防护用品之间的相互作用。最近，尼康（世界最大显微镜公司之一）向全球发布与LIG Nanowise公司合作，将我们的微球透镜技术与尼康光学显微镜结合，实现超分辨光学成像，推向主流市场。

5. As an editor of the *Light* journal, you have

witnessed the growth and development of *Light* from the beginning. What are your expectations and suggestions for *Light*, as well as its new sister journals *eLight* and *Light: Advanced Manufacturing*?

5. 作为*Light*的编委，您一路见证了*Light*的成长与发展，对于*Light*及其子刊*eLight*、*Light: Advanced Manufacturing*在未来几年的发展您有哪些期望和建议？

Prof. Jianlin Cao, Editor-in-Chief of the journal, awarded the letter of appointment as a *Light* editor to Prof. Lin Li in 2014
2014年*Light*期刊主编曹健林为李琳院士颁发编委聘书

Lin Li: *Light* has made history in establishing its high reputation in the field worldwide. The new *Light* series journals will certainly attract more scientists and engineers to publish. I sincerely wish the new *Light* series journals success in the coming years.

李琳：*Light*期刊在其领域享有很高的国际声誉。*Light*的系列子刊必定会吸引更多的科学家和工程师投稿并发表文章。衷心祝愿*Light*系列子刊早日成功。

6. You are a fellow of the Royal Academy of Engineering, and also have served as president of the Laser Institute of America (LIA), Association of Industrial Laser Users (AILU), and the International Academy of Photonics and Laser Engineering (IAPLE). You are also a fellow of the International Academy of Production Engineering (CIRP) and many other important organizations and have chaired many

conferences over the past decades. Could you please share with us some valuable experiences from your work in these associations, and what do board members of these associations value most?

6. 您是英国皇家工程院院士，同时您也担任过美国激光学会(LIA)、工业激光用户学会(AILU)和国际光子学与激光工程学会(IAPLE)的主席，也是国际生产工程学院(CIRP)等许多重要国际学术机构的会士，并且主持过很多激光加工和先进制造的会议。能否请您分享一下，您从这些协会工作中获得了哪些宝贵经验，这些协会的董事会成员最看重的是什么?

Lin Li: These international associations and societies are serving the international professional communities in the lasers, optics, and advanced manufacturing fields. My participation in these professional societies enabled me to serve the communities to promote laser science and engineering and knowledge exchange. I have learned a lot from colleagues and friends. The key elements in serving in these professional societies are enthusiasm, sacrifice, dedication, responsibility, and fairness.

李琳：上述国际学会和组织都是与激光、光学及先进制造领域有关。参与这些专业协会使我能够服务于行业同仁并加强激光科学和工程方面的知识交流。通过交流，我在同行和朋友那里收获良多。在协会工作中最重要的因素就是热情、牺牲、奉献、责任和公平。

7. You have supervised more than 60 Ph.D. students who are now working in different countries and different fields. You always encourage students to innovate and stand at the forefront of scientific development. What qualities do you think young researchers should possess? Do you have any advice for them?

7. 您非常注重人才教育与培养，指导毕业的博士生已有60多位，遍布各个国家和各个领域。您总是鼓励学生要开拓创新，站在科学发展的最前沿。您认为青年科研工作者应该具备哪些素养？您能提些建议给他们吗？

Lin Li: Training Ph.D. students is a transformation process. We do not expect them to know everything and be able to solve all the problems at the start. What we expect is that the students should be willing to work hard, willing to face failure and not to be deterred by failure, and have hopes and a desire to succeed. Research is fun and can also be boring. There is a will there is a way. Some of the important inventions may be the result of failed work of the planned research goals. Failure is the mother of success.

李琳：培养博士生是一个转变的过程。我们并不期望学生们从一开始就无所不知，能够解决所有问题。我们希望学生们能够好学不倦，敢于面对失败，常怀希望之心和成功的梦想。搞研究是一项既有趣又无聊的工作。有志者，事竟成。一些重要的发明可能就是你既定科研目标失败的成果。因此，要牢记失败是成功之母。

8. Before you joined The University of Manchester, you obtained your Ph.D. degree from the Imperial College London on the topic of laser processing, and you worked with your supervisor Professor William Steen at The University of Liverpool for six years, assisting him in building a new laser processing laboratory. What made you interested in the research of laser processing when you started your Ph.D. program? How did those six years at The University of Liverpool affect your academic career?

8. 您加入曼彻斯特大学之前，在伦敦帝国理工学院攻读了关于激光加工的博士学位，之后跟随您的老师William Steen在利物浦大学一起工作了6年，协助他创建新的激光加工实验室，最初读博期间是什么让您对激光加工的研究产生了浓厚兴趣？在利物浦大学工作的那6年对您未来学术生涯产生了怎样的影响？

Lin Li: My first degree at the Dalian University of Technology was in automatic control. My initial Ph.D. research topic at Imperial College was on output feedback control theory in the Department of Electrical Engineering. Although the pure theoretical study was useful, and I completed the theoretical work within a few months, I thought more practical, hands-on experience would be more beneficial for a Chinese researcher. One day I met a friend, Mr. Zhenda Chen, who was a Ph.D. student on laser alloying in Dr. Bill Steen's laser group. I was fascinated by the magic power of lasers, little known at the time for material processing. I applied to the university to change my Ph.D. topic and the supervisor to start my Ph.D. on the adaptive control of the laser cladding process. My Ph.D. thesis title was "Design and Construction of an Intelligent Laser Cladding Control System", with supervisors from the Department of Materials and Department of Mechanical Engineering. In my Ph.D. study, I applied artificial neural networks and in-process sensors for the control of laser cladding processes between 1985 and 1989. This topic is still a challenge today after 35 years in laser material processing. My postdoctoral research at Liverpool played a very important part in my career. I worked in a number of different projects including in-process monitoring of high-speed (1 m/s) laser welding process for packaging collaboration with a company and laser-based nuclear decommissioning, collaborating with industry. These projects opened up my minds to wider laser processing fields which allowed me to establish my research group in laser processing later on at Manchester.

李琳：我本科毕业于大连理工大学的自动控制专业。最初，我在帝国理工学院电气工程系读博士时的研究课题是输出反馈控制理论，并在几个月内完成了导师规定的理论工作。虽然纯理论的学习大有裨益，但我认为对于一名中国学者来说实践经验可能更为重要。有一天我遇到了一位好友——陈振达先生，他在Bill Steen博士领导的激光加工研究实验室做激光表面合金化博士课题研究。激光的魔力着实令我着迷，当时激光在材料加工中的应用还鲜为人知。于是我向学校申请更改博士论文题目和导师，开始攻读激光熔覆过程自适应控制的博士学位。我的博士论文题目是《智能激光熔覆控制系统的设计与构建》，指导我博士研究的两位导师来自材料系和机械工程系。在攻读博士学位期间（1985—1989年），我提出并研究将人工神经网络和在线传感器应用于激光熔覆过程的控制，35年后的今天这个课题对于激光材料加工来说仍然是一个挑战。在利物浦大学的博士后研究经历对我的职业生涯至关重要。我参与了许多不同种类的科研项目，包括与公司合作的用于包装行业的高速(1m/s)激光焊接过程的实时监控以及与工业界合作的基于激光的核退役技术。这些项目开阔了我的眼界，带我走进了更为广阔的激光加工领域，为我后来能够在曼彻斯特大学建立自己的激光加工研究团队奠定了基础。

9. You are often invited as a plenary speaker to various academic seminars and conferences held in China. Could you please talk about the similarities and differences in laser processing research in and outside of China in recent years?

9. 您经常会应邀回中国作为主讲嘉宾参加各种学术研讨会。可否请您谈一谈近年来国内外激光加工的研究存在哪些相同点和区别?

Lin Li: China's laser processing research is world-class and we see a large number of publications in this field coming from China. Between the 1980s and 1990s China had been working mainly in laser cladding, surface treatments, and laser welding and had the highest number of publications in laser cladding. Over the last 20 years, with the availability of more advanced laser facilities in university laboratories and increased international communications, China has quickly progressed into the fields of ultrafast laser micro/nano processing and additive manufacturing. Industrial applications of laser cutting, laser welding, laser marking, and additive manufacturing have boosted the Chinese laser processing industry and research. Internationally, research is mainly in welding, cutting of CFRP composites, welding of aluminum for battery and car production, additive manufacturing of metallic materials, and micro/nano processing of brittle materials such as glass, ceramic and silicon, and synthesis of nano-materials. In many laser processing fields, China is internationally leading. For example, additive manufacturing of very large metallic components by blown powder process, applications of two-photon polymerization for micro/nano device manufacture, laser shock peening, ultra-fast laser surface micro/nano texturing and applications, understanding of electron dynamics in ultra-fasting laser processing, electric current stir assisted laser welding, magnetic field-assisted laser surface cladding and alloying, ring beam laser cladding and multiple laser beam powder bed fusion large metallic component additive manufacturing.

李琳：中国的激光加工科研水平是世界级的，大量该领域的文章都来自中国。1980年至2000年间，中国主要开展激光熔覆、表面处理以及激光焊接方面的研究，并且在激光熔覆领域发表的论文最多。过去20年，随着各大学实验室先进激光设备的不断增多以及国际交流的不断加强，中国在超快激光微纳加工和增材制造领域取得了迅猛发展。激光切割、激光焊接、激光打标、增材制造等工业应用极大促进了中国激光加工行业和研究的发展。当前国际上激光加工研究主要集中在CFRP复合材料的焊接、切割、电池和汽车用铝的焊接、金属材料的增材制造、玻璃、陶瓷、硅等脆性材料的微纳加工和纳米材料的合成。在许多激光加工领域，中国处于国际领先地位。例如：通过激光熔覆增材制造大型金属组件，双光子聚合的微纳/纳米元件制造，激光冲击强化，超快激光表面微纳/纳米结构制造和应用，超快激光加工中的电子动力学、电流辅助激光焊接、电磁搅拌磁场辅助激光熔覆合金、环形激光熔覆以及多束激光粉床熔覆大型金属部件增材制造。

10. COVID-19 has caused a huge impact on our lives. Many scientific research projects have been interrupted or delayed. Students have had to take online courses. What are your feelings about these changes brought by the pandemic? Could you give some suggestions or advice to help researchers go through this extraordinary period?

10. 去年由于疫情原因，各行各业都受到了极大影响。在科研圈，由于疫情影响，许多科研项目迟迟无法开展，同时我也了解到很多国外大学的课程变成了线上教学。您如何看待疫情给科研带来的变化？能否提一些建议帮助科研人员渡过这个非常时期？

Lin Li: The UK has suffered badly during the Covid-19 pandemic. We have had several national and regional lockdowns. With the wide administration of vaccines, I hope the world will overcome this pandemic soon. We have to change our teaching to online delivery and discussions. We would have to quickly learn and use online teaching tools and develop new online teaching materials and student assessments. We have adopted quickly by working harder. In research and communications, the scale of laboratory work is reduced due to extra safety and social distancing requirements. We have to learn the new operating measures, rules, and limitations. Online meetings are getting more frequent. It is also a lot easier to attend and arrange online meetings. There is no traveling and we have saved a lot of time and it is good for the environment too. This may be integrated into the future mode of communication that more full or partial online meetings and conferences may become normal for international conferences and meetings.

李琳：在新冠肺炎疫情期间，英国遭受了沉重的打击。曾几次进行全国或局部封锁。我希望全世界能够通过大规模疫苗接种战胜这一流行病。受此影响，我们不得不将教学改为线上授课和讨论。我们需要快速学习并使用在线教学工具，开发新的线上授课教材以及制定学生考核标准。此外，我们需要更加努力地工作，以适应这些变化。在科学研究和学术交流方面，由于政府要求保持社交安全距离，因此实验室的人数也相应减少了很多。我们不断学习新的措施，掌握新的规则和要求，比如越来越多地采用线上会议的形式。参加和组织线上会议似乎更容易一些，因为它不需要出差，这样就节省了很多时间，同时也减少环境污染。我认为，未来部分或者全部采用线上交流将会成为召开国际会议的一种常态化方式。

11. In addition to being a celebrated scientist, a good teacher, and a hardworking team leader, I learned that you are also an outstanding musician who can play a multitude of musical instruments. Your regular BBQ gatherings with your students are also famed. What tips would you give young scientists on how to balance work and life?

11. 您不仅是著名的科学家、优秀的导师、勤奋的团队带头人，我知道您还擅长演奏许多乐器，也会定期和学生举行烧烤等活动，对于如何平衡工作和生活，您有什么建议给年轻科学家吗？

Prof. Lin Li plays the Chinese flute
李琳教授演奏竹笛

Lin Li: After all, we are human beings and not machines. We have feelings and have lives outside work. I play Chinese flute and erhu as a hobby. I was in the school music band during my middle and high school studies. I participated in the London Chinese Orchestra during my Ph.D. study from 1985 to 1988 and performed regularly in the public and now in the Oriental Breeze Chinese music band in Manchester, performing regularly in public. My advice to young people is that enjoy what life has offered and success in work is not always proportional to the time devoted. Balance in work and life will make both work and life more enjoyable.

李琳：毕竟我们是人，不是机器。我们在工作之外还有感情和生活。于我而言，我比较喜欢竹笛和二胡。在初中和高中时我就是学校乐队的成员。1985至1988年我在伦敦攻读博士学位时，参加了华人乐团，定期演出。现在，我在曼彻斯特东方丝竹民乐队，经常演出。我给年轻人的建议是好好享受生活给予的一切，工作的成功并不总是与投入的时

In February 2011, Prof. Lin Li (fourth from left) performed in the Oriental Breeze Chinese music band in Manchester

2011年2月李琳教授（左四）在英国曼彻斯特东方丝竹民乐队演出

间成正比。平衡好工作和生活会使工作和生活都更加美好。

12. Your daughter apparently is an excellent student at Imperial College London majoring in medicine. As an alumnus of your daughter, did you give her any advice when she chose university? How do you help her with study and life?

12. 您的女儿非常优秀，目前在帝国理工大学学习医学专业。作为女儿的大学校友，您在她择校时给出建议了吗？您是如何在女儿的学习和生活中给予帮助的呢？

Lin Li: We did not influence her choice of universities and discipline of study for university. We respected her own choice. She was born, grown, and educated entirely in the UK. Both the schools and the parents encouraged her to independent thinking and decision making. She was determined to do medicine to save lives and care for others, although the education will take a much longer time (6 years instead of 3-4 years for other subjects) and cost more money (She will have to borrow more from the UK government and pay back later). Fortunately, she did well in her A-level examinations with A*s in all the subjects. We are glad that she got what she wanted. She is now very happy and busy studying medicine at Imperial College London where I graduated. In life, we also respect her own choices and give our moral support for her decisions. We still, however, provide some financial support to her study, which is necessary, as the government loan only covers tuition fees and

Prof. Lin Li's daughter in her childhood
李琳教授女儿的童年时期照片

accommodation costs. She communicates with her mum every day by phone.

李琳：对于女儿学校和专业的选择，我们尊重她个人的意愿。她在英国出生、成长并接受教育。从小学校和家长都灌输给她独立思考和自主决定的理念。相比其他的学科只需要3~4年的学习时间，学医则需要花费6年，而且费用更高（她不得不从英国政府处借更多的钱，工作后偿还）。即便如此，她依然希望通过学医来拯救人的生命和帮助他人。幸运的是，她在A-level（高考）考试中表现得很好，所有科目都是A*s。我们很高兴她梦想成真。她现在就读于我毕业的帝国理工大学，虽然忙于学业但是很开心。生活中我们也尊重她的个人选择，并且对于她的决定给予精神支持。由于政府贷款只能涵盖学费和住宿费，所以我们作为家长也给她提供必要的生活费。现在她每天都会跟她妈妈电话沟通。

Reference
参考文献

[1] LI L, GUO W, YAN Y Z, et al. Label-free super-resolution imaging of adenoviruses by submerged microsphere optical nanoscopy. Light: Science & Applications, 2013,3:104.

Professor Tarik Bourouina

编者按

2015年，联合国195个国家提出了可持续发展目标，以缓解气候变化和全球污染问题。在法国，有一位科学家致力于通过使用MEMS、片上实验室和超材料为上述问题提供解决方案，他就是巴黎古斯塔夫艾菲尔大学ESYCOM实验室的Tarik Bourouina教授。他致力于微传感器和超材料的研究，不断探索将它们应用在“可持续”和“智慧”城市的未来蓝图中。另一方面，自创刊之日起，他就与*Light: Science & Applications* (*Light*) 结下了不解之缘，并在巴黎成立了*Light*海外办公室，这是*Light*在欧洲设立的第一个海外办公室。本期我们非常荣幸能够与Tarik Bourouina教授交流，他将在访谈中分享他的研究经历以及他与*Light*的故事。

For an Intelligent and Sustainable Future
筑梦远航“智慧城”，至臻至善可持续

Special Guest: Xiaoyi Liu　Science Editor: Hui Wang
特邀嘉宾 刘小翼　科学编辑 王卉

Editorial:

In 2015, 195 countries of the United Nations proposed Sustainable Development Goals so as to alleviate the problems of climate change and global pollution. In France, there is a scientist dedicated to contribute providing solutions for above issues by virtue of MEMS, Lab-On-Chip and metamaterials. This expert is Prof. Tarik Bourouina, a Professor of Physics at ESIEE Paris, Université Gustave Eiffel. He devoted himself to the investigations on micro sensors and metamaterials, and kept seeking their applications in the future blueprint of "Sustainable" and "Smart" cities. On the other hand, he has formed an indissoluble bond with *Light: Science & Applications* (*Light*) since the very beginning of the journal. He also set up the *Light*'s Paris office, which is the first *Light*'s overseas office in Europe. We are much honored to have an opportunity to exclusively communicate with Prof. Tarik Bourouina, who will share his research experience and stories with *Light* in this interview.

Light People

Biography: Tarik Bourouina is Professor of Physics at ESIEE Paris, Université Gustave Eiffel. He is affiliated to the French National Center for Scientific Research (CNRS) within the ESYCOM laboratory UMR9007. He was a Senior Research Fellow at The University of Tokyo, Institute of Industrial Sciences, Japan, an associate professor at Université Paris-Saclay, France and Director of a dual-degree Master program in MEMS Engineering with Nanyang Technological University (NTU) in Singapore. His current interests include nano-structured materials, micro-opto-fluidics and their applications to sustainable development. In 2017, he was the recipient of the Chinese Academy of Sciences President's International Fellowship Initiative.

Bourouina actively contributed to the launch and development of several companies with his former students and colleagues, which include MEMSCAP, Si-Ware Systems/Neospectra, MEMS-Schlumberger, Fluidion, and Izonics. He has several contributions in Photonic MEMS, among which the smallest MEMS-based FTIR Optical Spectrometer,NEOSPECTRA, developed within the spin-off company Si-Ware-Systems, and was awarded the "Prism Award for Photonics Innovation"in 2014, and the "Technology Showcase Award"in 2017 at the SEMI European MEMS and Sensor Summit.

专家简介：Tarik Bourouina，巴黎古斯塔夫艾菲尔大学物理学教授。他隶属于ESYCOM实验室

UMR9007的法国国家科学研究中心 (CNRS)。他曾任日本东京大学工业科学研究所高级研究员、法国巴黎萨克雷大学副教授和新加坡南洋理工大学MEMS工程双学位硕士项目主任。目前他的研究方向包括：纳米结构材料、微光流体及其在可持续发展中的应用。2017年他入选中国科学院国际人才计划（PIFI）。

Tarik Bourouina与他之前的学生和同事积极推动并成立多家公司，其中包括MEMSCAP、Si-Ware Systems/Neospectra、MEMS-Schlumberger、Fluidion、Izonics。他对MEMS光子学领域的发展作出了多项贡献，如与Si-Ware-Systems联合开发了最小的基于MEMS的傅里叶变换红外光谱仪NEOSPCTRA，该成果在2014年获得了“光子学创新棱镜奖”，并在2017年国际半导体产业协会欧洲MEMS/传感器峰会上荣获“技术展示奖”。

1. When did you first learn about the journal *Light: Science & Applications* (*Light*)? Why did you agree to

be the editor of *Light* before it became internationally well-known?

1. 您第一次听闻*Light*是什么时候？为什么在其尚未具备国际知名度时您就同意担任期刊的编委？

Prof. Tarik: It was in 2012 that I learned from European colleagues that the journal was launched and that there was a very interesting strategy in establishing a top journal dealing with all aspects of light, from the fundamentals to applications. The fact that this journal was co-branded by Nature Publishing Group and CIOMP, which is among the biggest institutes of Chinese Academy of Science was a very good sign that this journal will be eventually very successful. So, when I was nominated to join the editorial board, I immediately accepted and jumped-in. At that time my main activities were related to optical MEMS and metamaterials including black silicon and other silicon-based

Prof. Jianlin Cao, Editor-in-Chief of journal, awarded the letter of appointment to Prof. Tarik in 2016

2016年*Light*期刊主编曹健林为Tarik教授颁发编委聘书

Being awarded the "Outstanding Editors in the Year 2018"

获得“2018年度期刊优秀编委”

metasurfaces. But I was also looking for new research directions. From that perspective, the "Light conference" was an ideal discussion platform gathering international experts covering a very wide spectrum of optics-related research.

Tarik 教授：2012 年，我在欧洲同事那里听闻新成立了一本期刊，它的目标是成为光学领域涵盖各主题从基础到应用全方位的顶级期刊。该期刊由英国自然出版集团与中国科学院最大的研究所之一——中国科学院长春光学精密机械与物理研究所合作出版，这是一个非常好的信号，预示着该期刊必将指日成功。因此，当我得知自己被提名为期刊编委会成员时，我毫不犹豫地接受了邀请并立即投入工作。当时我主要从事光学 MEMS 与超材料，包括黑硅和其他硅基超表面相关的研究工作，但是我一直都在试图寻找新的研究方向。因此 Light 会议是一个理想的交流平台，国际光学各领域的专家在此聚集，共同就光学领域的各种问题探讨并交换意见。

2. You published a paper on *Light: Science & Applications* in 2013[1], regarding a novel monolithically integrated silicon micromirror with controlled three-dimensional curvature, which is capable of manipulating optical beams propagating in the plane of the silicon substrate. Could you please give a brief introduction of this work? What are the advantages of the proposed silicon micromirror compared with others?

2. 您于2013年在*Light*上发表了一篇题目为“具有三维可控曲率的硅基微镜片可实现无透镜的自由空间光束耦合”的论文[1]，内容是关于一种新型的单片集成的硅基微镜片，具有可控的三维曲率，它能够操纵光束在硅衬底平面上传播。您能否简单介绍一下这项工作？您提出的硅基微镜片与其他微镜片相比有哪些优势？

Prof. Tarik: Yes, this is actually my only paper published in *Light: Science & Applications* to date. The topic deals indeed with the design of 3D-curved mirror whose shape and size can accommodate for multiple applications dealing with free-space propagation of light, especially when considering small spot size and small radii of curvatures of the mirror. One of these applications that we reported later in the same year (in *Optics Express*) is the ability to produce wide angle spatial optical scanning without deforming the spot size and shape. Our findings were also very useful for the second generation of NEOSPECTRA spectrometer, which operates now with free-space light with no need of optical fiber connectors. This also allowed extending the spectral range up to the Mid-Infrared, which was not possible using optical fibers.

Tarik教授：是的，到目前为止这是我在*Light*上发表的唯一一篇论文。此课题实际上是设计一种三维曲面镜，其形状和大小可以适合处理自由空间光传播的多种应用，特别是当考虑小光斑尺寸和小曲率半径的镜面的时候。同年，我们在《光学快报》上报道了其应用之一是能够在不改变光斑尺寸和形状的情况下进行广角的空间光学扫描。我们的研究结果对第二代NEOSPECTRA光谱仪研究提供了非常重要的参考价值，现在它可以凭借自由空间的光束来操作而不需要光纤连接器。这也使得其光谱范围可以扩展到中红外波段，而这是使用光纤无法实现的。

3. The *Light*'s overseas office that you set up in your university is its first office in Europe, so could you tell us what kind of work this office is responsible for? What do you think is the significance of setting up *Light*'s overseas offices all over the world?

3. 您在您工作的大学设立了*Light*期刊在欧洲的第一个海外办公室，那么您能否介绍一下办公室具体负责哪些工作？您认为在世界各地设立*Light*期刊海外办公室的意义是什么？

Prof. Tarik: I am proud of being responsible of *Light* office in Paris. It is indeed hosted by my university. Among the most important events that we had in the recent years is a participation of *Light* with delegates among the editors and a booth during the international Year in of Light Opening Ceremony hosted in Paris UNESCO headquarters and then during the International Day of Light at UNESCO headquarters in Paris in 2018. Both Prof. Tianhong Cui and Dr. Yuhong Bai attended this event. We had a booth for *Light* at that occasion and we had the opportunity to meet two Nobel Prizes, Prof. Kip Thorne and Prof. Claude Cohen-Tannoudji. Besides, we also hosted 12 editors of *Light* in Paris during the last few years as well as the Vice-President of CIOMP, as part of dissemination actions of *Light* conducted in France and in Europe.

Tarik教授：我很自豪能够成为*Light*期刊巴黎海外办公室的负责人。近年来，我们做的最重要的事情是协助*Light*期刊的编委，包括崔天宏教授和白雨虹博士参加2018年联合国教科文组织在巴黎举办的国际光年开幕式和每年的国际光日活动。当时，我们有幸在活动中见到诺贝尔奖物理学奖获得者Kip Thorne教授和Claude Cohen-Tannoudji教授。除此

Light Editors Tarik Bourouina and Tianhong Cui and Yuhong Bai near the *Light* booth at International Day of Light, UNESCO, Paris 2018

*Light*期刊编委Tarik Bourouina与崔天宏教授、白雨虹博士在联合国教科文组织举办的国际光日活动*Light*展台上的合影（2018年法国巴黎摄）

Nobel Prize winner Kip Thorne with *Light* Editors Tarik Bourouina, Tianhong Cui and Yuhong Bai during International Day of Light, UNESCO, Paris 2018

诺贝尔物理学奖获得者Kip Thorne（右二）与*Light*出版中心主任白雨虹博士（左一）、编委Bourouina教授（左二）、执行主编崔天宏教授（右一）在联合国教科文组织举办的国际光日活动上的合影（2018年法国巴黎摄）

Editors of *Light* gathering after the opening ceremony of International Year of Light in Paris 2015

*Light*期刊编委在国际光年开幕式后的合影（2015年法国巴黎摄）

From left to right: Prof. Jean Mairesse, Dr. Yuhong Bai, Prof. Tarik Bourouina, and Prof. Cécile Delolme
从左往右依次为：Jean Mairesse教授、白雨虹博士、Tarik Bourouina教授、Cécile Delolme教授

之外，近年来，作为*Light*期刊在法国和欧洲宣传活动的重要分支，我们接待了10余位*Light*期刊的编委和长春光机所的领导。

4. You join the "Light Conference" almost every year, so would you like to comment this conference?

4. 您几乎每年都会来参加Light会议，您对该会议有何评价？

Prof. Tarik: "Light conference" is definitely a key event for sustaining the Light community. That's why I attended regularly this annual event except last year. I am eager to join the next "Light Conference" in a very next future as soon as possible.

Tarik教授：毫无疑问，Light会议是维系Light大

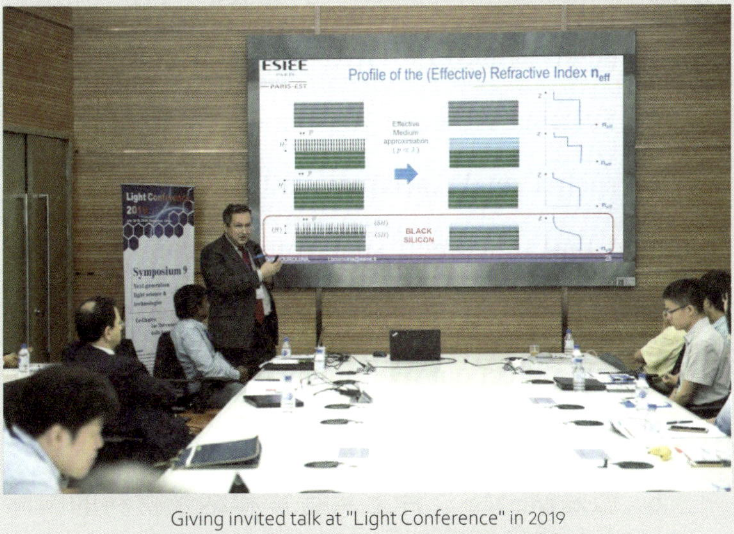

Giving invited talk at "Light Conference" in 2019
2019年Tarik教授受邀在Light会议分会场作报告

家庭成员交流的一项非常重要的活动，这就是为什么我除了去年（由于疫情）每年都会参加该会议的原因。我非常渴望下一届Light会议能够尽快举办，我也会积极参与。

5. You are an internationally renowned expert in MEMS, Lab-On-Chip and nanomaterials who has obtained a lot of achievements and awards. You won the Prism Award on photonics innovation in 2014 by virtue of the smallest MEMS-based FTIR Optical Spectrometer-NEOSPECTRA, jointly developed with Si-Ware Systems. How did you come up with the idea to develop such a small spectrometer? How does it work? I noticed that this small spectrometer can be further miniaturized, e.g. integrated into our mobile terminals. How will this affect our lives in the future?

5. 您是MEMS、片上实验室和纳米材料的国际知名专家，获得了诸多成就和奖项。您与Si–Ware

Systems联合开发了最小的基于MEMS的傅里叶变换红外光谱仪NEOSPECTRA，该成果在2014年获得了光子学创新棱镜奖。开发这种小型光谱仪的想法是如何萌生的？它是如何工作的？我注意到这个小型光谱仪可以进一步小型化，例如：它能够集成到我们的移动终端中。您能谈谈它对未来的生活将产生什么影响吗？

Prof. Tarik: Indeed, besides my academic research activities, I am also engaged since 14 years in Si-Ware Systems, a company established by a former Ph.D. student of my group, Dr. Bassam Saadany. This is very exciting to see the fruit of research efforts turning into a significant impact to the society with this MEMS-based FTIR spectrometer, which is now commercialized under the brand NEOSPECTRA, with tens of thousands units dispatched all over the world. The story started more than 15 years ago with a technology challenge that we tackled using Deep Reactive Ion Etching (DRIE) for the purpose of producing vertical Bragg mirrors, which consists of multiple Silicon-Air layers. In order to satisfy the strict optics requirements, those layers had to be strictly vertical, better than 0.01°, very smooth and deep enough to accommodate with a light spot of 100 microns. After succeeding with this first step, we started exploring the applications. We first made several Fabry-Pérot micro-cavities that were intended to produce tunable filters and refractometers, for instance. Then, during the last year of Bassam's PhD thesis, we worked on a Michelson interferometer that has a high potential of applications, especially in the FTIR spectrometer architecture. First patent applications were then filed. After that, we have been approached by Hamamatsu Photonics in Japan, considered as the world leading company in photonics and it went very fast to establish a collaboration project that was very beneficial for the young company to develop the first generation of NEOSPECTRA series product line, which is totally owned by Si-Ware

Systems. Yes indeed, this product won the Prism Award in photonics innovation, which was awarded in San Francisco during Photonics West 2014.

Tarik教授：的确，除了学术研究之外，我还参与Si-Ware Systems公司的工作，距今已有14年，该公司由我课题组之前的博士生Bassam Saadany博士创立。令人激动的是，这款基于MEMS的傅里叶变换红外光谱仪的研究成果对社会产生了巨大的影响，已经以NEOSPECTRA品牌成功商业化，并在全球范围内实现了上万台的出货量。这个故事始于15年前，当时我们面临着一项技术挑战——如何通过使用深反应离子刻蚀（DRIE）来制备垂直的布拉格反射镜，该反射镜由多个硅-空气层组成。为了满足严格的光学要求，胶管层必须严格垂直（倾斜角要小于0.01°），需要非常光滑且足够深，以适应100微米的光斑。第一步成功之后，我们开始探索应用的可能性。例如，我们首先制造了几个Fabry-Pérot微腔，旨在生产可调谐的滤光片和折射计。随后，在Bassam博士论文的最后一年，我们研制出具有巨大应用潜力的迈克尔逊干涉仪，尤其是在傅里叶变换红外光谱仪的架构中。第一项专利申请也随之提交。之后，世界领先的光子学公司——日本滨松电子很快联系了我们，并表示希望与我们进行合作，

2014 Photonics Innovation Prism Award Ceremony
2014年光子学创新棱镜奖颁奖仪式

这对于刚开始开发第一代NEOSPECTRA系列产品生产线的我们起到了极大的促进作用，该生产线完全归Si-Ware Systems所有。不久后该产品获得了光子学创新棱镜奖，于2014年在旧金山举办的Photonics West会议举行了颁奖典礼。

6. You have been involved in the investigations of Sustainable and Smart Cities based on Lab-On-Chip and micro sensors for several years. What are the definitions of "sustainable" and "smart" here? How can the MEMS and nanomaterials technologies serve in this process? On the other hand, you have always valued the transfer of academic results to industry and market. Could you please tell us your perspective of the potential applications and market prospects of MEMS and nanotechnologies based products?

6. 近年来，您一直在参与基于片上实验室和微型传感器的可持续和智慧城市的研究。这里的“可持续”和“智慧”的定义是什么？MEMS和纳米材料技术如何在这个过程中发挥作用？另一方面，您一直重视学术成果向产业和市场的转化。请您谈谈您对基于MEMS和纳米技术产品的潜在应用和市场前景的看法。

Prof. Tarik: Indeed, Sustainable and Smart Cities is my main focus area of applications. There are several reasons for that. One of them is that this is also the flagship focus of my university, so I have to contribute to the collective effort in the frame of the I-Site 'FUTURE' Excellence Program supported by the ANR research agency. Second, when you look to the past at the previous success stories of MEMS technologies, you can see that automotive area and smart phones were the main drivers of the huge deployment of MEMS sensors. Based on the current rise of Internet-of-Things (IoT) the next big application areas are definitely Smart Cities and Smart Manufacturing. The corresponding markets are huge and there are a plenty of room for new innovative sensors that do not exist yet. Among these sensors, those dealing with the environment, that is water, air, soil and other natural resources including energy and food. There is a huge avenue for innovation here, with multiple technological challenges and a lot of opportunities for optics technologies before reaching sensors that has to be functionally performant, reliable and low-cost. If one can make them energy-autonomous and biodegradable, this will definitely contribute to both the Smart and Sustainable facets of our efforts. With this, not only MEMS but also Lab-On-Chip and functional nanomaterials can help reaching this contribution to the Sustainable Development Goals, which led to an international Agreement under the United Nations on the Agenda of Sustainable Development for 2030. By the way, this agreement was adopted in Paris in 2015 and it is known as the "Paris Agreement".

Tarik教授：的确，可持续和智慧城市是我研究的主要应用领域。这有几个原因。其一，这是我所在大学的旗舰项目，所以我必须为此做出自己的贡献。二是回顾过去MEMS技术以往的成功案例，汽车领域和智能手机是MEMS传感器大范围普及应用的主要动力。基于目前物联网（IoT）的兴起，下一个大体量应用领域必定是智能城市以及智能制造。未来新型创新传感器的市场需求空间必定非常广阔。在这些传感器中，有些需要与环境进行交互，即水、空气、土壤和其他自然资源，包括能源和食物。这提供了一个巨大的创新途径，即在实现传感器层面之前，首先在光学技术层面上各种挑战和机会并存，必须要实现特定的功能，解决可靠性，降低成本。如果能让其实现能源自主和生物可降解，这必将有助于我们智慧和可持续两方面的研究工作。因此，不仅是MEMS、片上实验室和功能性纳米材料都可以为实现可持续发展目标做出贡献，这也是联合国为2030年实现可持续发展议程上达成的国际协议。顺便说一下，该协议于2015年在巴黎通过，它就是我们熟知的“巴黎协定”。

7. Recently you mainly focused on the studies on nanomaterials and metasurfaces such as Zinc-oxide and black silicon. What kind of remarkable characteristics do they possess? How will they integrate with MEMS and microfluidics systems to develop novel devices which can be utilized in drinkable water generation and purification?

7. 最近您聚焦于纳米材料和超表面材料的研究，如氧化锌和黑硅。它们具有怎样的显著特点？它们将如何与MEMS和微流控系统相结合，开发出可用于饮用水生产和净化的新型设备？

Prof. Tarik: Yes indeed, Zinc-oxide nanowires are among the nanomaterials that we have interest in. This material has multiple optical properties according to its semiconducting properties, wide-gap and crystalline high quality. For instance it is photochromic and photocatalytic. It is this last property that we have investigated in my group, together with my colleague, Prof. Yamin Leprince-Wang. Recently we reported on the integration of ZnO nanowires inside a microfluidic chip for the purpose of water purification. We demonstrated fast removal of Volatile Organic Compounds from water in less than 5 second transit time and also the capability to purify 1 liter of water per day with such tiny chip whose size is one centimeter-square. This work was published in 2018 in *Microsystems & Nanoengineering*. This work received a best paper award in 2020 from the journal, among the most cited papers within 2 years.

Tarik教授：的确，氧化锌纳米线是我们感兴趣的纳米材料之一。由于它具有半导体特性、宽间隙和较高的晶体质量，使得这种材料具有多种光学特性。例如，它具有光致变色和光催化的功能。我和我的同事Yamin Leprince-Wang教授一起研究的就是后者。最近，我们报道了将氧化锌纳米线集成到微流控芯片中用于净化水的研究成果，展示了在5秒转运时间内快速去除水中挥发性有机化合物的能力以及这种1厘米见方的微小芯片每天净化1升水的能力。该研究成果于2018年在*Microsystems & Nanoengineering*期刊上发表，荣获该杂志2020年最佳论文奖，并成为该期刊2年内被引用次数最多的论文之一。

8.Could you tell us your expectation for *Light*?

8. 您能谈谈对*Light*有哪些期待吗?

Prof. Tarik: *Light* is a wonderful platform, mainly due to the top-level network of experts that are gathering every year during the "Light conference". This allows one establishing ties for long-term collaboration. I personally had multiple opportunities to initiate several collaborations after meeting people during the "Light conference". This includes collaborations with CIOMP. I had a two-month appointment in 2017 as a laureate of the CAS President International Fellowship Initiative. I was hosted by Dr. Zhongzhu Liang in the State Key Laboratory of Applied Optics (SKAO Lab) of CIOMP. More recently, since January 2019, I hosted Dr. Xiaoyi Liu in my lab for a two-year post-doctoral fellowship. Those two experiences were very enriching and also very fruitful in terms of results.

My expectation from *Light* is that the "Applications" word which is in the name of the journal could be developed further, not only during the "Light conference" but also in the journal itself. Indeed, I noticed that recently there were less and less papers being published in *Light* dealing with Applications. Maybe one way to promote this aspect further is to launch special issues on different themes dealing with applications of Light.

Tarik教授：*Light*是一个高水平的学术交流平台。每年光学界顶尖科学家都会参加Light会议，这为彼此间的长期合作搭建了桥梁和纽带。我本人就是受益者，Light会议期间，我发起了一些合作，其中就包括与长春光机所的合作。2017年在中国科学院国际人才计划(PIFI)的资助下，我与长春光机所应用光学国家重点实验室梁中翥博士展开了为期2个月的合作。2019年1月，刘小翼博士来我们实验室展开了为期2年的博士后研究工作。这两段经历对我来说意义重大，收获满满。

我对 *Light* 的期望是，期刊名称中的“Applications”一词可以得到进一步的落实，不仅仅在 Light 会议期间，更要落实在期刊本身。我发现最近 *Light* 发表的应用型论文数量越来越少，所以我认为也许推出光的应用方向不同主题的特刊是进一步促进 *Light* 期刊关注应用研究的一个办法。

Comment to the No. 8 Answer

Thanks a lot for Prof. Bourouina's suggestion for *Light*. In fact, *Light* has already noticed that when it comes to publishing articles about applications, it's more difficult than basic or frontier research. In order to solve this problem, *Light* launched a sister journal in 2020 called *Light: Advanced Manufacturing* (LAM, http://www.light-am.com/), which aims to publish scientific research and application results in the field of advanced manufacturing. *Light* will try its best to serve the community as always.

对第8个回答的回答

非常感谢 Tarik 教授对 *Light* 期刊的建议。事实上，*Light* 期刊已经注意到，发表应用类文章比基础或前沿研究要更难。为了解决这个问题，*Light* 期刊于 2020 年推出姊妹刊 *Light: Advanced Manufacturing*（LAM, http://www.light-am.com/），旨在发表先进制造领域的科学研究和应用成果。*Light* 期刊将一如既往地为社区服务。

Reference
参考文献

[1] SABRY Y M, SAADANY B, et al. Silicon micromirrors with three-dimensional curvature enabling lensless efficient coupling of free-space light. Light: Science & Applications, 2013,3:94.

Professor James C.Wyant

编者按

究竟是怎样的一个人，能够担任美国三大光学中心之一亚利桑那大学光学研究中心的首任院长，能够当选为光学领域中两个权威国际学术组织——美国光学学会(OSA)与国际光学工程学会(SPIE)的双会主席，能够成为众多科技公司的创始人？所有这些问题的答案就是——James C. Wyant。他身上有太多标签：光学大师、企业达人、慈善名人等。他是上帝的幸运儿，将儿时理想变为现实；他是努力拼搏的科学家，将光学事业做到极致，实现了多项成果转化；他是慷慨的慈善家，捐赠大额资产资助光学事业发展；他是热衷于体育的运动爱好者，经常户外徒步或跑步。本期James C. Wyant与我们相遇“Light人物”，他将与我们分享与光结缘的故事以及自己在光学领域学术上和国际组织活动中的感悟和体会等，我们将看到“硬汉”心底最柔软的地方，探知从科学概念到产品诞生的过程，学会如何能成为一名优秀的科学家和企业家。接下来，让我们一起走近James C. Wyant。

To Light and Beyond
光学工匠，向光而行

Special Guest: Cun Yu　Science Editor: Hui Wang
特邀嘉宾 于存　科学编辑 王卉

Editorial:

He is the founding dean of the University of Arizona's College of Optical Sciences. He was elected president of the OSA and the SPIE, two of the most respected international academic organizations in the world of optics. He is the founder or co-founder of multiple hi-tech companies. He is Prof. James C. Wyant. Prof. Wyant is many things: master of optics, entrepreneur and philanthropist, but above all, he is one of those rare lucky people who see their childhood dreams come true. He is the hardworking scientist who pushes optical science to the limit. He is the successful entrepreneur whose Midas touch turns research achievements into lucrative commercial projects. He is the generous philanthropist who has given a large fortune to help promote the development of optical science. He is the avid athlete who enjoys the outdoors and takes pleasure in hiking and running. From tender memories to cutting-edge research and hard-nosed business advice, Prof. Wyant will share with us how he became fascinated with optics and what he thinks about academic life and organizations.

Light People

Biography: James C. Wyant is a professor emeritus and founding dean at the College of Optical Sciences at the University of Arizona, where he was director (1999–2005), dean (2005–2012), and a faculty member since 1974. He received a B.S. in physics from Case Institute of Technology and M.S. and Ph.D. in optics from the University of Rochester. He was a founder of the WYKO Corporation and served as its president and board chairman from 1984 to 1997 and he was a founder of the 4D Technology Corporation and served as its board chairman from 2002 to 2018. Wyant is a member of the National Academy of Engineering, the National Academy of Inventors, a Fellow of OSA (Optical Society of America) and SPIE (International Society of Optics and Photonics), a distinguished fellow of the Optical Society of India, an honorary member of the Optical Society of Korea, and former editor-in-chief of the OSA journal *Applied Optics*. He was the 2010 president of OSA and the 1986 president of SPIE. Wyant has received several awards for his technical work, including the OSA Joseph Fraunhofer Award; SPIE Gold Medal; SPIE Technology Achievement Award; SPIE Chandra Vikram Award; SPIE Visionary Award; and five R&D 100 Awards. He received the University of Rochester College of Engineering Distinguished Alumnus Award, the Case Alumni Association Gold Medal Award, Case Western Reserve University Athletic Hall of Fame, the University Medal from Case Western Reserve University, and an Honorary Doctor of Science from the University of Rochester. For his entrepreneurial activities, Wyant has received several awards, including

Arizona's "Innovator of the Year" Product Award; the Tom Brown Excellence in Entrepreneurship Award; and the University of Arizona Technology Innovation Award. The University of Arizona renamed the College of Optical Sciences the James C. Wyant College of Optical Sciences in 2019.

专家简介：James C. Wyant，美国亚利桑那大学光学科学学院荣誉教授和创始院长，自1974年起担任职工、主任（1999—2005）、院长（2005—2012）。本科毕业于凯斯理工学院（CIT）（现为凯斯西储大学）物理专业，于美国罗切斯特大学取得光学硕士及博士学位。他是WYKO公司的创始人，并于1984年至1997年担任该公司总裁兼董事会主席，此外他还是4D科技公司创始人，并于2002年至2018年担任该公司董事会主席。Wyant教授是美国国家科学院和美国国家发明家科学院院士，美国光学学会（OSA）、国际光学工程学会（SPIE）会士，印度光学学会杰出会士，韩国光学学会荣誉会员，美国光学学会期刊《应用光学》前主编。他曾担任2010年美国光学学会主席和1986年国际光学工程学会主席。因其杰出的工作，他曾荣获：美国光学学会 Joseph Fraunhofer 奖、SPIE 金奖、SPIE 技术成就奖、SPIE Chandra Vikram 奖、SPIE Visionary 奖以及5项“R&D 100”奖。他还获得罗切斯特大学工程学院杰出校友奖、凯斯校友会金奖、凯斯西储大学奖章和罗切斯特大学荣誉理学博士。因其杰出的创业活动，Wyant 教授获得了多项荣誉，包括：亚利桑那州“年度创新者”产品奖和汤姆布朗卓越创业奖、亚利桑那大学技术创新奖。2019年亚利桑那大学光学科学学院正式更名为 James C. Wyant 光学科学学院。

1. In November 2018, the University of Arizona received an historic pledge of $20 million from you and your family to support 10 new faculty positions in its College of Optical Sciences. This is not the first time you have donated large sums of money to optics research and education, and as far as I know, you've been donating in many ways and giving back to the community as

much as you can. Could you talk a little bit about what motivates your generosity?

1. 2018年11月，您和您的家人向亚利桑那大学承诺捐赠2000万美金，用以资助光学科学学院10个教授岗位。这已经不是您第一次为光学研究和光学教育捐赠如此高额的资金了。据我所知，多年来您一直以各种方式和途径尽可能地回馈社会。您能谈一谈捐赠的初心吗？

Prof. Wyant: My primary reason for donating is to show my gratitude for everything my career in optics has given me and to honor my mentors who have helped shaped who I am today. I also hope that my commitment to support optics education will inspire others to do the same.

Wyant教授：我捐赠的主要原因是想感谢光学职业生涯所给予我的一切，并向我的老师们表达感谢，是他们塑造了今天的我。我也希望自己支持光学教育的行为能够鼓舞其他人也这样做。

2. As a successful entrepreneur with significant expertise in launching and growing industry corporations you have received several awards for your entrepreneurial activities, including Arizona's "Innovator of the Year" Product Award and the Tom Brown Excellence in Entrepreneurship Award. Could you talk about why you wanted to start the business? What do you think are the biggest challenges for scientists trying to commercialize their research achievements? Any tips or warnings?

2. 作为一名成功的企业家，您在公司创建和发展方面经验丰富且荣获多项荣誉，包括：亚利桑那州“年度创新者”产品奖和汤姆布朗卓越创业奖。您能谈谈创业的原因吗？对于科学家而言，在研究成果商业化的过程中您认为面临的最大挑战是什么？您有什么建议或者忠告吗？

Prof. Wyant: From an early age, I knew I wanted to do three things when I grew up—become a professor, be an inventor, and start a company. As a young professor/researcher, I put together an excellent student research group, and we became very excited about the possibility of turning some of our research into a commercial product.

One of the biggest challenges involved was accessing need and designing a unique product that many people would buy. In addition, we had to have a product that would still operate properly day-after-day-after-day after being shipped halfway around the world and operated by people with many different skill levels.

The best tip I can give anyone trying to commercialize their research is to accept that you cannot do everything well. Acknowledge your strengths and weaknesses, and hire people with skills that you do not have. When I started WYKO, I quickly realized I lacked marketing, writing, and accounting skills, so I hired talented people for those areas.

Wyant教授：从小我就励志长大后要做3件事：做一名教授，成为一名发明家和开公司。当我还是一名年轻的教授或者说研究人员时，我便组建了一支由优秀学生组成的研究小组，我们非常希望能够将研究的成果转化为商业产品。

这个过程中面临的最大挑战之一是设计能够满足需求且会让大多数人愿意购买的独特产品。此外，我们必须要有一款产品，它能够在漂洋过海运输将近半个地球后依然可以日复一日地良性运行，并且不同技能水平的人都能够操作并使用它。

对于那些想要实现研究成果商业化的人，我

最好的建议是学会接受自己无法做到事事完美的事实，认识自己的长处和短处，学会雇佣专业人士来弥补自己的不足。当我创建WYKO公司时，我很快意识到自己缺乏市场营销、写作和会计的技能，因此我聘用这些领域的专业人才。

Prof. Wyant with his OSA group met CIOMP delegation at the 8th Pacific Rim Conference on Lasers and Electro-Optics (CLEO) in Shanghai in 2009
2009年Wyant教授及其OSA代表团成员与中科院长春光机所代表团在上海举办的第八届环太平洋激光与光电子国际会议上合影

3. Your entrepreneurial success is firmly rooted in your excellent scientific and technological achievements. Would you care to share with us any moments of joy when you made scientific breakthroughs in your

research?

3. 您创业成功是基于您优秀的科研和技术成果。您愿意与我们分享一下在科研中取得突破性成果的一些振奋人心的精彩瞬间吗？

Prof. Wyant: There were many moments throughout my academic and professional career when a particular concept I was working on just clicked and I suddenly understood the concept in great detail—making a previously unsolved problem clear and obvious. I will give two examples—one technical and one business-related.

One technical example occurred during my time at ITEK in Boston, Massachusetts, in the late 1960s when I was working with computer-generated holograms (CGHs) to test aspheric optics. While I understood mathematics well, I did not totally understand the physics of a CGH. One day I realized that a CGH was just a computer-drawn binary representation of a regular interferogram. After that, I made very rapid progress using CGHs to test aspheric surfaces. In hindsight the solution was obvious, and I often wonder why I did not think of it earlier. I think I spent too much time on the math because I liked math, but it was really important to not just understand the math, but to also think about the physics of what was happening. Without really understanding the physics, I could have never really understood what I was doing. Math by itself, was not enough.

The second example concerns a business decision. When we started the WYKO Corporation the major market we intended to sell metrology equipment to was optical fabrication, and we did sell them a lot of equipment. The magnetic data storage industry also came to us and bought some equipment, but we continued to concentrate our efforts on interferometric metrology equipment for optical manufacturing. One day, while mowing the lawn at my home, I suddenly realized that the market of selling metrology equipment to manufactures of magnetic hard disk drives for the new personal computers was many times greater than the potential market for the optics industry—in particular for measuring the shape of magnetic recording heads used in hard disk drives. After that, we concentrated on designing interferometers and software for the magnetic data storage industry. The hard disk drive industry grew at a fantastic rate, and our business was able to take advantage of this growth. In hindsight, it is obvious that we needed to take advantage of the rapid growth in the hard disk drive industry because they needed metrology equipment very similar to what we were already selling, but at the time we were concentrating on the market that had been good to us in the past, rather than the market that had the best potential future.

Wyant教授：在我的学术和职业生涯中，有很多时候当我在研究某个特定的概念时，感觉自己好像被什么东西猛地一击，突然间就理解了这个概念，先前无法解决的问题一下子就变得豁然开朗了。在这里我举两个例子，一个与技术相关，一个与业务相关。

20世纪60年代我在美国马萨诸塞州首府波士顿ITEK公司工作，主要研究如何通过计算机生成的全息图来测试非球面光学。虽然我数学不错，但是并不能完全理解计算机生成的全息图方面的物理知识。有一天，我意识到计算机生成的全息图只是一台计算机绘制的常规干涉图采用二进制来表示。后来，我通过计算机生成的全息图来检测非球面取得了非常快速的进展。事后看来，解决方法是显而易见的。我经常在想，为什么我没有早点儿想到这一点。我知道自己因为热爱数学，所以在它身上花费了大量的时间，但是有一个忽略的事实也很重要，那就是数学本身需要理解，但是思考事物发生过程中蕴含的物理也同样重要。如果不能真正地理解物理学，那我就永远不可能真正理解自己到底在做什么。只依靠数学是不够的。

第二个例子有关业务决策方面。当我们开始成立WYKO公司时，市场定位是要将计量设备卖给光学制造公司，此前我们也确实卖给过他们很多设备。磁数据存储行业也购买过我们的一些设备，但是我们还是专注于做光学制造的干涉计量设备。有一天，当我在家里修剪草坪时，我突然意识到，计量设备在新型个人电脑硬盘驱动器制造方面的市场要比光学行业的潜在市场大许多倍，尤其是在测量硬盘驱动器磁头形状方面。所以在那之后，我们开始专注于磁数据存储行业的干涉仪和软件设计。硬盘驱动器行业以惊人的速度在增长，我们的业务也凭借这一优势取得了大幅增长。回过头来看，我们利用硬盘驱动器行业快速增长的优势，而他们需要的测量设备也恰巧与我们正准备出售的设备相似，但是当时我们只关注对我们有利的市场，而忽略了最具未来潜力的市场。

4. Your major research interests involve using interferometric techniques combined with computers and modern electronics to produce "state of the art" solutions for a variety of metrology problems. What were the most significant scientific and technological challenges?

4. 您主要的研究领域是使用干涉技术将计算机与现代电子技术相结合，以得到不同种计量问题的“最先进的”解决方案。在这个过程中最大的科学技术挑战是什么？

Prof. Wyant: Back in the early 1980's when we first started our company, WYKO, the main challenge was the lack of powerful "out-of-the-box" technology that is easily obtained today. Computers were slow with little memory, so we had to write very efficient software to do calculations, Commercial graphic display boards were not available, so we built bit-mapped display boards to accurately show our results. And we had no way to interface solid-state detector arrays to a computer, so we had to build our own electronics to interface between the computers and detectors. I would have loved to have had one of today's smartphones back then!

Wyant教授：早在1980年我们初创WYKO公司时，面临的主要挑战是缺乏今天非常容易获得的“开箱即用”技术。计算机运行缓慢且内存不足，因此我们不得不编写高效的软件来进行计算，加之无法获得商业图形显示板，因此我们构建了位图显示板来准确展示我们的结果。此外，由于我们无法将固态探测器阵列连接到计算机，我们不得不构建专属的电子设备以便在计算机和探测器之间建立接口。那时我真想拥有一部现在的智能手机！

5. It is often said that the stars seen on earth are actually what they looked like millions of years ago. If

the distance is 100 light years, then what we see is the light emitted by the constellation 100 years ago. So, are lights seen with high-power telescopes and those seen with naked eyes emitted at the same time? (This question is chosen from a selection of questions from the CIOMP graduate students.)

5. 人们常说，现在地球上能够看见的星星实际上是它们几百万年前的样子。如果距离是100光年，那么我们现在所看到的就是100年前星座发出的光。所以大功率望远镜看到的光和肉眼看到的光是同时发出的吗？（该问题由长春光机所研究生提问）

Prof. Wyant: Large aperture telescopes collect more light than our small aperture eyes so they can detect stars that are fainter due to being farther away. If the star is 100 light-years away, the light was emitted 100 years ago and has been traveling at the speed of light for 100 years to reach us. Therefore, some of the light seen with high-power telescopes was emitted long before the light seen with naked eyes.

Wyant教授：与小口径望远镜相比，大口径望远镜能够收集更多的光，因此可以检测因距离较远而较暗的恒星。如果恒星距离我们100光年，那么它的光是100年前发出的，并且以光速行进了100年抵达。因此，大功率望远镜看到的光要早于用肉眼看到的光。

6. You have served as the president of OSA and SPIE, two world-renowned and influential organizations in the field of optics. What are their similarities and differences please?

6. 您曾担任过美国光学学会（OSA）与国际光学工程学会（SPIE）的主席，这两个组织在光学领域均享誉盛名。请问它们之间有什么相似和不同之处？

Prof. Wyant: OSA and SPIE are more similar now than they were many years ago. Both organizations are financially sound and managed very well, with excellent leaders and extremely competent staff. While traditionally OSA has been known to be more focused on science and SPIE on engineering, both organizations are now very strong in both science and engineering. Also, both organizations are proud to be international societies, with members, officers, and meetings around the world.

Wyant教授：与过去相比，现在美国光学学会（OSA）与国际光学工程学会（SPIE）两者间的相似度要高很多。这两个组织无论是在财务方面还是管理方面，表现得都非常优秀，而且它们都有出色的领导和能干的员工。虽然从传统意义上看，OSA更关注科学，SPIE更关注工程，但是现在它们不论是在科学，还是在工程方面实力都很强。此外，它们在国际上都盛名远播，在全世界都有属于自己的会员、工作人员和国际会议等。

7. As the 1986 SPIE President and the 2010 OSA President, you have had significant experiences with the leadership, awards, and major meetings of both societies. What responsibilities did these positions involve and what influence did this kind of volunteer work have on your career?

7. 作为1986年SPIE主席和2010年OSA主席，您在领导、获奖和大型会议方面都有着丰富的经验。主席这个职位都有哪些责任？这项工作对您日后的职业有什么影响？

Prof. Wyant: Before becoming President of SPIE or OSA, I served on numerous committees; was active in both SPIE and OSA journals including being the Editor-In-Chief for OSA's *Applied Optics*; and was involved with organizing meetings for both OSA and SPIE. As President of SPIE, I helped to increase our involvement in meetings held outside the United States and worked to expand the size of the exhibits at SPIE meetings. While I was President of OSA, we began publishing a greater number of specialized optics journals and we increased our international activities and membership. I was fortunate to visit many new OSA student chapters around the world.

Wyant教授：在担任SPIE和OSA主席前，我曾在多个委员会任职，活跃于这两个组织创办的期刊，包括担任美国光学学会*Applied Optics*（中文：《应用光学》）的主编，参与组织两个学会的多场

Prof. Wyant with his OSA executives met CIOMP delegation in 2012
2012年Wyant教授与OSA高管一同会见中科院长春光机所代表团

会议。作为国际光学工程学会(SPIE)的主席，我使会议的举办地不再限于美国，并努力扩大会议上展览的规模。在我担任美国光学学会(OSA)期间，我积极推动出版大量的光学专业期刊，并且不断增加国际活动和会员的数量。我很荣幸访问了许多设立在世界各地的OSA学生分会。

8. The College of Optical Sciences at the University of Arizona is one of the best optical engineering/science institutes in the world. As the founding dean and a professor emeritus of the College, what qualities do you look for when recruiting new faculty and graduate students?

8. 亚利桑那大学是世界上最好的光学工程/科研院所之一。作为这所大学光学科学学院的创始院长和荣誉退休教授，您在招募教师和学生时，最看重什么?

Prof. Wyant: It is so important for both faculty and graduate students to be passionate about the field they have chosen, along with being smart and ambitious. Good communication skills are a must, as well as the ability to work well with others. Personally, I have found that graduate students that are also committed to a hobby, such as sports or music, tend to be motivated and have a strong work ethic.

Wyant教授：不论是职工还是学生，对自己所选择的事情充满激情，同时又有才智和雄心是非常重要的。此外，好的沟通技巧以及与他人合作的能力同样也是必不可少的。就我个人而言，我发现那些有个人爱好的学生（比如爱好运动或者音乐），往往会更加积极并且有着很强的职业操守。

9. As I know, you have paid three visits to the Changchun Institute of Optics, Fine Mechanics and Physics (CIOMP), Chinese Academy of Sciences, what

Prof. Wyant participated in the ICO 2005 organized by CIOMP in Changchun
2005年Wyant教授参加由长春光机所承办的第20届国际光学委员会大会

Prof. Wyant participated in the academic conference for celebrating the 60th anniversary of CIOMP
2012年Wyant教授参加长春光机所60周年所庆学术会议

are your impressions of it?

9. 据我所知，您曾经 3 次访问中国科学院长春光学精密机械与物理研究所（简称“长春光机所”），您对长春光机所的印象是什么？

Prof. Wyant: I enjoyed my visits to CIOMP and was very impressed with the facilities, faculty, and students. Everyone was very welcoming and went out of their way to show me their labs and introduce me to their research. I found the labs and equipment to be state-of-the-art and the people extremely dedicated.

Wyant教授：我非常享受访问长春光机所的过程，长春光机所的设施、教职工给我留下了非常深刻的印象。每个人都很热情，积极地向我展示实验室，并介绍他们所做的研究工作。我发现长春光机所实验室的设备都非常先进，员工也非常敬业。

Prof. Wyant participated in the summer school jointly organized by CIOMP and OSA in 2013

2013年Wyant教授参加长春光机所与美国光学学会联合组织的夏令营活动

Hiking with students during summer school in 2013

2013年参加夏令营徒步活动

10. You once said, "Optics is a wonderful career where you can be a physicist, an engineer, an entrepreneur, or a combination of the three." So, when and how did you become interested in optics?

10. 您曾经说过:“光学是一项美好的职业，在这里你可以成为物理学家、工程师、企业家或身兼多职。”那么您是何时或者说是如何对光学感兴趣的?

Prof. Wyant: I first started thinking about optics between my junior and senior years at Case Institute of Technology (CIT). I got a summer job at Libby-Owens-Ford Glass Company in Toledo, Ohio, where I was given an optics project to develop an instrument that would inspect automobile window glass to determine the amount of surface scatter. The project was such a success that the instrument was installed in their factory.

Then during my first senior physics lab at CIT, I saw my first laser and my first hologram. My professor illuminated a cloudy glass plate with a Helium-Neon laser. A stapler appeared that looked so realistic, I actually tried to grab it. I remember thinking that I just had to learn the science behind creating this amazing 3-D image!

Wyant教授：在凯斯理工学院(CIT)（现为凯斯西储大学）读本科三年级和四年级时，我开始思考研究光学。暑假时我到俄亥俄州托莱多市利比-欧文斯-福特玻璃公司工作，在这里公司给我分配了一项光学项目，该项目旨在开发一种能够检测车窗玻璃以确定表面散射量的仪器。这个项目最后大获成功，以至于后来他们工厂也安装了这个设备。

在CIT高级物理实验室学习期间，我看到了我人生中第一台激光器和第一张全息图。教授用氦氖激光器照亮了一块浑浊的玻璃板，一个装订器形象就出现了，它是如此逼真，我都想去抓住它。我清晰地记得当时我就决定要学习能够创造这张惊人的3D图像背后的科学！

11. From a student to a scientist, a teacher, and an

academician, how do you think your attitude toward scientific research has changed over the years?

11. 从学生到科学家，从教师到院士，您认为这些年您对科研的态度发生了哪些转变?

Prof. Wyant and Dr. Yuhong Bai, the director of Light Publishing Group
Wyant教授与*Light*出版中心主任白雨虹博士合影

Prof. Wyant: When I was a young researcher, I remember there being times when I discarded certain research ideas because they were not practical or useful, but since then I have learned that what might not be practical or useful at the present time may become highly practical when other technology becomes available. And these ideas may be useful for new applications we have not thought of yet.

Wyant教授：当我还是一名年轻的研究员时，我记得很多次都有想要放弃某些研究想法的时候，因为它们不切合实际或者说没有用处，但是也是从那时起，我意识到现在没有用的东西在某些技术成熟可用的时候有可能会具有实际作用。这些想法对新应用可能是有用的，只是当时我们还没有想到而已。

12. I read that you were captain of the cross-country team at Case Institute of Technology (CIT) for which you ran outdoors in winter, even falling down a few times on ice. Is running a hobby of yours? Do you have any other

hobbies?

12. 我听说，您曾是CIT越野赛队的队长，您冬天在户外跑步，甚至在冰上还摔倒过几次。跑步是您的爱好吗？您还有其他的爱好吗？

James C. Wyant was running as a junior in college in 1963
1963年，当时大学三年级的James C. Wyant在户外跑步

Prof. Wyant: During my undergraduate years at CIT, I was part of the track and field team, as well as the cross-country team where we ran races outside over natural terrain. Participating in athletics those 4 years was one of the best experiences of my academic career. I learned valuable skills such as how to be part of a team and how to collaborate. The experience also helped me develop a habit of exercise that I still maintain today, although mostly walking and hiking now.

Wyant教授：当我在CIT读本科时，曾是田径队的一员，同时也是越野赛队的一员，我们在户外的天然地势上赛跑。参加体育运动的那4年是我学术生涯中最美好的一段经历。我学到了很多宝贵的经验，比如如何成为团队的一员，如何与他人合作。这些经历也帮助我养成锻炼的好习惯，直到今天我仍然坚持锻炼，尽管大部分时候我会选择走路和徒步。

My other big hobby is ham radio. I have been a ham radio operator for more than 60 years which I find interesting because there are many similarities between radio communications and optics. When I first became interested in holography as an undergraduate student, I realized how much my knowledge of radio communications helped me understand the concepts of optics. Then, during this past year, when I had to stay home more due to the pandemic, I knew I was going to need a project. For several years, I had been thinking about putting together an Earth-Moon-Earth (EME, "Moon Bounce") station to bounce radio waves off the moon to communicate with operators around the world. While designing this station, I realized that my knowledge of optics now helped me understand many aspects of EME.

我的另一大爱好就是业余无线电。我从事业余无线电操作员已经60余年了，这项工作非常有趣，因为无线电通信与光学之间有很多相似之处。当我第一次对全息照相感兴趣时是在本科阶段，我意识到无线电通信知识能够帮助我理解光学的概念。过去的一年里，受疫情影响，我不得不待在家时，我知道自己需要做一个项目。几年来，我一直思考建立一个地球—月球—地球站（“月球反弹”）实现无线电波从月球反弹，与世界各地的运营商建立通信。当我在设计测试站时，我意识到光学知识帮助我从多维度理解地球—月球—地球。

13. If you could travel in time, which period in history or in your life would you like to go back to? Why?

13. 如果时间可以穿梭，您最想回到生命中的哪个时期？为什么？

Prof. Wyant: My father was killed in a farming accident when I was 5 years old, therefore most of my memories of him are ones told to me by my mother and other family members. I think it would be great to go back to the time before he died (prior to 1948) so I could commit to memory his personality and interactions with me during those first years of my life, especially since I am often told that I am very much like my father. Before his death, he was known for his clever inventions used on our farm.

Wyant教授：在我5岁时，父亲死于一场农场事故，所以我对他的大部分记忆都是母亲和其他家人告诉我的。如果时间可以穿梭，我希望回到他去世之前（1948年前），那样我就可以记住他的性格和小时候与他互动的瞬间，尤其是我经常听到有人说，我非常像我的父亲。在他去世前，他因在农场上使用自己的很多发明而闻名。

14. Could you tell us who you consider as your mentor in your career and how he/she has influenced you?

14. 在您的职业生涯中，您将谁奉为您的导师？他/她是如何影响您的？

Prof. Wyant: I always say that the one person that influenced my career choices the most was Bob Shannon. I first met him when I was a graduate student at the University of Rochester and, upon graduation, he hired me as an optical engineer at ITEK Corp. in

Boston, Massachusetts. Shortly afterward, Bob left ITEK to become a professor at the Optical Sciences Center (OSC) at the University of Arizona. Five years later, Bob encouraged me to leave the industry and join the faculty at OSC. Bob also encouraged my involvement with the professional societies OSA and SPIE.

Wyant教授：我经常说对我职业选择影响最大的人就是鲍勃·香农。我第一次见到他是我在罗切

Group photo at the College of Optical Sciences Renaming event (from left to right: Harry Barrett, James C. Wyant, Dick Powell, Bob Shannon, and Tom Koch).
光学科学学院更名活动合影（从左到右：Harry Barrett、James C. Wyant、Dick Powell、Bob Shannon和Tom Koch）

斯特大学读书的时候。毕业后，他聘请我在美国马萨诸塞州首府波士顿的ITEK公司担任光学工程师。不久之后，鲍勃·香农离开了ITEK公司，成为了亚利桑那大学光学科学学院的教授。5年后，他鼓励我离开企业，加入到光学科学学院。此外，他也激励我加入美国光学学会(OSA)和国际光学工程学会(SPIE)这样的专业组织。

15. How do you balance your work and family life?

15. 如何平衡工作和家庭生活?

Prof. Wyant: To be honest, when I was young and in the prime years of my career, I probably did not balance work and family life as well as I could have. For years, I worked 7 days a week, almost never taking a vacation. Now that I am retired, I realize all that hard work paid off and I can now "play" 7 days a week, but I still in some ways wish I had always had a better life/work balance.

Wyant教授：老实说，当我年轻的时候，也就是在我职业生涯的黄金时期，我可能并没有平衡好工作和家庭之间的关系。多年以来，我每周工作7天，几乎从未有过假期。现在我退休了，我意识到所有辛苦的工作都得到了应有的回报，现在一周7天都是我的假期，但是在某种程度上我仍然希望我过去能够更好地做到工作和生活的平衡。

16. What advice do you have for young researchers?

16. 您对年轻科研工作者有什么建议?

Prof. Wyant: Find your passion and, once you do, surround yourself with smart people who will teach and inspire you to push yourself. A lot of the time, a student that has just received their degree will accept a job with the company that offers them the most money. While money certainly should be a consideration, it is far more important at that point in their career to accept the job that offers challenging projects you would be excited to be working on.

I also think it is very important to join and be involved with professional societies. Contacts you make by attending meetings and being on committees may prove to be invaluable for networking. In addition, some of those you meet may become professional mentors or lifelong friends.

Wyant教授：找到自己的激情所在，一旦投入到一件事，多与聪明人在一起，他们将会教导并激励你不断前进。很多时候，刚毕业的学生在找工作的时候会选择能够给他们提供高薪资的企业，尽管钱是考虑的因素之一，但是在职业生涯中，接受一份让你感到兴奋且具有挑战性的工作要重要得多。

我认为参与并加入专业社团也是非常重要的。通过参加会议，成为委员会一员对于职业社交网络的搭建是非常有益的。此外，你遇到的一些人未来可能会成为你的专业导师或一辈子的朋友。

[Note: The Optical Society of America (OSA) has been rebranded as OPTICA since September 20, 2021.]

［注：美国光学学会（OSA）已于2021年9月20日更名为OPTICA。］

Professor Aydogan Ozcan

编者按

2016年，基于深度学习原理的谷歌人工智能机器人AlphaGo战胜围棋前世界冠军、韩国九段名将李世石的消息轰动了AI届与围棋届，为深度学习的发展带来了划时代意义。深度学习是一种复杂的机器学习算法，它使用多层人工神经网络来自动分析信号或数据。目前，深度学习已经渗透到我们的日常生活中，比如人脸识别、语音识别等智能应用。科学家们也基于深度学习研究取得了许多瞩目的科研成果。来自美国加州大学洛杉矶分校（UCLA）的Aydogan Ozcan教授带领他的团队深入研究深度学习算法，为光学计算成像与传感技术的研究提供了新的思路，引入的图像生成和重建方法为相关领域的发展带来了重大的技术革新，促使光学设计与设备从硬件革新朝着数据驱动的方向发展。本期，我们非常荣幸邀请到美国发明院院士、UCLA校长教授Aydogan Ozcan为我们解读他的最新科研成果与对相关领域未来发展的远见卓识，分享他的追光心路历程、与*Light*的不解之缘，以及在人才培养方面的心得体会。让我们一起来聆听这位世界领军科学家的精彩故事。

Meet Extraordinary Temperament by Light—Professor Aydogan Ozcan
因光而遇，风采卓然

Science Editor: Tingting Sun 科学编辑 孙婷婷

Editorial:

In 2016, the news that Google's artificial intelligence (AI) robot AlphaGo, based on the principle of deep learning, won the victory over Lee Sedol, the former world Go champion and the famous 9th Dan competitor of Korea, caused a sensation in both fields of AI and Go, which brought epoch-making significance to the development of deep learning. Deep learning is a complex machine learning algorithm that uses multiple layers of artificial neural networks to automatically analyze signals or data. At present, deep learning has penetrated our daily life, such as the applications of face recognition and speech recognition. Scientists have also made many remarkable achievements based on deep learning. Professor Aydogan Ozcan from the University of California, Los Angeles (UCLA) led his team to research deep learning algorithms, which provided new ideas for the exploring of optical computational imaging and sensing technology, and introduced image generation and reconstruction methods which brought major technological innovations to the development of related fields. Optical designs and devices are moving from being physically driven to being data-driven. We are much honored to have Aydogan Ozcan, Fellow of the National Academy of Inventors and Chancellor's Professor of UCLA, to unscramble his latest scientific research results and foresight for the future development of related fields, and to share his journey of pursuing Optics, his indissoluble relationship with *Light: Science & Applications*, and his experience in talent cultivation.

Light People

Biography: Prof. Aydogan Ozcan is the Chancellor's Professor and the Volgenau Chair for Engineering Innovation at UCLA and an HHMI Professor with the Howard Hughes Medical Institute, leading the Bio- and Nano-Photonics Laboratory at UCLA School of Engineering and is also the Associate Director of the California NanoSystems Institute. Prof. Ozcan is elected Fellow of the National Academy of Inventors (NAI) and holds >45 issued/granted patents and >20 pending patent applications, is also the author of one book and the co-author of >700 peer-reviewed publications in major scientific journals and conferences. Prof. Ozcan is the founder and a member of the Board of Directors of Lucendi Inc., Hana Diagnostics, Pictor Labs, as well as Holomic/Cellmic LLC, which was named a Technology Pioneer by The World Economic Forum in 2015. Prof. Ozcan is also a Fellow of the American Association for the Advancement of Science (AAAS), the International Photonics Society (SPIE), the Optical Society of America (OSA), the American Institute for Medical and Biological Engineering (AIMBE), the Institute of Electrical and Electronics Engineers (IEEE), the Royal Society of Chemistry (RSC), the American Physical Society (APS) and the Guggenheim Foundation, and has received major awards including the Presidential Early Career Award for Scientists and Engineers, International Commission for Optics Prize, Biophotonics Technology Innovator Award, Rahmi M. Koc Science Medal, International Photonics Society Early Career Achievement Award, Army Young Investigator Award, NSF CAREER Award,

NIH Director's New Innovator Award, Navy Young Investigator Award, IEEE Photonics Society Young Investigator Award and Distinguished Lecturer Award, National Geographic Emerging Explorer Award, National Academy of Engineering The Grainger Foundation Frontiers of Engineering Award and MIT's TR35 Award for his seminal contributions to computational imaging, sensing and diagnostics. Dr. Ozcan is also listed as a Highly Cited Researcher by Web of Science, Clarivate, and serves as the co-Editor-in-Chief of *eLight*.

专家简介：Aydogan Ozcan 教授是美国加州大学洛杉矶分校（UCLA）的校长教授和 Volgenau 工程创新主席，以及霍华德 · 休斯医学研究所（HHMI）教授，领导 UCLA 工程学院的生物和纳米光子实验室，同时也是加州纳米系统研究中心（CNSI）的副主任。Ozcan 教授为美国国家发明院（NAI）院士，持有 45 项已授权专利和 20 多项专利申请，并著有一本专著，在主要科学期刊和会议上发表 700 余篇经同行评议的论文。

Ozcan 教授是 Lucendi Inc.、Hana Diagnostics、Pictor Labs、Holomic/Cellmic LLC 的创始人和董事会成员，Holomic/Cellmic LLC 于 2015 年被世界经济论坛评为技术先驱。Ozcan 教授还是美国科学促进会（AAAS）、国际光学工程学会（SPIE）、美国光学学会（OSA）、美国医学与生物工程院（AIMBE）、电气电子工程师学会（IEEE）、英国皇家化学学会（RSC）、美国物理学会（APS）和古根海姆基金会会士，并获得了重要奖项，包括美国青年科学家与工程师总统奖、国际光学委员会奖、生物光子学技术创新者奖、Rahmi M. Koc 科学奖章、国际光学工程学会早期职业成就奖、陆军青年研究者奖、美国国家科学基金会职业奖、美国国立卫生研究院主任创新者奖、海军青年研究者奖、IEEE 光电学会青年研究者奖和杰出讲师奖、国家地理新兴探索者奖、美国国家工程院 Grainger 基金会前沿工程奖和麻省理工学院 TR35 奖，以表彰他在计算成像、传感和诊断方面的开创性贡献。他还被列为 Web of Science、Clarivate 的高引用研究人员，并担任 *eLight* 期刊的联合主编。

1. Can you please briefly define with your own words the focus of your research lab?

1. 能不能简要概括一下您实验室的研究重点?

Prof. Ozcan: My lab is composed of 3 sub-areas:

Computational microscopy includes e.g., deep learning-enabled microscopy, holography, lensless imaging, on-chip microscopy, 3D microscopy, imaging flow-cytometry, among others.

Sensing: point-of-care sensors, mobile-phone enabled sensors, field-based sensing and measurement systems with applications in mobile health and telemedicine, environmental monitoring (for example, air/water quality sensing).

Optical computing and inverse design: diffractive networks, diffractive optical processors, and deep learning-designed free-space optics.

While conducting exciting, cutting-edge applied

research on photonics and optics, we are also training the next generation of engineers, scientists, and entrepreneurs through our research programs. Some of our trainees have started up their own labs in the United States, China, and other parts of the world, some went to industry, leading their teams, and some started up companies.

Ozcan教授：我们实验室由3个研究领域组成：

计算显微技术：包括深度学习显微镜、全息成像、无透镜成像、片上显微镜、3D显微镜、成像流式细胞术等。

传感：即时护理传感器、移动电话传感器、应用于移动医疗与远程医疗的实地传感和测量系统、环境监测(如空气质量/水质的监测)。

光学计算与反向设计：衍射神经网络、衍射光学处理器和深度学习设计的自由空间光学。

在光子学和光学领域进行激动人心的前沿应

用研究的同时，我们还通过研究项目培养下一代工程师、科学家和企业家。我们的一些学员已经在美国、中国和世界其他地方建立了自己的实验室，一些人进入了产业界，领导着自己的团队，还有一些人创办了公司。

2. Optical Coherence Tomography (OCT) is a widely used imaging method that provides three-dimensional information about the optical scattering properties of biological samples. One of your recent publications in *Light* focused on improving image reconstruction in OCT[1]. Could you please introduce the research idea and main advantages of your method as well as its impact on the OCT field?

2. 光学相干断层扫描（OCT）是一种广泛应用的成像方式，可以提供生物样品光学散射特性的三维信息。您最近在*Light*上发表了一篇关于改进OCT图像重建的文章[1]，您能介绍一下该方法的研究思路与主要优势吗？这对于OCT领域有怎样的重要意义？

Prof. Ozcan: Indeed, OCT is widely used in diagnostic medicine, for example in ophthalmology, to noninvasively obtain detailed 3D images of the retina and underlying tissue structure. In our latest paper[1] published in *Light*, we have developed a deep learning-based OCT image reconstruction method that can successfully generate 3D images of tissue specimens using significantly less spectral data than normally required. Using standard image reconstruction methods employed in OCT, undersampled spectral data, where some of the spectral measurements are omitted, resulting in severe spatial artifacts in the reconstructed images, obscuring 3D information and structural details of the sample to be visualized. In our new approach, we trained a neural network using deep learning to rapidly reconstruct 3D images of tissue samples with much less spectral data than normally acquired in a typical

OCT system, successfully removing the spatial artifacts observed in standard image reconstruction methods.

The efficacy and robustness of this new method were demonstrated by imaging various human and mouse tissue samples using 3-fold less spectral data captured by a state-of-the-art swept-source OCT system. Running on graphics processing units (GPUs), the neural network successfully eliminated severe spatial artifacts due to undersampling and omission of most spectral data points in less than 1 ms for an OCT image that is composed of 512 depth scans (A-lines).

These results that we have recently published in *Light* highlight the transformative potential of this neural network-based OCT image reconstruction framework, which can be easily integrated with various spectral-domain OCT systems, to improve their 3D imaging speed without sacrificing resolution or signal-to-noise of the reconstructed images.

Ozcan教授：OCT确实被广泛应用于诊断医学，例如眼科，可以无创获取视网膜和底层组织结构的精细三维图像。我们在*Light*发表的这篇论文中，描述了我们开发的一种基于深度学习的OCT图像重建方法，该方法可以用比通常明显更少的光谱数据生成组织样本的3D图像。若使用OCT的标准图像重建方法，欠采样的光谱数据（其中一些光谱测量被省略）会导致重建图像中存在严重的空间伪影，遮蔽待测样本的三维信息和结构细节。在我们

Prof. Ozcan presenting at 2017 "Light Conference"
Ozcan教授在2017年“Light Conference”上作精彩报告

的新方法中，使用深度学习训练神经网络来快速重建组织样本的三维图像，其光谱数据比在典型OCT系统中获取的光谱数据要少得多，并成功地去除了标准图像重建方法中观察到的空间伪影。

为了证明这种新方法的有效性和稳定性，我们通过使用先进的扫频源 OCT 系统，对各种人类和小鼠组织样本进行成像,并获取了 3 倍欠采样光谱数据。对于由 512 个深度扫描（A–line 信号）组成的 OCT 图像，借助使用图形处理单元（GPUs），神经网络仅在不到 1 ms 的时间内即可成功地消除由于欠采样和大部分光谱数据点遗漏而导致的严重空间伪影。

我们最近发表在*Light*上的这些结果突出了这种基于神经网络的图像重建框架的潜力，它易于与各种光谱域OCT系统集成，以提高他们的三维成像速度却不牺牲重建图像的分辨率或信噪比。

3. In 2017, your paper "Phase Recovery and

Holographic Image Reconstruction using Deep Learning in Neural Networks"[2] published in *Light* has got 359 citations on the Web of Science, and also won the "Light annual Outstanding Paper", Highly Cited Paper, Popular Downloaded Paper, which became a major breakthrough in the field of optical computational imaging. Can you talk about the development status and future trends of computational imaging? What are the potential applications?

3. 2017年，您在*Light*出版的论文“Phase Recovery and Holographic Image Reconstruction using Deep Learning in Neural Networks”[2]在Web of Science已获得359次引用，也获得了*Light*年度优秀论文、高被引论文、热门下载论文，成为光学计算成像领域的重大突破。您能谈一下计算成像的未来发展趋势吗？有哪些潜在的应用领域？

Prof. Ozcan: This seminal *Light* paper of our team

was published online in October 2017, and it was placed in arXiv by our team in May 2017. These results demonstrate the first use of deep neural networks for holographic image reconstruction and phase recovery. In this paper, we demonstrated that a convolutional neural network (CNN) can learn to perform phase recovery and holographic image reconstruction after appropriate training. This deep learning-based approach provides a fundamentally new framework to conduct holographic imaging by rapidly eliminating twin-image and self-interference related spatial artifacts, which have been part of holography since its invention by Dennis Gabor (leading to the Nobel Prize in Physics, 1971). Compared to existing holographic phase recovery approaches, this neural network framework is significantly faster to compute and reconstructs much improved phase and amplitude images of the objects using a single hologram, i.e., requires less number of measurements in addition to being computationally faster. Remarkably, this deep learning-based dual image elimination and phase recovery have been achieved without any model of light-matter interactions or solutions of the wave equation.

Ozcan教授：这篇开创性的*Light*论文于2017年10月在线上发表，是表明深度神经网络首次用于全息图像的重建和相位恢复。在这篇论文中，我们证明了卷积神经网络(CNN)在经过适当的训练后可以学习相位恢复和全息图像重建。这种基于深度学习的方法提供了一个全新的框架，可以快速消除自Dennis Gabor（1971年诺贝尔物理学奖获得者）发明全息术以来，一直伴随全息术产生的孪生像和自干涉相关的空间伪影问题。与现有的全息相位恢复方法相比，这种基于神经网络框架的方法仅需使用单个全息图，即可高速计算并重建高质量的相位和振幅图像，也就是说，除了计算速度更快之外，测量次数的需求也更低。值得注意的是，这种基于深度学习的孪生像消除和相位恢复的方法，不需任何借助对光—物质相互作用的建模或波动方程的求解就已经得以实现。

After this 2017 *Light* publication, our team has further expanded these results in many unique ways. In an *Optica* paper[3] published in 2018, we demonstrated an innovative application of deep learning to significantly extend the imaging depth of a hologram. We demonstrated a CNN-based approach that simultaneously performs auto-focusing and phase-recovery to significantly extend the depth-of-field (DOF) in holographic image reconstruction. For this, a CNN is trained by using pairs of randomly de-focused back-propagated holograms and their corresponding in-focus phase-recovered images. After this training phase, the CNN takes a single back-propagated hologram of a 3D sample as input to rapidly achieves phase-recovery and reconstructs an in focus image of the sample over a significantly extended DOF. Furthermore, this deep learning based auto-focusing and phase-recovery method are non-iterative, and significantly improves the algorithm time-complexity of holographic image reconstruction from O(nm) to O(1), where n refers to the number of individual object points or particles within the sample volume, and m represents the discrete focusing search space, within which each object point or particle needs to be individually focused.

2017年在*Light*的文章发表之后，我们团队用许多独特的方式进一步扩展了这些结果。2018年在*Optica*上发表的那篇论文中，我们展示了一种深度学习的创新应用，显著扩展了全息图的成像深度[3]。我们演示了一种基于CNN的方法，该方法可以同时进行自动聚焦和相位恢复，显著扩展全息图像重建中的景深（DOF）。为此，我们将全息图反向传播至随机的非聚焦平面，并将其与聚焦的相位恢复后的图像进行匹配，得到图像对，用以训练CNN。在这个训练阶段之后，CNN可以以一个三维样本的单一反向传播全息图作为输入，以快速实现相位恢复，并在显著扩展的DOF上重建该样本的聚焦图像。此外，这种基于深度学习的自动聚焦和相位恢复方法是非迭代的，使全息图像重建算法的时间复杂度从O(nm)提高到O(1)，其中n为样本体积内单个目标点或粒子的数量，m表示离散聚焦搜索空间，其中每个目标点或粒子都需要单独聚焦。

Another breakthrough result, in my opinion, that is at the intersection of deep learning and holography was published in *Light* in 2019, and this work was placed in arXiv in 2018 by our team. In this publication[4], we introduced the use of a deep neural network to perform cross-modality image transformation from a digitally back-propagated hologram corresponding to a given depth within the sample volume into an image that is equivalent to a bright-field microscope image acquired at the same depth. Because a single hologram is used to digitally propagate to different sections of the sample to virtually generate bright-field equivalent images of each section, this approach bridges the volumetric imaging capability of digital holography with speckle- and artifact-free image contrast of bright-field microscopy. After its training, the deep neural network learns the statistical image transformation between a holographic imaging system and an incoherent bright-field microscope, and intuitively it brings together "the best of both worlds" by fusing the advantages of holographic and incoherent bright-field imaging modalities.

在我看来，另一个突破性成果是在深度学习和全息术的交叉融合上（于2019年发表在*Light*上）。在这篇文章中，我们介绍了使用深度神经网络实现了对样本的跨模态成像，即将三维样本某特定深度的反向传播全息图转化成其在明场显微镜下观测到的同深度下的图像[4]。由于反向传播图像至不同聚焦平面仅需单个全息图作为输入，这种可以得到对应明场下无散斑无伪影的图像的方法，体现了全息术的立体成像能力。经过训练，深度神经网络学习了全息成像系统和非相干明场显微镜之间的统计图像转换，并通过融合全息和非相干明场成像方式的优点，直观地将“两全其美”的东西融合在一起。

For this holographic to bright-field image transformation, we used a generative adversarial network (GAN), which was trained using pollen samples imaged by an in-line holographic microscope along with a bright-field incoherent microscope (used as the ground truth). After the training phase, which needs to be performed only once, the generator network blindly takes as input a new hologram (never seen by the network before) to infer its bright-field equivalent image at any arbitrary depth within the sample volume. We experimentally demonstrated the success of this powerful cross-modality image transformation between holography and bright-field microscopy, where the network output images were free from speckle and various other interferometric artifacts observed in holography, matching the contrast and depth-of-field of bright-field microscopy images that were mechanically focused onto the same planes within the 3D sample. We also demonstrated that the deep network also correctly colorizes the output image, using an input hologram acquired with a monochrome sensor and narrow-band illumination, matching the color distribution of the bright-field image.

对于这种全息到明场图像的转换，我们使用生成对抗网络（GAN）对全息显微镜和明场非相干显微镜拍摄的花粉样本进行训练。只需要训练一次，训练结束后，生成网络将一个新的全息图（之前网络从未见过）作为输入，推断出其在样本体积内任意深度的明场等效图像。我们通过实验成功地证明了这种在全息术和明场显微镜之间强大的跨模态图像转换能力，其中网络输出图像不受全息术中观察到的散斑和各种其他干涉伪影的影响，与聚焦在3D样品中相同平面上的明场显微镜图像的对比度和景深相匹配。我们还证明，深度神经网络还可以使用单色传感器和窄带照明获得的输入全息图，正确地为输出图像着色，与明场图像的颜色分布相匹配。

This deep learning-enabled image transformation between holography and bright-field microscopy replaces the need to mechanically scan a volumetric sample, as it benefits from the digital wave-propagation framework of holography to virtually scan through the sample, where each one of these digitally propagated fields is transformed into bright-field microscopy equivalent images, exhibiting the spatial and color contrast as well as the depth-of-field expected from an incoherent microscope.

这种基于深度学习的全息术和明场显微镜之间的图像转换取代了机械扫描体积样本的需求，因为它得益于全息术的数字波传播框架，可以虚拟扫描样本，每一个数字传播的场都被转换成明场显微镜等效图像，显示出空间和颜色对比以及非相干显微镜预期的景深。

Prof. Aydogan Ozcan in the lab
Aydogan Ozcan教授在实验室

4. You lead your team to research Diffraction Deep Neural Network and moved the Neural Network from the chip to the real world, which realized deep learning with almost zero energy consumption and zero delays by relying on light propagation. The results were also successfully published in *Science*[5]. Can you talk about the subtlety of this research work? For the further development of this technology, what are the key

problems to be solved currently?

4. 您带领自己的团队研究的衍射深度神经网络（Diffractive Deep Neural Network），把神经网络从芯片上搬到了现实世界中，依靠光的传播，实现几乎零能耗、零延迟的深度学习[5]。该成果也成功发表在*Science*上。您能谈谈该研究的精妙之处吗？对于该技术的进一步发展，还有哪些关键问题有待突破？

Prof. Ozcan: Diffractive Optical Networks have been introduced by my lab as a machine learning framework that unifies deep learning-based training of matter with the physical models governing the light propagation and diffraction to enable optical inference through a set of diffractive layers (published in *Science*, 2018)[5]. The forward model of a diffractive optical network can be mathematically formulated as a complex-valued matrix operator that multiplies an input field to create an output field at the detector plane/aperture. This operator is designed/trained using deep learning to transform a set of complex fields (forming, e.g., the object data classes) at the input aperture of the optical network into another set of corresponding fields at the output aperture (forming, e.g., the data classification signals) and is physically created through the interaction of the input light with the designed diffractive surfaces as well as free-space propagation within the network. The training stage of a diffractive network is performed using a computer and relies on deep learning and iterative error backpropagation methods to tailor the light-matter interaction across a set of diffractive layers that collectively perform a given machine learning task, such as object classification. After this numerical training phase is implemented in a computer, the diffractive network design is fixed and the transmission or reflection coefficients of the neurons of all the layers are determined. This diffractive design, once physically fabricated using e.g., 3D printing, lithography, etc., can then perform at the speed of light, the specific task that it is trained for, using only optical diffraction and passive optical layers, creating an efficient and fast way of implementing optical inference.

Ozcan教授：我们实验室开创了衍射神经网络作为机器学习框架。衍射神经网络结合了深度学习训练方法以及描述光学衍射及传播的物理模型，从而通过一组衍射层来实现光学推断。衍射光网络的前向模型在数学上可以表示为一个复矩阵算子，通过与输入场相乘在像平面/孔径处生成输出场。通过基于深度学习的设计/训练，这个复算子可以将一系列复杂入射光场（例如形成某一类物体的图像）转化为像平面上的一系列对应复杂光场（例如物体对应的类别信息），这一算子的实现是通过输入光与设计的衍射表面的交互作用以及网络中的自由空间传播而生成。衍射网络的训练通过计算机进行，并依靠深度学习和迭代误差反向传播来设定一组衍射层之间的光-物质相互作用。这些衍射层将共同执行给定的机器学习任务，例如对象分类。在计算机上完成这一训练后，衍射网络及各衍射层上的神经元的透射或反射系数就已被确定。这种衍射设计一旦使用 3D 打印、光刻等进行制造，就可以以光速执行它所训练的特定任务，仅使用光学衍射和无源光学层，创造一种高效、快速的实现光学推断的方法。

Our previous studies on diffractive optical networks have demonstrated the generalization capability of these multi-layer diffractive designs to new, unseen image data. For example, using a 5-layer diffractive network architecture, all-optical blind testing accuracies of >98% and >90% have been reported for the classification of the images of handwritten digits (MNIST dataset) and fashion objects (Fashion-MNIST dataset) that were encoded in the amplitude and phase channels of the input object plane, respectively. For more complex and much harder to classify image datasets such as

CIFAR-10, a substantial improvement in the inference performance of diffractive networks was demonstrated using ensemble learning[6] published in *Light* in 2021. After independently training >1250 individual diffractive networks that were diversely designed with a variety of passive input filters, a pruning algorithm was applied to select an optimized ensemble of diffractive networks that collectively improved the image classification accuracy. Through this pruning strategy, an ensemble of N=14 diffractive networks collectively achieved a blind testing accuracy of 61.14% on the classification of CIFAR-10 test images, providing an inference improvement of 16.6% compared to the average performance of the individual diffractive networks within each ensemble, demonstrating the "wisdom of the crowd".

我们之前对衍射光网络的研究已经证明了这些多层衍射设计对新的、不可见的图像数据的泛化能力。例如，采用五层衍射网络架构，对编码在输入光场的振幅通道中的手写数字（MNIST数据集）和相位通道中的时尚对象（Fashion-MNIST数据集）进行分类，其全光盲测试精度分别大于98%和90%。对于更复杂和更难分类的图像数据集，如CIFAR-10，使用2021年发表在*Light*上的集成学习能够显著提升衍射网络的推理性能[6]。在独立训练了超过1250个使用不同被动滤波器对输入图像进行预处理的独立衍射网络后，我们采用一种剪枝算法来选择一个优化的衍射网络集合，从而整体提高了图像分类的精度。通过这种剪枝策略，N=14个衍射网络的集合对CIFAR-10图像分类的盲测精度达到了61.14%，比单个衍射网络的平均性能提高了16.6%。这一结果展现了“群众智慧”。

Successful experimental demonstrations of these all-optical image classification systems have been reported using 3D-printed diffractive layers that conduct inference by modulating the in-coming object wave at terahertz (THz) wavelengths. In addition to statistical inference, the same optical information processing framework of diffractive networks has also been utilized to design deterministic optical components, for e.g., ultra-short pulse shaping[7], spectral filtering and wavelength division multiplexing[8]. In these latter examples, the input field was known a priori and was fixed, i.e., unchanged, where the task of the diffractive network was to perform a deterministic, desired transformation for a given/known optical input.

我们通过实验使用3D打印的衍射层通过调制太赫兹（THz）波段的入射波进行全光图像分类，验证了衍射网络的正确性。除了统计推断外，衍射网络这一光学信息处理框架也被用于设计确定性光学元件，如超短脉冲整形[7]、光谱滤波和波分复用[8]。在这些例子中，输入场是先验不变的，其中衍射网络的任务是对给定/已知的光输入执行一个预期的变换。

Despite the lack of nonlinear optical elements in these previous implementations, diffractive optical networks have been shown to offer significant advantages in terms of (1) inference/classification accuracy, (2) diffraction efficiency, and (3) output signal contrast, when the number of successive diffractive layers in the network design is increased. We published an important work in *Light* detailing some of these characteristics of diffractive optical networks, which is titled: "All-Optical Information Processing Capacity of Diffractive Surfaces"[9].

尽管这些先前的工作中缺少非线性光学元件，但我们已证明当增加衍射网络的衍射层数时，衍射光学网络在推理/分类精度、衍射效率、输出信号对比度方面具有显著优势。我们在*Light*上发表的一篇重要论文详细介绍了衍射光学网络的一些特征，其标题为“All–Optical Information Processing Capacity of Diffractive Surfaces”[9]。

Diffractive optical networks have also been extended to harness broadband input radiation to design spectrally-encoded single-pixel machine vision systems, where unknown input objects were classified and reconstructed through a single-pixel detector[10]. This single-pixel machine vision framework achieved >96% blind testing accuracy for optical classification of handwritten digits (MNIST dataset) based on the spectral power detected at ten distinct wavelengths, each assigned to one digit/class. In addition to the optical classification of objects through the spectral encoding of data classes, a shallow electronic neural network with two hidden layers was trained (after the diffractive network training) to rapidly reconstruct the images of the classified objects based on their diffracted power spectra detected by a single-pixel spectroscopic detector. Using only 10 inputs, one for each wavelength, this shallow network successfully reconstructed the images of the input, unknown objects, even if they were (rarely) incorrectly classified by the trained diffractive network. Considering the fact that each image of a handwritten digit is composed of ~800 pixels, this shallow image reconstruction network, with an input vector size of 10, performs a form of image decompression to successfully decode the task-specific spectral encoding of the diffractive network.

衍射光学网络也已扩展到利用宽带输入来设计光谱编码的单像素机器视觉系统，其中未知输入对象可通过单像素探测器进行分类和重建[10]。该单像素机器视觉框架检测10个分别分配给不同数字的波长的光谱功率对手写数字（MNIST数据集）进行光学分类，得到了大于96%的盲测精度。除了基于光谱编码进行光学分类外，我们还训练一个带有两个隐藏层的浅层电子神经网络，根据单像素光谱探测器检测到的衍射功率谱快速重建被分类对象的图像。仅用10个输入，每个波长一个，该浅层网络成功地重建了输入未知对象的图像，即使它们被训练过的衍射网络错误分类（虽然这种错误并不常见）。考虑到每个手写数字的图像都由约800像素组成，该浅层图像重建网络事实上使用大小为10的输入矢量，进行了一种图像解压，从而成功解码衍射网络的特定光谱编码。

In one of our latest papers published in *Light*[11], we also report the design of diffractive surfaces to all-optically perform arbitrary complex-valued linear transformations between an input and output field of view. Stated differently, we demonstrated in this recent work the universal approximation capability of diffractive networks for all-optically synthesizing any arbitrarily-selected linear transformation with independent phase and amplitude channels. Our methods and conclusions in this recent *Light* work can be broadly applied to any part of the electromagnetic spectrum to design all-optical processors using spatially-engineered diffractive surfaces to universally perform an arbitrary complex-valued linear transformation. Therefore, these results have wide implications and can be used to design and investigate various coherent optical processors formed by diffractive surfaces such as metamaterials, plasmonic or dielectric-based metasurfaces, as well as flat optics-based designer surfaces that can form information processing networks to execute a desired computational task between an input and output aperture.

我们最近发表在*Light*上的一篇论文中还报道了

Prof. Ozcan communicating with Prof. Olav Solgaard (left) and Prof. Tianhong Cui (right) at 2017 "Light Conference" in Changchun
Ozcan教授与Olav Solgaard教授(左)、崔天宏教授(右) 在长春举行的2017年"Light Conference" 上交流讨论

用于在输入和输出视场之间进行任意复线性变换[11]的衍射表面设计。换句话说，我们在最近的工作中证明了衍射网络拥有对任意振幅和相位独立的复线性变换进行全光学近似的能力。论文中的方法和结论可以广泛应用于电磁频谱的任何部分，以设计使用衍射表面进行任意复线性变换的全光处理器。因此，这些结果具有广泛的意义，可用于研究和设计由诸如超材料、等离子或电介质超表面及基于平面光学的设计表面等衍射表面形成的各种相干光处理器，从而形成在输入和输出孔径之间执行所需的计算任务的信息处理网络。

5. Deep learning is a class of machine learning techniques that use multiple layers of artificial neural networks to automatically analyze signals or data. The introduction of deep learning brings new opportunities for the development of optical microscopy. Can you talk about the current status of optical microscopy? What revolutions has deep learning brought to optical

microscopy techniques? What are the application prospects?

5. 深度学习是机器学习技术的一类，使用多层人工神经网络来自动分析信号或数据。深度学习的引入为光学显微技术的发展带来了新的机遇。您能否谈谈光学显微技术的发展现状吗？深度学习为光学显微技术带来了哪些变革？应用前景如何？

Prof. Ozcan: In addition to holography, phase recovery, and holographic image reconstruction that I described earlier, another area that our lab has made seminal contributions to is deep learning microscopy. In fact, the first use of deep neural networks for advancing the resolution, field-of-view, and depth-of-field of optical microscopy has been demonstrated by our team in 2017. This work of our lab titled "Deep Learning Microscopy"[12] was published in *Optica* in November 2017 and was put in arXiv by our team in May 2017, receiving so far >400 citations. This seminal work was followed by many research labs, bringing in new computational tools to the microscopy field, powered by deep learning.

Ozcan教授：除了我之前描述的全息术、相位恢复和全息图像重建，我们实验室的另一个重要贡献是深度学习显微镜。事实上，早在2017年，我们团队便首次使用深度神经网络来提高光学显微镜的分辨率、视场和景深。这项名为“Deep Learning Microscopy”[12]的工作于2017年11月发表在*Optica*期刊上，迄今为止引用次数已超过400。这项开创性的工作得到了许多研究室的跟进，在深度学习的推动下，将新的计算工具引入显微镜领域。

In a follow-up work by our team, we published another very important result[13] in *Nature Methods* demonstrating super-resolution imaging in fluorescence microscopy and beating the diffraction limit of light through cross-modality image transformations from e.g. confocal microscopy to STED or TIRF to SIM. Perhaps one of the most surprising results that we have got on this line of research was on 3D virtual refocusing of fluorescence microscopy images using deep learning[14], also published in *Nature Methods*. In this work, we introduced a new framework (termed Deep-Z) that is enabled by deep learning to statistically learn and harness hidden spatial features in a fluorescence image to virtually propagate a single fluorescence image onto user-defined 3D surfaces within a fluorescent sample volume. This is achieved without any mechanical scanning, additional optical hardware/components, or a trade-off of imaging resolution, field-of-view, or speed. Stated differently, we introduced, for the first time, a digital propagation framework that learns (through only image data and without any assumptions or theoretical models) the spatial features in fluorescence images that uniquely encode the 3D fluorescence wave propagation information in an intensity-only 2D recording without additional hardware.

后来，我们在*Nature Methods*上发表了另一项非常重要的研究成果[13]，展示了荧光显微镜的超分辨率成像能力。该方法通过从共聚焦（Confocal）显微镜到STED或从TIRF到SIM的交叉模态图像转换，实现了对光的衍射极限的突破。也许，我们在这方面研究中最令人惊讶的结果之一是利用深度学习对荧光显微镜图像进行3D虚拟聚焦，该技术也发表在*Nature Methods*期刊上[14]。在这项工作中，我们引入了一个新的框架，称为Deep-Z。该框架通过深度学习，以统计的方式学习并利用了荧光图像中隐藏的空间特征，从而实现了将单个荧光图像虚拟地传播到荧光样本体积内用户定义的任意3D表面上。这种方法无需使用任何机械扫描，或增添额外的光学硬件/组件，抑或在分辨率、视场和成像速度间做出权衡。换句话说，在不借助额外硬件的帮助下，我们首次引入了一种数字传播框架，用以学习并转化(仅通过图像数据，无需任何假设或理论模型)编码于2D荧光图像的3D空间特征。

There are various powerful features of Deep-Z that make it transformative for fluorescence imaging at all scales and across various disciplines that use fluorescence. A unique capability of the Deep-Z framework is that it enables digital propagation of a fluorescence image of a 3D surface onto another 3D surface, user-defined by the pixel mapping of the corresponding digital propagation matrix (DPM). An analog of the same capability exists in holography under the paraxial approximation. In this sense, the Deep-Z framework brings the computational 3D image propagation advantage of holography or other coherent imaging modalities into fluorescence microscopy. Such a unique capability can be useful, among many applications, for e.g., simultaneous auto-focusing of different parts of a fluorescence image after the image capture, measurement, or assessment of aberrations introduced by the optical system as well as for correction of such aberrations by applying a desired nonuniform DPM. To exemplify the power of this additional degree of freedom enabled by Deep-Z, we experimentally demonstrated the correction of the planar tilting and curvature of different samples after the acquisition of a single 2D fluorescence image per object.

Deep-Z拥有着强大的适应性，使其能在不同场合、学科中按不同的需求对荧光成像进行转换。Deep-Z框架的一个独特功能是能够将一个3D表面上的荧光图像转化到另一个由用户通过相应的数字传播矩阵（DPM）定义的3D表面上。在近轴近似下，全息术也有类似的能力。从这个意义上讲，Deep-Z框架将原本存在于全息或其他相干成像模式中的数字3D图像传播优势引入到了荧光显微镜中。这种独特的能力可应用于许多场合中，例如，在捕获荧光图像后对其不同部分进行数字对焦，测量或评估光学系统引入的像差，以及通过利用DPM来校正像差。为了证明Deep-Z带来的额外自由度优势，我们通过实验证明了该方法可以在获取2D荧光图像后，对图像进行由样本倾斜和曲率造成的离焦校正。

Yet another unique feature of this Deep-Z framework is that it permits cross-modality digital propagation of fluorescence images, where the neural network is trained with gold standard label images obtained by a different fluorescence microscopy modality to teach the generator network to digitally propagate an input image onto another plane within the sample volume, but this time to match the image of the same plane that is acquired by a different fluorescence imaging modality compared to the input image. We term this related framework Deep-Z+. To demonstrate the proof of concept of this unique capability, we trained Deep-Z+ with input and label images that were acquired with a wide-field fluorescence microscope and a confocal microscope, respectively, to blindly generate at the output of this cross-modality network, digitally propagated images of an input fluorescence image that match confocal microscopy images of the same sample sections, i.e., performing axial sectioning (similar to the contrast that a confocal microscope has) and digital propagation of a fluorescence image, both at the same time.

Deep-Z框架的另一个特点是它允许对荧光图像进行跨模态数字转换。在此框架中，神经网络被用于将一种荧光显微镜下拍摄到的样本图像，转化到另外一种荧光显微镜下拍摄到的相同样本在不同平面中的图像。我们称这个相关框架为Deep-Z+。为了证明这种独特能力，我们分别使用宽视野荧光显微镜和共聚焦显微镜获取了的输入图像和目标图像，用以对Deep-Z+进行训练。训练后，该网络即可在盲测中将宽视野显微镜下拍摄到的图像，转化为相同样本共聚焦显微镜下拍摄到的不同平面的图像。

After its training, Deep-Z remains fixed, and its non-iterative inference requires no parameter estimation or search. The inference is performed in a rapid fashion, as it outputs the desired digitally-propagated fluorescence image without any changes to the optical microscopy set-up or a trade-off of its spatial resolution or field-of-view. As such, it allows rapid volumetric imaging (limited only by the detector speed) without any axial scanning or hardware modifications. In addition to fluorescence microscopy, the Deep-Z framework might be applied to other incoherent imaging modalities, and in fact, it provides a bridge to close the gap between coherent and incoherent microscopes by enabling computational 3D imaging of a volume using a single 2D incoherent image.

Deep-Z在经过训练后，参数即被固定，在其非迭代推演的应用过程中，无需进行参数的估计或搜索。该推演过程可被高效地应用并执行，因为它输出我们所需要的荧光图像而不依赖于对光学显微镜硬件上的修改，也不影响其空间分辨率或视场。因此，它允许快速的体积成像（仅受探测器速度的限制），而不需要任何轴向扫描或硬件修改。除了荧光显微镜，Deep-Z框架还可以应用于其他非相干成像模式，事实上，通过使用单个2D非相干图像对体积进行计算3D成像，Deep-Z框架提供了一座弥合相干和非相干显微镜的桥梁。

6. Prior to joining UCLA in 2007, you received your Ph.D. and completed postdoctoral fellowship at Stanford University and were appointed as a research faculty at Harvard Medical School, Wellman Center for Photomedicine. How did this experience influence your subsequent scientific career? Why did you later consider to join UCLA?

6. 在2007年加入UCLA之前，您在斯坦福大学获得了博士学位并完成了博士后研究工作，并被任命为哈佛医学院Wellman光医学中心的研究教员。这段经历对您之后的科研生涯产生了怎样的影响？后来您为什么考虑加入UCLA?

Prof. Ozcan: After an engineering Ph.D. at Stanford, moving to a medical school to conduct research was an eye-opening experience for me. At Harvard Medical School, I learned how an MD looks at innovation from the perspective of impact — not novelty. An engineer, sometimes, can get obsessed with the novelty and "coolness" of an invention or idea — but biomedical research first and foremost cares about impact, especially from the perspective of improving human health. My experience at Stanford and Harvard Medical School (Wellman Center for Photomedicine) taught me the importance of the intersection set between Impact and Novelty. That shaped how I look at science and engineering from the perspective of "innovations that matter". Gary Tearney and Brett Bouma, pioneers in the OCT field have been my mentors at Harvard and I would like to acknowledge them for their contributions to my training.

Prof. Ozcan receiving the Rahmi M. Koc Science Medal from Koc University and Vehbi Koc Foundation. This Science Medal carried the name of Rahmi M. Koc, one of the most prestigious businessmen and philanthropists in Turkey. Prof. Ozcan was an inaugural recipient of this prestigious award in 2016 and received it in Istanbul right after his 38th birthday

Ozcan教授获得KOC大学和Vehbi Koc基金会的Rahmi M. Koc科学奖章。这枚奖章以土耳其最负盛名的商人和慈善家Rahmi M.Koc的名字而命名。Ozcan教授在2016年首次获得这一著名奖项，并在其38岁生日后在伊斯坦布尔接受颁奖

Ozcan教授：在斯坦福大学获得工程博士学位后，到医学院进行研究对我来说是一次大开眼界的经历。在哈佛医学院，我学到了医学博士如何从影响的角度而不是新颖的角度看待创新。有时，工程师可能会沉迷于一项发明或想法的新颖性和“酷

感”——但生物医学研究首先关心的是影响，尤其是从改善人类健康的角度来看。我在斯坦福大学和哈佛大学医学院(Wellman光医学中心)的经历让我明白了影响和创新融合的重要性。这塑造了我如何从“创新意义”的角度看待科学和工程。Gary Tearney和Brett Bouma是OCT领域的先驱，他们是我在哈佛的导师，我很感谢他们对我的培养。

7. You've been working on optics for many years and have become a world lead scientist in related fields, so we are wondering, what are your plans for your future development of scientific research?

7. 多年来，您一直从事光学研究，已经成为相关领域的世界领军科学家，我们很想知道，您对于以后的科研事业发展有怎样的规划?

Prof. Ozcan: A very exciting development in my career right now is a new spin-off company from my lab that aims to transform a century-old field and redefine histopathology and how it is practiced.

Ozcan教授：目前我职业生涯中一个非常令人兴奋的发展是从我的实验室衍生出的一家新公司，旨在改造一个百年历史的领域并重新定义组织病理学及其实践方式。

Approximately 2 years ago, my lab published a paper in *Nature Biomedical Engineering* which introduced a deep learning-based method to "virtually stain" autofluorescence images of unlabeled histological tissue sections, eliminating the need for chemical staining[15]. This technology was developed to leverage the speed and computational power of deep learning to improve upon century-old histochemical staining techniques which can be slow, laborious and expensive. In this seminal paper, we showed that this virtual staining technology using deep neural networks is capable of generating highly accurate stains across a wide variety of tissue and stain types. It has the potential to revolutionize the field of histopathology by reducing the cost of tissue staining, while making it much faster, less destructive to the tissue and more consistent/repeatable.

大约2年前，我的实验室在*Nature Biomedical Engineering*上发表了一篇论文，介绍了一种基于深度学习的方法，可以对未标记的组织切片的自荧光图像进行“虚拟染色”，从而消除了化学染色的必要性[15]。这项技术的开发是为了利用深度学习的计算速度和能力，来改进已有百年历史的缓慢、费力且昂贵的组织化学染色技术。在这篇开创性的论文中，我们展示了这种使用深度神经网络的虚拟染色技术能够在各种组织和染色类型中进行高精确染色。通过降低组织染色成本，它有可能彻底改变组织病理学领域，同时使染色速度更快，对组织的破坏性更小。

Since the publication of our paper, we have had a number of exciting developments moving the technology forward. We have continued to find new applications for this unique technology, using the computational nature of the technique to generate stains that would be impossible to create using traditional histochemical staining. For example, we have used what we refer to as a "digital staining matrix" which allows us to generate and digitally blend multiple stains using a single deep neural network, by specifying which stain should be performed on the pixel level. Not only can this unique framework be used to perform multiple different stains on a single tissue section, it can also be used to create micro-structured stains, digitally staining different areas of label-free tissue with different stains. Furthermore, this digital staining matrix enables these stains to blend together, by setting the encoding matrix to be a mixture of the possible stains. This technology can be used to ensure that pathologists can receive the most relevant information possible from the various virtual stains being performed. This work[16] was published in *Light* in 2020 and has opened up the path for a very exciting new opportunity: stain-to-stain transformations, which enable transforming existing images of tissue biopsy stained with one type of stain into many other types of stains, almost instantaneously. Published in *Nature Communications*[17], this stain-to-stain transformation process takes less than one minute per tissue sample, as opposed to several hours or even more than a day when performed by human experts. And, this speed differential enables faster preliminary diagnoses that require special stains, while also providing significant savings in costs.

这篇论文发表以来，我们取得了许多令人兴奋的进展。我们一直在为这项独特的技术寻找新的应用，利用该技术的计算特性来生成传统组织化学染色无法生成的染色剂。例如，我们使用了一种称之为“数字染色矩阵”的方法，该方法允许我们使用单个深度神经网络对单一样本进行像素级的混合染色。这种独特的框架不仅可以在单个组织切片上进行多种不同的染色，还可以用于创建微结构染色，用不同的染色对无标记组织的不同区域进行数字化染色。此外，这个数字染色矩阵将不同的染色进行编码，使这些染色能够混合在一起。该技术可用于确保病理学家从各种虚拟染色中获得尽可能多的相关信息。这项工作[16]于2020年发表在*Light*期刊上，为一个非常激动人心的新机会开辟了道路：染色到染色的转换，这使一种染色的组织活检图像几乎在瞬间转换为许多其他类型的染色。我们发表在*Nature Communications*期刊上的一篇文章[17]曾表明，这种染色到染色的转化过程在每一个组织样本上，仅需要不到一分钟，而人工获取特殊染色往往需要几个小时甚至一天以上的时间。这种时间差能够更快地对需要特殊染色的疾病进行快速初步诊断，同时还能显著节省成本。

Motivated by the transformative potential of our

virtual staining technology, we have also begun the process of its commercialization and founded Pictor Labs, a new Los Angeles-based startup. Pictor in Latin means "painter" and at Pictor Labs, we virtually "paint" the microstructure of tissue samples using deep learning. In 2020, we were successful in raising seed funding from venture capital firms including M Ventures (a subsidy of Merck KGaA), Motus Ventures, as well as private investors.

基于虚拟染色技术的变革潜力，我们也开始了商业化的进程，并成立了Pictor Labs，一家位于洛杉矶的新公司。Pictor在拉丁语中的意思是“画家”，在Pictor Labs，我们使用深度学习来“绘制”组织样本的微观结构。在2020年，我们成功地从包括M Ventures、Motus Ventures等风险投资公司与私人投资者筹集到了启动资金。

Through Pictor Labs, we aim to revolutionize the

histopathology staining workflow using this virtual staining technology, and by building a cloud computing-based platform that facilitates histopathology through artificial intelligence, we will enable tissue diagnoses and help clinicians manage patient care. I am very excited to have this unique opportunity to bring our cutting-edge academic research into the commercialization phase and

Prof. Ozcan receiving the World Technology Award on Health & Medicine, presented by the World Technology Network in association with TIME, CNN, AAAS, Science, Technology Review, Fortune and Kurzweil (2012)
Ozcan教授在2012年获得由全球技术网络、《时代》、CNN、AAAS、《科学》《技术评论》《财富》和Kurzweil联合颁发的世界卫生与医学技术奖

look forward to more directly impacting human health over the coming years using this transformative virtual staining technology.

通过Pictor Labs，我们旨在使用这种虚拟染色技术彻底改变组织病理学染色工作流程，通过AI促进组织病理学，构建基于云计算的平台，我们将实现组织诊断并帮助临床医生管理患者护理。我非常高兴有这个独特的机会将我们的前沿学术研究带入商业化阶段，并期待在未来几年中使用这种变革性的虚拟染色技术对人类健康产生更直接的影响。

8. The scientific research should finally serve to improve people's livelihood and economic development, and the transformation from academic to industrial is an important process. At present, which ones of your research works have realized achievement transformation? What are the social benefits?

8. 科学研究最终要服务改善民生与促进经济发展，从学术到产业的转化是一个重要的过程。目前，您的哪些科研工作已经实现成果转化？带来了怎样的社会效益？

Prof. Ozcan: My research on computational imaging, mobile sensing, and diagnostics created widely-scalable mobile technologies for e.g., blood analysis, sensing of pathogens/toxins in bodily fluids, food and water samples, diagnosis of infectious diseases, screening of antimicrobial resistance, pathology analysis, as well as particulate matter and bio-aerosol detection for air quality measurements, which altogether have the potential to dramatically increase the reach of advanced biomedical technologies to developing countries and resource limited settings. My work has been broadly helping to democratize biomedical measurement science by enabling advanced measurements to be cost-effectively performed even in field settings using mobile instruments powered by computational optics and machine learning.

Ozcan教授：我在计算成像、移动传感和诊断方面的研究创造了可广泛扩展的移动技术，例如血液分析、体液中的病原体与毒素传感、食物和水样本、传染病诊断、抗菌药物耐药性筛选、病理分析、以及用于空气质量测量的微粒物质和生物气溶胶检测，这些都有可能大幅提升先进生物医学技术对发展中国家和资源匮乏环境的影响。通过使用由计算光学和机器学习支持的移动仪器，即使在现场环境中也能经济高效地执行测量，从而帮助普及生物医学测量科学。

These innovative measurement technologies led to >45 issued patents, several licensed by different companies including Honeywell, GE, Northrup Grumman (Litton), Arcelik, NOW Diagnostics and my own start-ups, targeting multi-billion $ markets, with products used in

>10 countries, also earning one of my own companies a "Technology Pioneer" Award given by The World Economic Forum in 2015.

这些创新的测量技术带来了超过45项专利，其中多项获得了不同公司的授权，包括Honeywell、GE、Northrup Grumman (Litton)、Arcelik、NOW Diagnostics和我自己的初创公司，目标是数十亿美元的市场，产品用于超过10个国家及地区，我自己的一家公司还获得了2015年世界经济论坛颁发的“技术先锋”奖。

My work on mobile microscopy entered introductory level biology textbooks by e.g. *National Geographic*, *Cengage*, and is being used by numerous academic groups worldwide, including in developing countries, also through my lab's massive collaborations with >25 labs.

我在移动显微镜方面的工作进入了*National Geographic*、*Cengage*等入门级生物教科书，被世界各地包括发展中国家的众多学术团体使用，并用于我们与超过25个实验室的大规模合作中。

My lab was one of the first teams that utilized the cellphone as a platform for advanced measurements, microscopy, and sensing covering various applications. For example, we were the first group to image and count individual viruses, individual DNA molecules using mobile phone-based microscopes. We were one of the first groups to utilize the smartphone as a platform for quantitative sensing, for example, quantification of lateral flow tests. Our mobile diagnostic test readers are still being used in the industry through a licensee of one of our patents. Lucendi, a start-up that I cofounded, has commercialized a mobile imaging flow cytometer for water quality analysis, including for example alga toxic blooms. In fact, this seminal work[18] was also published

Prof. Ozcan receiving the Popular Mechanics Breakthrough Award
Ozcan教授获得大众力学突破奖

Prof. Ozcan explaining his mobile microscopy technology to Michael Bloomberg.
Ozcan教授向Michael Bloomberg解释他的移动显微镜技术

in *Light*.

我们实验室是第一批利用手机作为先进测量、显微镜和传感平台的团队之一，涵盖了各种应用。例如，我们是第一个使用手机显微镜对单个病毒和单个DNA分子进行成像和计数的团队。我们是首批利用智能手机作为定量传感平台的团队之一，例如对横向流动测试的量化。工业界仍在使用我们的专利授权的移动诊断测试读取器。我创立的Lucendi公司已经将一种用于水质分析的移动成像流式细胞仪商业化，包括有毒藻类水华等。事实上，这项开创性的工作也发表在了*Light*上[18]。

As another example, our team has introduced the first point of care sensor that is designed by machine learning and that runs and makes decisions based on a neural network[19][20]. This is a vertical flow assay that can look at >80 immunoreactions in parallel. We have shown its efficacy for the detection of early stage Lyme disease patients based on IgG and IgM panels (profiling the immunity of the patient), published in *ACS Nano*. We are also considering a similar approach for COVID-19 — especially important to understand e.g., the efficacy of vaccines and when a booster shot is needed.

另一个例子是，我们团队推出了第一个基于神经网络运行和决策的护理点传感器[19][20]。这是一种垂直流分析，可以同时观察80个以上免疫反应。我们已经证明了基于IgG和IgM检测早期莱姆病患者的有效性（分析患者的免疫），发表在*ACS Nano*上。我们也在考虑对COVID-19采取类似方法，这对于了解疫苗的效力以及何时需要加强注射尤其重要。

9. We officially launched *eLight* journal in June 2021, which aims to attract the finest manuscripts, broadly covering all sub-fields of optics, photonics and electromagnetics, in particular focusing on those emerging topics and cross-disciplinary researches related

to optics. As the Editor-in-Chief, can you talk about the development orientation and direction of *eLight*? How can this new journal stand out from its peers? What is your vision and expectation for *eLight*?

9. 2021年6月*eLight*正式创刊，致力于挖掘覆盖光学、光子学和电磁学的各个子领域的创新工作，尤其关注光学相关的新兴课题和交叉学科研究。您作为卓越行动计划高起点新刊*eLight*的主编，能谈谈*eLight*的发展定位与方向吗？这本新刊如何能在同行期刊中脱颖而出？您对*eLight*有怎样的愿景和期待？

Prof. Ozcan: *eLight* is the new kid in the block. Together with Chengwei Qiu, I am serving as the co-EIC of *eLight* and I am also the father of its name. *Light* is an amazing success story in Optics/Photonics field, with an impact factor of 17.782 — it is a global leading journal in optics, and CIOMP should be proud of it. *eLight* will be powered by the same team that has made *Light* an amazing success. Approximately 50 publications will be targeted per year. So my message to all the researchers who are focusing on Optics/Photonics field, broadly defined: Think of your best work in a given year — that would provide an excellent fit to *eLight*. Please consider submitting your best work to *eLight*.

Ozcan教授：*eLight*是这个领域的新刊，也是我给它起的名字，由我和仇成伟教授一起担任主编。*Light*是光学与光子学领域的一个令人惊叹的传奇故事，目前影响因子为17.782，是世界顶尖的光学期刊，长春光机所应该为此感到自豪。*eLight*期刊将由使*Light*取得惊人成功的同一团队提供强大动力。每年将出版大约50篇文章。因此，我想对所有关注光学及光子学领域的研究人员说：您在一年中最好的工作将非常适合*eLight*期刊。请考虑将您最好的作品提交给*eLight*。

10. In our impression, you are working almost all the

time, and it seems that whenever send you a message, we can get a response at once. We really admire your professionalism a lot. How do you maintain your robust energy and positive attitude at work? In your opinion, what characters should an excellent scientific researcher possess?

10. 在我的印象里，您几乎是一直在工作，似乎无论何时，我们发出的消息都能得到迅速回应。我

Prof. Ozcan is the inaugural recipient of the SPIE Biophotonics Technology Innovator Award

Ozcan 教授是SPIE生物光子学技术创新奖的首届获奖者

们对您的敬业精神十分钦佩，您如何在工作中保持充沛的精力与积极的态度？在您看来，一个优秀的科研工作者应该具备哪些素养？

Prof. Ozcan: You have got to constantly learn new things. My lab is not focusing on a narrow area, and effectively it has 3 different labs come together. This gives us the big picture and the ability to connect things because we can see how different areas can come together by looking at the big picture. This also makes it much bigger than the sum of its parts.

Running a large engineering lab with a broad focus is a lot of effort, but to succeed in all of these areas you need to build interdisciplinary teams with a culture of sharing and learning from each other. My team is very diverse, covering many areas of engineering, and everyone can learn from everyone else. At the same time, we have many interdisciplinary collaborators. This makes our publications high impact and relevant — meaning, we solve problems that really matter — at the intersection of impact and novelty.

In summary: Never stop learning. Be open-minded to new directions. Learn from your students, team members and colleagues. And understand that everyone can be wrong, including yourself. No one is perfect and understanding your weaknesses is important.

Ozcan教授：必须不断学习新东西。我的实验室并不专注于一个狭窄的领域，它将3个不同的实验室有效结合在一起。这给了我们一个宏大的视野和联通事物的能力，因为我们可以通过查看全局来了解不同的领域如何结合在一起。这比各部分的总和大得多。

运营一个关注广泛的大型工程实验室需要付出很多努力，但想要在所有这些领域取得成功，需

Ozcan Group former Postdocs Dr. Sungkyu Seo (top) and Dr. Euan McLeod (bottom) won the Chancellors Award for Postdoctoral Research at UCLA. Dr. Seo is currently a Professor at Korea University and Dr. McLeod is an Associate Professor at the College of Optical Sciences, University of Arizona

Ozcan团队的前博士后Sungkyu Seo（上）和Euan McLeod（下）获得UCLA博士后研究校长奖。Seo博士目前是高丽大学教授，McLeod博士是亚利桑那大学光学科学学院副教授要建立一种相互分享和学习的跨学科团队。我的团队非常多元化，涵盖了很多工程领域，每个人都可以向其他人学习。同时，我们有许多跨学科的合作者。这使得我们的文章具有很高的影响力和相关性——也就是说，我们旨在解决真正重要的问题——即影响力和创新性的交叉融合。

总之，永远不要停止学习。对新方向持开放态度。向你的学生、团队成员和同事学习。要明白每个人都可能犯错，包括你自己。没有人是完美的，了解自己的弱点很重要。

11. "Rising Stars of Light" is an annual international competition initiated by *Light* to select the brightest young scientists in optics-related fields. Due to the epidemic, 2020 Rising Stars was moved online. After two fierce and friendly contests totaling 8 hours, it was successfully concluded in the presence of more than 500,000 worldwide viewers. 2021 Rising Stars has set

sail, and we are honored to invite you again to be the chairman of this competition. What positive effects do you think such events achieve? If it will promote the international influence of *Light*?

11. 未来之星是*Light*发起的一年一度的评选活动，旨在选拔国际光学相关领域的顶尖后浪。由于疫情原因，2020年未来之星改为线上评选，历经2场累计8小时激烈而友好的比拼，在全球50多万观众的见证下圆满落幕。2021未来之星已经起航，我们也很荣幸地再次邀请您成为本次评选活动的主席。您认为这项评选活动会产生哪些积极影响?

Prof. Ozcan: I think the Rising Stars Awards has already become a very prestigious recognition among junior researchers in fields related to optics and photonics. This year's cohort of applications was amazingly well qualified and it was very difficult for the award committee to make a selection for the next round.

Researchers do not work for awards — we are motivated by our curiosity and our passion for "change" — making the world better and advancing our understanding of the universe through the impact of our science and engineering. Having said this, these awards can sometimes motivate researchers to continue in their careers, and help them accelerate their progress, reminding them of the importance of their research and broader impact. In this sense, I find the Rising Stars Awards very important and timely.

Ozcan教授：我认为未来之星奖已经获得光学和光子学相关领域的年轻研究者的高度认可。今年的申请名单质量很高，因此评委会很难为下一轮做出选择。

研究人员不为奖励而工作——我们的动力来自我们对“改变”的好奇心和热情——通过我们对科学和工程的影响，让世界变得更美好并推进我们对宇宙的理解。话虽如此，这些奖项有时可以激励研究人员继续他们的职业生涯，并帮助他们加速进步，提醒他们的研究的重要性和更广泛的影响。从这个意义上说，我觉得未来之星奖的意义重大。

2020 "Rising Stars of Light" online
2020年未来之星线上评选

2021 "Rising Stars of Light" online
2021年未来之星线上评选

12. In 2017, you were invited by OSA/SPIE Student Branch of Changchun Institute of Optics, Fine Mechanics and Physics (CIOMP) to bring a wonderful OSA Travelling Lecture, which atmosphere on-site was quite warm. What's your impression of CIOMP? What aspects do you think should be noticed in talent training?

12. 2017年，您曾应长春光机所OSA/SPIE学生分会邀请，为长春光机所研究生带来一场精彩的OSA Travelling Lecture，现场气氛十分热烈。您对长春光机所印象如何？您认为人才培养应该注重哪些方面？

Prof. Ozcan: This was my first time visiting CIOMP. I am very impressed with Optics and Photonics research coming out of China, and over the last 2 decades, I have seen Chinese universities in general, together with their students and scholars, making amazing progress. In my lab, I have got several generations of Chinese students, from Tsinghua University, Peking University, Zhejiang University and others, and some of my best students are from China. I always eagerly look to see new applications from Chinese universities. The students have an amazing package. They come with an excellent research background, strong publications and are always eager to work hard and learn deeper. Also I personally find Chinese students provide an excellent fit to my lab and its dynamic style — they are very collegial, respectful and hardworking.

Prof. Aydogan Ozcan giving a lecture at CIOMP
Aydogan Ozcan教授在长春光机所作精彩报告

Ozcan教授：这是我第一次访问长春光机所。中国的光学和光子学研究给我留下了非常深刻的印象，在过去的20年里，我看到中国的大学以及学生和学者取得了惊人的进步。在我的实验室里有几届中国学生，来自清华大学、北京大学、浙江大学等，我有些最好的学生也是来自中国。我总是很期待看到来自中国大学的新申请。他们拥有出色的研究背景，优秀的文章，总是渴望努力工作和深入学习。此外，我个人认为中国学生非常适合我的实验室及其充满活力的风格——他们非常团结、懂得尊

Prof. Aydogan Ozcan with participants at CIOMP
Aydogan Ozcan教授与参会者合影留念

重和勤奋。

13. How do you relieve pressure at work? Do you have any interests except for your job?

13. 您平时如何缓解工作的压力？除了工作，您有什么兴趣爱好？

Prof. Ozcan: I like cooking and inventing new dishes, which mostly end up very tasty (according to my wife), but sometimes perhaps end up with a tasteless invention. I am not afraid of failures in this sense. I also like basketball very much — played at a competitive level until I seriously injured my knees — both of them, one ACL torn after another, one year apart, playing basketball in each case. This also tells something more about me: perseverance and the tendency to learn (slowly) through experiments. I stopped playing basketball after losing all the ACL in my knees.

Ozcan教授：我喜欢烹饪和发明新菜式，这些菜式大多都很美味（据我妻子说），但有时也可能会以难吃而告终。在这个意义上，我并不害怕失败。我也非常喜欢篮球——一直打竞技级别的比赛，直到我的两个膝盖严重受伤，时隔一年，两个膝盖的前交叉韧带在打篮球时接连撕裂。这也教会我更加了解自己：通过实验（慢慢地）学习的毅力和倾向。在膝盖韧带受伤后，我就不再打篮球了。

Prof. Ozcan baking bread
Ozcan教授烘焙面包

References

参考文献

[1] ZHANG J Y, LIU T R, et al. Neural network-based image reconstruction in swept-source optical coherence tomography using undersampled spectral data. Light: Science & Applications,2021,10:155.

[2] RIVENSON Y, ZHANG Y B, et al. Phase recovery and holographic image reconstruction using deep learning in neural networks. Light: Science & Applications,2018,7:17141.

[3] WU Y C, RIVENSON Y, et al. Extended depth-of-field in holographic imaging using deep-learning-based autofocusing and phase recovery. Optica,2018,5(6):704-710.

[4] WU Y C, LUO Y L, et al. Bright-field holography: cross-modality deep learning enables snapshot 3D imaging with bright-field contrast using a single hologram. Light: Science & Applications,2019,8:25.

[5] XING L, RIVENSON Y, et al. All-optical machine learning using diffractive deep neural networks. Science, 2018,361(6406):1004-1008.

[6] LI J X, RIVENSON Y, et al. Ensemble learning of diffractive optical networks. Light: Science & Applications,2021,10:14.

[7] VEIL M, MENGU D, et al. Terahertz pulse shaping using diffractive surfaces. Nature Communications,2021,12:37.

[8] LUO Y, MENGU G, et al. Design of task-specific optical systems using broadband diffractive neural networks. Light: Science & Applications,2019,8:112.

[9] KULCE O, MENGU D, et al. All-optical information-processing capacity of diffractive surfaces. Light: Science & Applications,2021,10:25.

[10] LI J X, MENGU D, et al. Spectrally encoded single-pixel machine vision using diffractive networks. Science Advances,2021,7(13).

[11] KUCLE O, MENGU D, et al. All-Optical Synthesis of an Arbitrary Linear Transformation Using Diffractive Surfaces. Light: Science & Applications,2021,10:196.

[12] RIVENSON Y, ZHANG Y B, et al. Deep learning microscopy. Optica,2017,4(11):1437-1443.

[13] WANG H D, RIVENSON Y, et al. Deep learning enables cross-modality super-resolution in fluorescence microscopy.

Nature Methods, 2019,16:103–110.

[14] WU Y C, RIVENSON Y, et al. Three–dimensional virtual refocusing of fluorescence microscopy images using deep learning. Nature Methods,2019,16:1323 - 1331.

[15] RIVENSON Y, WANG H D, et al. Virtual histological staining of unlabelled tissue–autofluorescence images via deep learning. Nature Biomedical Engineering,2019,3:466–477.

[16] ZHANG Y J, RIVENSON Y, HAAN K D, et al. Digital synthesis of histological stains using micro–structured and multiplexed virtual staining of label–free tissue. Light Science & Applications, 2020,9:78.

[17] ZHANG Y J, HAAN K D, ZUCKERMAN J E. et al. Deep learning–based transformation of H&E stained tissues into special stains. Nature Communications,2012,12:4884.

[18] TAMAMITSU M, BIANCO V, WOLF P, et al. A deep learning–enabled portable imaging flow cytometer for cost–effective, high–throughput, and label–free analysis of natural water samples. Light Science & Applications,2018,7:66.

[19] BALLARD Z S, JOUNG H A, Point–of–care serodiagnostic test for early–stage Lyme disease using a multiplexed paper–based immunoassay and machine learning. ACS Nano,2020,14(1):229–

240.

[20] BALLARD Z S, JOUNG H A, GONCHAROV A, et al. Deep learning-enabled point-of-care sensing using multiplexed paper-based sensors. npj Digital Medicine,2020,3:66.

Professor John Dudley

编者按

超连续谱产生（SCG）中的极限光谱展宽往往被认为是非线性光学的精华。在本次采访中，*Light: Science & Applications*邀请了超连续谱产生及其异常波和超快激光的先驱——John Dudley教授，分享超连续谱产生在过去一段时间的演变及其发展方向。同时，作为联合国教科文组织国际光日、国际光年（IDL & IYL）的委员会主席，John Dudley教授还和我们分享了他对光学将会如何影响疫情后的科研世界的见解。

Professor John Dudley Spoke about Supercontinuum Generation and International Day of Light
光谱展宽路修远，吾将上下而求索

Science Editor: Chenzi Guo 科学编辑 郭宸孜

Editorial:

The extreme spectral broadening of light in supercontinuum generation (SCG) is considered by many as the ultimate legacy of nonlinear optics. In this interview, *Light: Science & Applications* invited John Dudley — pioneer of supercontinuum generation, rogue waves, and ultrafast lasers—to share insight on how supercontinuum generation have evolved over the past decades and where it is heading. Also as the Steering Chair of UNESCO's International Day of Light & International Year of Light (IDL & IYL), John is asked to share his comments on how light may influence post-pandemic world.

Light People

Biography: Dr., Prof. John Dudley received his Ph.D. from the University of Auckland and is currently a Professor at the University of Franche-Comté in Besançon, France. He is a Fellow of OSA, SPIE, IEEE, EOS, and an Honorary Fellow of the Royal Society of New Zealand Te Aparangi. Prof. Dudley's research covers a wide range of topics in ultrafast and nonlinear optics. In addition to early work in source development, he pioneered the use of advanced measurement techniques to characterize complex pulse propagation in nonlinear fiber optics, and contributed especially to the development of a clear understanding of the physics of fiber supercontinuum generation. He has published over 500 contributions in journals & conference proceedings and delivered over 120 invited talks at major conferences. He served as the President of the European Physical Society from 2013 to 2015, and has served on a number of editorial boards and conference committees. Prof. Dudley is also known for initiating the International Year of Light and chairing the Steering Committee of IYL and IDL. He is a keen educator in teaching undergraduate lectures and specialised graduate courses with both English and French. Prof. Dudley is the recipient of the IXCore Fondation pour La Recherche Prize, the Grand Prix de l'Electronique Général FERRIÉ of the Société des Electriciens et Electroniciens, the Médaille d'Argent of the national French research agency CNRS, the SPIE President's Award, the OSA Hopkins Leadership Award, the IOP President's Medal and the

APS Dwight Nicholson Medal for Outreach. In 2019 he was awarded the Harold E. Edgerton Award of SPIE recognizing his contributions to ultrashort pulse measurements in nonlinear fibre optics. In 2020 he was awarded the R. W. Wood Prize of OSA recognizing his contributions to explaining and interpreting the physics of fibre supercontinuum generation, and was elected an Honorary Fellow of the Royal Society of New Zealand Te Aparangi.

专家简介：John Dudley教授于新西兰奥克兰大学获得博士学位，目前是法国弗朗什—孔泰大学的教授。他是OSA、SPIE、IEEE、EOS等多个学会的会士，也是新西兰Te Aparangi皇家学会的荣誉会士。Dudley教授的研究领域主要涉及超快和非线性光学，其在光源开发方面做了很多早期的奠基工作，并率先使用先进的测量技术来表征非线性光纤中的复杂光脉冲传播，同时他也为光纤超连续谱产生中的物理过程阐释做出了重要贡献。Dudley教授在期刊和会议论文集上发表了500多篇论文，受邀在学术大会上作报告120余次。他于2013至2015年间担任欧洲物理学会主席，并在多家期刊担任主编、编委。Dudley教授还因发起国际光年，担任国际光年、国际光日的委员会主席而闻名。他也是一位热衷于用英语和法语教授本科和研究生课程的教育家。Dudley教授曾荣获IXCore Fondation pour La Recherche Prize，the Grand Prix de l'Electronique Général FERRIE of the Société des Electriciens et Electroniciens, the Médaille d'Argent of the national French research agency CNRS，the SPIE President's Award，the OSA Hopkins Leadership Award，the IOP President's Medal和APS Dwight Nicholson Medal for Outreach等重要奖项。2019年，他被授予SPIE Harold E. Edgerton奖，以表彰他对非线性光纤中超短脉冲测量的贡献。2020年，他被授予OSA R. W. Wood 奖，以表彰他在阐释光纤超连续谱产生的物理学中的贡献。

1. What is the present situation with supercontinuum

generation? What are the current major challenges?

1. 超连续谱产生研究的现状如何？当前的主要挑战是什么？

Prof. Dudley: The supercontinuum is a remarkable light source where multiple nonlinear processes in an optical waveguide combine to transform a narrowband input into a broadband spectrum, capable of spanning from the ultraviolet to the infrared. The way in which the frequency conversion processes occur depends critically on the dispersion engineering of the waveguide, so extensive work is now using advances in waveguide engineering and fabrication to design supercontinuum spectra optimized at specific wavelengths for specific applications.

The overall physics is now well understood, but a number of new challenges are emerging in trying to understand how cascading different waveguides can be used to sequentially seed different nonlinear processes. A great deal of work continues to studying supercontinuum noise in order to determine the fundamental limits to coherence, with continued interest in the development of frequency comb technology. And researchers are also moving beyond the single mode fiber platform to consider the additional degrees of freedom afforded from control of multimode interactions.

Dudley教授：超连续谱是一种具有独特特性的光源，通过光波导中的多个非线性过程相结合，将窄带光谱输入转换为跨越紫外–红外波段的宽带光谱输出。其频率转换过程产生方式的关键取决于波导的色散工程，因此大量的工作正在利用波导工程和制造技术的快速发展来设计针对特定应用在特定波长优化的超连续谱。

现如今，人们对超连续谱产生的物理学过程已经有了比较好的理解，但是在试图理解如何使用级联波导来连续产生不同的非线性过程时，许多新的挑战出现了。大量工作继续研究超连续谱噪声以确定相干性的基本限制，并且对光频梳技术发展的兴趣与日俱增。研究人员也已经不再将目光局限于单模光纤平台，而是更多地考虑控制多模相互作用提供的额外自由度。

2. Supercontinuum generation has been demonstrated spanning the ultraviolet, visible and near infrared range. In the future, how broadband supercontinuum can be? What are the limiting factors?

2. 超连续谱产生已被证明可以跨越紫外、可见光和近红外波段。未来，宽带超连续谱能有多宽？可能的限制因素是什么？

Prof. Dudley: The obvious limits to achievable bandwidth are the factors such as material attenuation and the amount of power one can couple into the system before reaching the material damage threshold. A key advance that has managed to overcome these limits has been spectral broadening using soliton dynamics in hollow core fibres. This has actually been very significant in allowing access to the important ultraviolet spectral range approaching the boundary of attoscience. Results in the four-octave range have been reported, and these are really remarkable. In this regime, other limiting factors associated with plasma and related dynamics may also begin to play a role, which will evoke fascinating physics and inspire a lot of work in this field of gas-based nonlinear optics.

Dudley教授：带宽的显著制约因素包括材料衰减以及在达到材料损坏阈值之前可以耦合到系统的功率等。成功克服这些限制的一个关键进展是在空心光纤中使用光孤子动力学进行光谱展宽。这实际上对于探索attoscience尺度紫外光谱非常重要。近期，四个八度范围内的结果已经有被报道，这些结果非常了不起。在这种尺度下，与等离子体和相关动力学相关的其他限制因素也可能开始发挥作用，这将激发对于其中物理机制以及气体非线性光学的大量工作。

3. Photonic crystal fibers enabled supercontinuum generation without high power lasers. What are the other options for generating supercontinuum without high power lasers?

3. 光子晶体光纤无需高功率激光器即可产生超连续谱。有没有其他可能，在没有高功率激光器的情况下也能产生超连续谱?

Prof. Dudley: It depends on your application, because some applications will always require high spectral density to achieve good signal to noise and in such cases, the pump source will likely also need to satisfy minimum power requirements. But in general, the conversion efficiency into particular wavelength bands depends critically on the waveguide design and dispersion characteristics, and for any given pump, the key is to optimize the dispersion tailoring to favor the generation of spectral components where they are desired. The development of compact integrated waveguides with novel materials and precise dispersion engineering is proving especially effective here, and many impressive results are being reported.

Dudley教授：这取决于面向的应用，因为一些应用总是需要高频谱密度来实现良好的信噪比，在这种情况下，泵浦源还是需要满足最低功率要求。但总的来说，转换到特定波段的效率关键取决于波导设计和色散特性，对于任何给定的泵浦源，关键是通过优化色散特性以促进在需要的地方生成光谱分量。事实证明，开发具有新型材料和精确色散工程的紧凑型集成波导卓有成效，并且报道了许多令人印象深刻的结果。

4. How do Rogue waves affect supercontinuum?

4. 异常波（Rogue waves）如何影响超连续谱?

Prof. Dudley: Optical rogue waves are high intensity pulses of light that appear in a supercontinuum as a result of noise-sensitive soliton dynamics. Rogue waves in a supercontinuum are usually associated with shifting the bandwidth towards longer wavelengths, and although they are necessarily associated with shot-to-shot instability, for many applications this is not important when high repetition rate sources are used. A potential deleterious effect can also occur, however, if the rogue wave intensity at some point in the waveguide exceeds the damage threshold. One of the important open questions here is to try to determine how to exploit rogue wave dynamics in a controlled way to develop practical methods for supercontinuum spectral engineering.

Dudley教授：异常波是由于噪声敏感的孤子动力学而出现在超连续谱中的高强度光脉冲。超连续谱中的异常波通常会将带宽红移，尽管它们必然与脉冲间的不稳定性相关，但对于许多高重复率光源的应用而言，这并不重要。然而，如果波导中某个点的异常波强度超过损坏阈值，则可能产生有害影响。这里一个重要的开放性问题是尝试利用可控的异常波来实现超连续谱工程。

5. What changes will machine learning bring to supercontinuum?

5. 机器学习会给超连续谱带来哪些改变?

Prof. Dudley: Machine learning is already becoming part of the standard toolbox used in nonlinear optics. Optimization algorithms have already been used in experiments to modify initial conditions to generate supercontinnum with desired spectral properties, and this approach—using genetic algorithms and/or neural networks—is likely to become widespread. There is also tremendous potential in the real-time control of pump laser systems used in experiments, and from a theoretical perspective, neural networks have already proved to be very powerful in identifying patterns and correlations in supercontinuum dynamics.

Dudley教授：机器学习已经成为非线性光学中的一大标准工具。在实验中，我们已经可以将优化算法用于修改初始条件以生成具有所需光谱特性的超连续谱，并且遗传算法、神经网络等机器学习方法在超连续谱中的应用可能会变得越来越普遍。在实验中使用的泵浦激光系统的实时控制方面也有巨大的潜力，从理论的角度来看，神经网络已经证明了其在识别超连续谱动力学中的模式和相关性方面具有强大的功能。

6. Supercontinuum has found significant applications in spectroscopy and microscopy, what are the other possibilities for supercontinuum that has not been well aware of yet?

6. 超连续谱在光谱学和显微术中有着重要的应用，除此之外，还有哪些潜在的应用？

Prof. Dudley: The supercontinuum is a versatile and flexible light source and has potential applications anywhere light is used. Whether the emphasis is on generating light within a particular wavelength range or over a broad bandwidth, there is usually a supercontinuum source that provides what is needed. The issue here of course is compactness and cost! Amongst some of the emerging applications that are attracting wide interest are the applications of supercontinuum in the mid-infrared—in extending the bandwidths of fiber laser sources, and in developing frequency combs with very low amplitude and phase noise.

Dudley教授：超连续谱是一种多功能、灵活的光源，在任何使用光的地方都有潜在的应用。因为无论是在特定波长范围内还是在宽带范围产生光，通常都需要超连续光源。存在的问题主要是紧凑性和成本！例如，超连续谱在中红外领域的应用——扩展光纤激光源的带宽，以及开发具有极低幅度和相位噪声的频率梳——就引起了广泛的兴趣。

7. More broadly, what are the most promising directions in nonlinear optics and ultrafast lasers?

7. 更宽泛地说，您认为非线性光学和超快激光器领域里最有前途的方向是什么？

Prof. Dudley: What a question! Probably every researcher in the field will have their own favorite answer, but with my own interest in the field of more basic research, I am really interested in understanding how the techniques of machine learning can help us gain new insights into light–matter interactions. In addition to optimization approaches, machine learning brings in very advanced techniques for data analysis, and new ways to attempt to infer the underlying physics from data-driven discovery. I think there are some fascinating years ahead to see where this will take us.

Dudley教授：好问题！可能该领域的每个研究人员都会有自己的答案，但由于我自己偏好更基础的研究领域，我真的很想了解机器学习技术如何帮助我们获得光与物质相互作用的新见解。除了优化方法之外，机器学习还引入了非常先进的数据分析技术，以及尝试从数据驱动的发现中推断底层物理的新方法。我认为未来大有可为，我很期待它将引领我们去向何方。

8. We first met in 2017 at the IDL meeting at CLEO

Munich, where light, its applications and how IDL shall improve the impact of light were extensively discussed. Looking back the past few years, can you name a few things that IYL & IDL has brought changes to? Also, could you share insight on how light may influence the post-pandemic world and how our researchers can utilize the interplay?

8. 我们第一次见面是在2017年，CLEO慕尼黑的国际光日会议上，当时会上讨论了光、光的应用以及国际光日如何提升光学的影响力。现在已经过去几年了，您能列举一些国际光年和国际光日带来的变化吗？此外，您能否谈谈疫情之后，光会如何影响世界以及我们的研究人员该如何作为呢？

Prof. Dudley: IYL and IDL have succeeded beyond anything we initially hoped for. Concretely, since 2015 they have led to over 15,000 outreach events that have reached millions of people, all focused around light and photonics. On a societal level, I think we have raised awareness of the importance of light science for sustainable development, and many of the themes we have promoted have found their way into government and political statements. For example, in 2021 we focused on a campaign aiming to promote trust in science, and this was adopted by UNESCO and stressed explicitly by their Director General of UNESCO in an important public message in May. The central role played by science in society has been shown very clearly over the last 18 months, where we have clearly seen the importance of long-term investment in basic research and technology — from the science of vaccines to the infrastructure photonic-based communications networks. I think it is essential that researchers learn how to argue for more long-term investment in science. Our future depends on it.

Dudley教授：国际光年和国际光日取得了超出

我们最初期望的成功。具体而言，自2015年以来，他们已经发起了15,000多场外展活动，覆盖了数百万人，所有活动都围绕光和光子学展开。在社会层面，我认为我们已经提高了人们关于光学对可持续发展重要性的认识，我们宣传的许多主题已经进入了政府和政治声明。例如，在2021年，我们重点开展了一项旨在促进“信任科学”的运动，该运动被联合国教科文组织采纳，并由联合国教科文组织总干事在当年5月的一项重要的活动中重点宣传。在

Prof. Dudley spoke at the Opening Ceremony of IYL. Credit to: Dan Curticapean
Dudley教授在国际光日的开幕式致辞（版权属于Dan Curticapean）

2017 IDL Steering Committee in Munich
2017慕尼黑国际光日委员会议

Trust Science Event Banner. Credit to: IDL
“信任科学”运动的横幅（版权属于国际光日）

Homepage of IYL. Credit to: IYL
国际光年主页（版权属于国际光年）

过去的18个月里，科学在社会中发挥的核心作用已经非常清楚地展现出来，我们看到了对基础研究和技术进行长期投资的重要性——从疫苗科学到光子通信网络基础设施，我认为研究人员必须学会如何争取对科学进行更多的长期投资。而光学，将是我们未来不可或缺的一部分。

9. You have always been a dedicated educator, and quite creative in live-science lectures. What is the difference between conveying information to students and the general public, what different moves do you usually take?

9. 您一直是一位敬业的教育家，在直播科学讲座方面做了很多开创性探索。能否和我们分享一下，向学生和公众传达信息有什么区别，您通常采取哪些不同的举措?

Prof. Dudley: I have always found that independent of the audience, the essential thing is to ensure that you try to first explain the concepts in very general terms, and that these are linked quickly with concrete real-world applications. That is, you start by asking the question

"Why is this interesting and important", and you give a short answer to this question before getting into detail. Hopefully, this attracts people's interest and inspires them to want to learn more about the topic. For both the general public and students, I also try to use simple experiments to illustrate the point, and we are lucky in optics that we have such a visual subject. Of course the big difference when teaching students at university is that we extend conceptual explanations with mathematical modelling, trying to explain what we see quantitatively and hopefully predicting effects we hadn't expected. When this forces us to change our conceptual picture, then we have really succeeded!

Dudley教授：我一直认为，不管面向什么听众，最重要的是确保用非常通俗易懂的术语解释概念，并且这些概念能够迅速与具体的现实世界的应用联系起来。也就是说，你首先要问“为什么这很有趣和重要”这个问题，然后在进入细节之前简短地回答这个问题，从而吸引人们的兴趣并激发他们想要了解更多有关该主题的信息。对于普通大众和学生，我也尝试用简单的实验来说明这一点，幸运的是，由于我们从事的是光学，很多实验都是可视的。当然，在大学教授学生时，最大的不同在于我们会用数学建模来扩展解释概念，并试图定量地解释我们所观察到的，并希望预测我们没有预料到的结果。当这迫使我们改变我们的传统观念时，那么我们就真的成功了！

Prof. Dudley at teaching. Credit to: Coraline Lapre
Dudley教授的教学现场（版权属于Coraline Lapre）

10. With your years of experience in promoting popular science, can you use a few words to elaborate Rogue waves, supercontinuum and their correlation, to those who does not work in physics or even science?

10. 根据您多年的科普经验，能不能用简短的几句话给那些不从事物理学甚至科学研究的人解释一下异常波、超连续谱及其相关性？

Prof. Dudley: The picture we see in the movies of a laser as a powerful beam of light is correct, but lasers are sometimes limited in that they can produce light of one color. However, a wonderful discovery has been that if you focus a laser into a special kind of glass-based material, you can convert the laser into a powerful beam of light that spans all the colors of the rainbow. This is called a supercontinuum, and it finds all sorts of applications — from environmental detection that may help us monitor climate change, to new techniques in medical imaging, and even in the detection of planets around distant stars. Under some conditions, it is even possible to make a very unstable supercontinuum where the behavior of the light mimics the behavior of waves on the ocean! This has been important in allowing us to study how dangerous rogue waves form on the open sea, and also in giving us some ideas about how we might be able to predict them.

Dudley教授：我们在电影中常常看到激光可以提供强大的光束，但激光有时会受到限制，因为它们通常只能产生单色光。然而，奇妙的是，如果我们将激光聚焦到一种特殊的玻璃基材料上，就可以将激光转换成一束覆盖所有颜色的强大光束。这就是超连续谱，它有各种各样的应用——从帮助我们监测气候变化的环境检测，到医学成像的新技术，甚至是探测遥远恒星周围的行星。在某些条件下，我们甚至可以制造出非常不稳定的超连续谱，用光的行为来模仿海洋上的波浪现象！这对于我们研究海洋中危险巨浪的形成非常重要，也为我们提供了如何预测这些巨浪的灵感。

Professor Dayong Jin

编者按

他开创了一种新型纳米荧光探针，可将红外光上转换成高亮度的可见光，由此于2015年获得澳大利亚科研最高奖“尤里卡奖交叉学科创新奖”。他发明的超分辨显微镜，使我们能够追踪到单分子以及动态观察活细胞工作，并于2017年获得“澳大利亚总理奖——年度物理学家奖”。2016年，他被《澳大利亚人报》提名为“知识经济时代百名开拓人物”。2021年，42岁的他荣获了澳大利亚桂冠教授奖，并当选澳大利亚工程院院士。他就是悉尼科技大学杰出教授、南方科技大学讲席教授金大勇，同时也是*Light: Science & Applications*（*Light*）悉尼办公室负责人、*Light*“Perspective”专栏编辑。本期“Light人物”，我们非常荣幸邀请到金大勇院士与我们分享他在科研工作、学生培养和团队建设等方面的经历和体会。下面让我们一起走近金大勇院士的科研生活，领略他的杰出风采和他成功的故事。

Light up Street View of Living Cells with Super-resolution Imaging
超分辨率成像：点亮生物细胞的街景图

Science Editor: Ying Zhang 科学编辑 张莹

Editorial:

He pioneered a new family of nanoscopic probes that can up-convert infrared photons into intense visible light, and won the Australian Museum Eureka Prize for Interdisciplinary Scientific Research in 2015. He created new kinds of microscopes that allow us to watch molecules at work inside living cells, and won the Australian Prime Minister's Prize for Science Malcolm McIntosh Prize for Physical Scientist of the Year 2017. *The Australian* newspaper identified him among 100 "rock stars of Australia's new economy" as the Knowledge Nation 100. In 2021, at his age of 42, he won the Australian Laureate Fellowship and was elected to the fellowship of Australian Academy of Technology and Engineering. This is Dayong Jin, a Distinguished Professor at the University of Technology Sydney and a Chair Professor at Southern University of Science and Technology, as well as the editorial manager in Sydney office and the perspective column editor of *Light: Science & Applications*. "Light People" is a featured column of high-end interviews with outstanding scientists. On this issue, it is our great honor to invite Prof. Dayong Jin to provide his perspectives on his work, end-user driven research, student mentoring and team building philosophy. In the following, let's take a closer look at the research life of Prof. Dayong Jin, and appreciate his style and the story behind his success.

Light People

Biography: Dayong Jin is a Distinguished Professor at the University of Technology Sydney (UTS) since 2017 and a Chair Professor at Southern University of Science and Technology (SUSTech) since 2019. Prof Jin obtained his Ph.D. from Macquarie University in 2007. At Macquarie, he was promoted to Lecturer in 2010, Senior Lecturer in 2013, Associate Professor in 2014, and Professor in 2015.

At UTS, as the director, he established the Australian Industry Transformation Research Hub for Integrated Devices for End-user Analysis at Low Levels (ARC

IDEAL Hub), the Department of Industry, Science, Energy and Resources' Australia-China Joint Research Centre for Point of Care Testing (DISER POCT), the UTS-SUSTech Joint Research Centre for Biomedical Materials & Devices, and three major programs underpin the UTS Institute for Biomedical Materials & Devices (IBMD), to transform advances in photonics and materials into disruptive biotechnologies.

His research has been in the physical, engineering and interdisciplinary sciences, with expertise covering biomedical optics, nanotechnology, luminescent materials, microscopy, diagnostics, and microfluidics devices.

Prof. Jin is the winner of the Australian Museum Eureka Prize for Interdisciplinary Scientific Research in 2015, the Australian Academy of Science John Booker Medallist in 2017, and the Prime Minister's Prize for

Physical Scientist of the Year 2017. In the year of 2021, Prof. Jin won the Australian Laureate Fellowship and was elected to the fellowship of Australian Academy of Technology and Engineering.

专家简介：金大勇，2017年起担任悉尼科技大学杰出教授，2019年起任南方科技大学讲席教授。他于2007年在麦考瑞大学获得博士学位，并于2010年晋升为麦考瑞大学讲师，随后在2013年晋升为高级讲师，2014年晋升为副教授，2015年晋升为教授。

作为项目团队负责人，金大勇在悉尼科技大学建立了澳大利亚可集成生物医疗仪器与技术转化港、中澳科技部联合资助的便携式体外诊断技术联合研究中心，以及悉尼科技大学—南方科技大学生物医学材料和器件联合研究中心。他组建的悉尼科技大学生物医学材料及仪器研究所旨在将最前沿的光子学和先进材料转化为颠覆性的生物技术。

金大勇的研究工作涉及物理、工程和跨学科领域，专业涵盖了生物医学光子学、纳米技术、发光材料、显微镜方法学、生物医疗诊断、微流体器件等。

金大勇于2015年荣获澳大利亚科研最高奖尤里卡奖交叉学科创新奖；2017年荣获澳大利亚科学院颁发的约翰·布克工程科学奖章，同年获得澳大利亚总理奖——年度物理学家奖；2021年，金大勇获得澳大利亚桂冠教授奖，并当选澳大利亚工程院院士。

1. First of all, congratulations on your being awarded the Australian Laureate Fellowship and being elected to the fellowship of Australian Academy of Technology and Engineering. Would you like to tell us more about your research in relation to important achievements?

1. 首先，祝贺您荣获2021澳大利亚桂冠教授奖，并当选澳大利亚工程院院士。请您向我们介绍一下您的主要研究工作。

Prof. Jin: Indeed, these are the Australian highest recognitions of our works from basic research to applied science and engineering, and our significant contributions to the Australian research landscape by building core resources and consortiums in imaging, cytometry and point-of-care diagnostics, and leading international research programs that are transforming advances in photonics and materials into biotechnology.

The Laureate fellowship in Australia supports the world leaders to play a sustained leadership and significant mentoring role in building Australia's internationally competitive research capacity. Through the Fellowship, I will build a Laureate team and grow our strengths in super-resolution imaging and single molecular sensing, and develop technologies to map the structures and functions of subcellular compartments and single molecules, so that biologists can then drop-down to get a "street view" of the molecular traffic within cells to decode the complexities of life at work and the early signs of diseases.

金教授：今年获得两项荣誉，实际上是对我们团队多年来在生物光子学和纳米光子学领域长期努力的认可。我们在超分辨、单分子及单细胞成像和即时诊断技术等方面建立了核心资源与产学研联盟，并承担了许多国家级研究项目。我们的工作旨在将光学和材料的前沿进展转化为革新性的生物技术。

澳大利亚桂冠教授奖是澳大利亚为了培养具有国际竞争力的学科及学科带头人所设立的人才项目。我将充分利用这个平台继续加强我们在单分子检测和超分辨成像方面的科研能力，并通过技术开发，绘制出亚细胞互作和单分子功能全景图，从而构建活细胞成像和细胞器互作成像的“谷歌街景图”。有了这张图，生物学家就可以进一步深入获得细胞内分子交通的“街景”，这将有助于解码错综复杂的生命科学并指导我们认识疾病的形成。

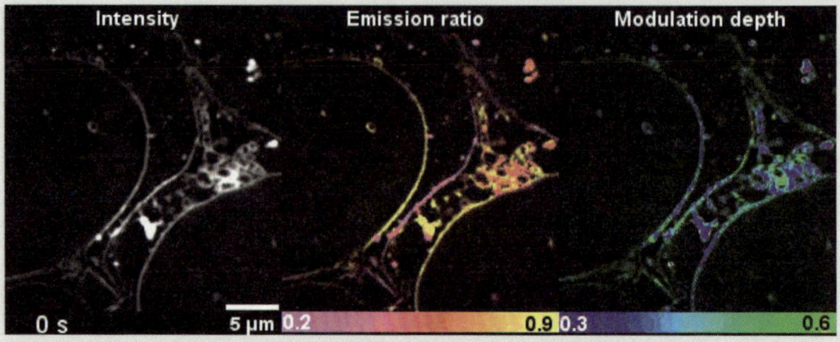

Time-lapse high-dimensional super-resolution imaging of the late-stage division of two U2-OS cells. Super-resolution "street view" microscopy hits the SPOT[1]
超分辨“街景”显微成像。两个U_2-OS细胞分裂后期的延时高维超分辨率成像[1]

The fellowship of the Australian Academy of Technology and Engineering recognizes our efforts in the translational research from basic science to new technology developments. Over the past decade, our profile is increasingly known among Australian biotechnology SMEs as a source of advice on photonics and biomedical imaging devices, nanotechnology and point of care testing technologies. We have developed disruptive technologies for Australian biotechnology, diagnostics, veterinary, agribusiness, and manufacturing firms. Through the fellowship, I will work with leaders in academia, industry and government, to provide innovative solutions across a range of areas in addressing issues of critical importance for Australia. In particular, we will focus on the endusers-driven research and impact-driven research to help the Australian community and international countries to recover from this current pandemic.

今年我当选澳大利亚工程院院士是对我们从基础科学到新技术发展与转化方面工作的认可。我们将更加强化从基础科学到应用科学的转化，加大与科研队伍、政府、产业及国际机构的合作力度，为解决澳大利亚关键问题提供跨领域的创新解决方案。在过去的10年中，我们在光子学与生物医学成像仪器、纳米技术和即时检测技术方向同众多澳大利亚中小企业合作。我们为澳大利亚的生物技术、诊断学、兽医、农业综合企业和制造企业开发颠覆性的技术。特别是我们将专注于终端用户需求和社会民生发展为驱动的研究，以帮助各国从当前的新冠肺炎疫情中恢复过来。

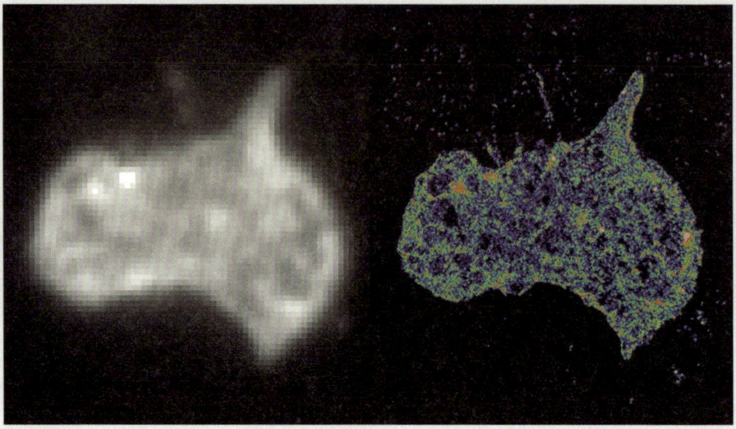
Joining the dots for "street view" of single human cells. A single platelet cell under a normal microscope (left) and viewed with super-resolution imaging (right)
单细胞“街景”显微成像。普通显微镜下观察单体血小板细胞（左图）及其超分辨成像（右图）

2. In 2003, you went to Macquarie University to pursue your Ph.D. Your Ph.D. supervisor Prof. Jim Piper is a renowned laser physicist. At that time, you chose an engineering science topic to develop a new flow cytometer. You then established the advanced cytometry laboratory. Would you like to tell us what made you interested in the research and development of biomedical instruments?

2. 2003年，您远赴澳大利亚麦考瑞大学攻读博士学位，师从国际著名激光物理学家Jim Piper教授。当时，您选择了工程科学课题，开发了一种新型流式细胞仪。随后，您建立了先进细胞仪实验室。请问是什么原因让您对生物医学仪器的研究和开发产生兴趣？

Prof. Jin: First of all, I would like to acknowledge my Ph.D. supervisor Prof. Jim Piper. He's a great supervisor, an excellent engineering scientist, and a highly respected laser physicist, who always encourages me to direct my fundamental research towards practical outcomes. Under his supervision, several generations of his students become national and international leaders, including Dr. Larry Marshall, the current CEO of the Commonwealth Scientific and Industrial Research Organisation.

金教授：首先，我要感谢我的博士生导师Jim Piper教授。他是一位优秀的导师，一位杰出的工程科学家，也是一位备受尊敬的激光物理学家。他总是鼓励我把基础研究引向实际应用。在他的指导下，他的多名博士生都已经成为科研领域的领袖，包括澳大利亚联邦科学和工业研究组织现任首席执行官Larry Marshall博士。

Photo with Ph.D. mentor Prof. Jim Piper in 2008. Photo with Prof. Jim Piper (Left) and Dr. Larry Marshall (Right) on the 2017 Prime Minister Prize for Science ceremony
2008年金大勇与他的博士生导师Jim Piper教授合影；2017年金大勇与Jim Piper教授和Larry Marshall博士在澳大利亚总理奖颁奖典礼现场合影

When I started my Ph.D. at Macquarie University in 2003, Prof. Jim Piper suggested two topic areas, to build more efficient lasers, or to develop biomedical devices for cell analysis. From my early trainings in physics and optical engineering, I was deeply inspired by translating laser science into biomedical device applications, and I chose to conduct research in developing flow cytometry. This allows me to learn the multidisciplinary skills, not only in optics, but also in microfluidics, electronics, data acquisition and programming, fluorescent probes, and cell biology.

I completed the three years of my Ph.D. research with an an international patent, which is a very valuable experience to my science career. You may find that most of the research contributions, later on I made in chemistry, material sciences and cell biology, directly benefit from my Ph.D. training as a technology developer and instrumentation builder.

2003年，我在麦考瑞大学攻读博士学位时，Jim Piper教授提出了两个课题供我选择：一个是研发更高效的激光器，另一个是开发用于细胞分析的生物医学仪器。基于我早期在物理学和光学工程的学习，我更喜欢将光学应用到生物医学仪器领域，于是我选择了后者，研究开发流式细胞仪。这使我能够学到多学科的技能，不仅是光学，还包括微流控、电子控制、数据采集、编程、荧光探针和细胞生物学等。

我完成了3年的博士研究并获得了一项国际专利，这是我科学生涯非常宝贵的经验。你可能会发现，我后来在化学、材料科学和细胞生物学方面的大部分研究贡献，都得益于我在博士学习阶段中仪器研制的经验。

3. In 2015, following your success in Macquarie University, you joined the University of Technology Sydney. In only five years, you have successfully established the Institute for Biomedical Materials & Devices, the Australian Industry Transformation Research Hub for Integrated Devices for End-user Analysis at Low Levels, and the Australia-China Joint

Research Centre for Point of Care Testing. Could you please share with us your successful experience in building these multidisciplinary research entities? Have you encountered any challenges? How did you overcome them?

3. 2015年，继您在麦考瑞大学取得成功后，您加入了悉尼科技大学。在短短的5年时间里，您成功建立了生物医学材料及仪器研究所、澳大利亚国家可集成生物医学器件与技术转化中心以及中澳联合便携式体外诊断技术联合研究中心。您能与我们分享一下您在建立多学科研究实体方面的成功经验吗？您遇到过哪些挑战，又是如何应对的？

Prof. Jin: It is all because of my "ambition"! UTS Vice-Chancellor and President, Prof. Attila Brungs, describes me as an ambitious "builder", which I agree, as I always look for new potentials, make designs and plans, and take the challenges to build new projects. After building the advanced cytometry lab and the node of ARC Centre of Excellence for Nanoscale Biophotonics at Macquarie University, I decided to give myself a new challenge.

My move to UTS provides me an opportunity to build a multidisciplinary research institute. I learn to mentor early career and mid career researchers, and look after other colleagues as well as building the external partnerships and connections. There are completely different challenges. In fact, these challenges also teach me finding the solutions to make the Institute financially sustainable. The mentorship of ECRs and MCRs led to more than ten fellowships externally funded, and our strategic partnership developments with industry and other universities have resulted in several major research centres being funded, including the Australian IDEAL research hub. The establishment of IDEAL Hub further gave us a new credit as the leader in point of care diagnostics, which was strengthened by the Australian

Department of Industry and its counterpart in China to fund the Joint Research Center in this area.

金教授：我取得的一些成功都是因为我的“进取心”！悉尼科技大学校长Attila Brungs教授说我是一个有抱负的“建设者”。我总是在寻找新的可能，不断进行设计和规划，并接受不同的挑战，开拓新的研究领域。在麦考瑞大学建立先进细胞仪实验室和澳大利亚纳米生物光子学卓越中心之后，我

An IDEAL way to connect with industry. In 2016, through the establishment of the IDEAL Hub, Prof. Jin puts Australian biophotonics research into a world leading position, with strong industry partners. The ARC highlights: "A good researcher thinks about collaborations and takes action to develop them as they build their research career"

2016 年，金教授建立澳大利亚可集成生物医疗仪器与技术转化港，使澳大利亚的生物光子学研究处于世界领先地位，并拥有强大的行业合作伙伴。澳大利亚研究理事会这样评价他：“一个好的研究人员会思考合作，并在发展自己的研究事业时建立合作”

决定给自己一个新的挑战。

悉尼科技大学为我提供了建立跨学科研究机构的机会。我学会了与同事和年轻学者共建战略合作伙伴关系，以及发展产学研联盟，这是完全不同的挑战。事实上，这些挑战也教会我如何找到方案使研究所可持续发展。对年轻学者的指导，使我们研究所获得了十余个国家级资助的人才项目。我们与工业界和其他大学的战略伙伴关系促成了我们几个主要研究中心的项目资助，包括澳大利亚可集成生物医疗仪器与技术转化港。该转化港的建立为我们赢得了在即时诊断领域领先发展的机会。两年后，在澳大利亚工业部和中国工信部资助下，我们成立了即时诊断技术开发的联合研究中心，从而进一步加强了我们在这个领域的研究实力。

4. You talked about your success in attracting major research funding in Australia and China. We are also interested in learning how you could manage to publish

more than 200 high-quality research papers, including more than 30 in *Nature* and its sister journals. Would you please share with us your experience and advice on securing research incomes and publishing the high-quality research outputs?

4. 您在澳大利亚和中国承担了多项重大科研项目，发表SCI高水平论文200余篇，其中包括*Nature*及其子刊30余篇。请您谈一谈在申请科研项目和发表高水平文章方面的经验和建议。

Prof. Jin: The short answer is to align the research to the end-users' needs. It becomes a lot of easier to sell the research significance, benefits and impacts to the funding agents, the editors and referees. I foster an environment that stimulates our young ECRs and postgraduate students to formulate their own big ideas, and encourage them to conduct high-risk and high-return projects. Most of our work has been designed to address the critical needs, and provide the potential solutions to the multidisciplinary research communities. This ensures the topic of each project not only very interesting in knowledge advancement, but also very trendy at the cutting edge of the emerging fields.

金教授：简短的回答是我们始终不忘联系基础研究和终端的应用需求。也就是说，在申请科研经费和发表高水平文章时要以应用为导向，既要做好“有趣的科学”，又在不断发展（潜在）“有用的技术”。这样在向资助机构、编辑和审稿人阐述研究目的、意义和重要影响时会更容易。我们IBMD研究所营造了一个环境，激励年轻学者和学生勇于提出自己的想法，并鼓励他们参与高风险和高回报的项目。我们的大部分工作都是为了解决领域中或者转化中关键瓶颈问题，并为多学科的研究提供潜在的解决方案。每个项目的主题不仅在知识先进性方面非常有趣，而且在新兴前沿领域也非常有用。

The second tip is to continuously build new instruments, though takes longer time to build, always return to us new capability, so that we could comprehensively investigate the science and suggest the new directions with sufficient depth. Majority of our high impact papers are based on the purpose-built instruments and instrumentation methods[2], which makes our research unique, well-planned, innovative, and comprehensive.

我们的另外一个特色就是，通过搭建新的仪器，拓展我们新的科研能力，从而能够全面地研究科学问题，并不断开辟具有深度的新方向。我们大部分的高影响力论文都是基于特制的仪器和新的仪器方法的开发，从而取得全新的研究成果，比如在单颗粒光学表征系统的建立[2]等，这使得我们的研究具有独特性、计划性、创新性和综合性。

I have a simple formula (Why – What – How – and

So what) for them to follow in their project planning, data presentation and publication preparations. "Why" your research is more important, and "why" the editors, the readers, and the reviewers should care about your research. "What" exactly you did, or what is exactly the idea? What's fundamentally new, what's fundamentally different from others' doing? "How" actually you achieve this? How do you design your research very comprehensively, so as to make sure there are sufficient steps to take from where we are to where we want to be. Then "so what"? how the research will impact the community?

在写作方面，我特别强调信息的有效传递。我通常采用四步法（Why—What—How—So what），供学者和学生在项目规划、开展实验和撰写论文等方面参考。首先要讲清楚你的科研工作为什么很有前景，它的主要瓶颈在哪里？为什么编辑、读者和审稿人应该关注你的研究？这就是第一步

“Why”。第二步“What”，需要一句话告诉大家，你的想法是什么，你在这个方向发现或者发明了什么，什么是根本性的新现象，与同行工作的根本性区别是什么？第三步“How”，你如何一步一步将这个问题研究清楚，按照逻辑顺序阐述完整。第四步“So what”，你的科研成果如何影响你的同行群体？

5. You spent the past three years strengthening international collaborations, and established the UTS-SUSTech Joint Research Center for Biomedical Materials & Devices at Southern University of Science and Technology since 2019. What are your views on the Joint Research Center model for international collaboration?

5. 您在过去3年中不断加强国际合作，并从2019年起在南方科技大学建立了悉尼科技大学—南方科技大学生物医学材料和器件联合研究中心。请问您对联合研究中心的国际合作模式有什么看法？

Prof. Jin: Biomedical research is a typical field requiring multidisciplinary skills and joint efforts from all the countries. As nobody could use a single technology to solve any single problem, you need a group of people to work together, and the research will benefit everyone in the world. I hope, through the scientific research, all the people around the world, all the nations, could reach a common understanding and recognition towards the mutual benefits.

金教授：生物医学研究是一个需要多学科技能和各国共同努力的研究领域。因为没有人可以用单一的技术来解决任何一个问题，你需要一群人一起工作，然后研究成果将使世界上的每个人都受益。我希望通过科学研究，世界各国及各国人民能够对互利共赢达成共识和认同。

From 2019, I took the new challenge again to explore the new model for international partnerships. I spent quite a lot of efforts in South Korea, Singapore, Germany, and China. The establishment of the JRC with SUSTech is a successful example. The JRC provides us with the scale we need to develop new technologies and prototype devices for tracking disease progression at the level of single cells. Bringing together the leading regional universities of technology, students spend 2 years in Shenzhen and 2 years in Sydney to gain the international experience, and researchers could develop sustainable model by jointly supervising Ph.D. students and academic exchanges.

从2019年开始，我再次接受新的挑战，探索国际伙伴关系的新模式。我在韩国、新加坡、德国和中国花了不少精力。与南方科技大学建立的联合研究中心就是一个成功的例子。联合研究中心为我们提供了开发新技术和样机所需的资源和条件，使我们能够在单细胞水平上跟踪疾病的发展。通过国际合作，我们汇集了这个区域领先的两所科技大学，学生在深圳和悉尼分别学习2年，获得国际教育及科研经历，双方导师可以通过联合指导博士生和学术交流，建立可持续的发展模式。经过过去两年的摸索，我们的模式日渐成熟，每年都会面向全世界招收10名联合培养博士生，欢迎大家的加盟！

NSW Governor, the Hon Margaret Beazley AO QC. (middle of photo) witnessed MOU signing with SUSTech

新南威尔士州州长Margaret Beazley见证了悉尼科技大学与南方科技大学签署合作备忘录

6. As a world leader in photon-upconversion materials and technologies, your research breakthroughs have been published by the top-tier journals, including *Nature*,

Nature Nanotechnology, *Nature Photonics*, *Nature Methods*, and *Light: Science & Applications*. And how the series of advances been made? Where the field will go as the next?

6. 近年来，您在上转换发光材料与技术领域取得重大突破，相关成果发表在*Nature*、*Nature Nanotechnology*、*Nature Photonics*、*Nature Methods*和*Light: Science & Applications*等国际顶级期刊。请您介绍一下这些代表性研究成果，并对这个领域的未来前景做一下展望。

Prof. Jin: Welcome to the backyield of my "dots" collection! They began with Super Dots, the world-first highly doped upconversion nanocrystals, that are three orders of magnitude more sensitive than quantum dots. In our 2013 *Nature Nanotechnology* paper[3], we showed that this limitation of concentration quenching can be overcome, so that we can significantly increase the brightness of single nanocrystal.

The dots that shine at different times were named Tau-Dots. In our 2014 *Nature Photonics* paper[4], by controlling each Dot to "take a turn" to shine, Tau-Dots could facilitate the high-throughput simultaneous detections of multiple target biological cells, subcellular components, and pathogen DNA molecules.

Then came Hyper Dots, in forming heterogeneously doped nanocrystals with the precise control in size, shape, surface, and composition placements (2016 *Nature Communications*[5]). We can build a single Dot into a nano machine.

We then unveiled a photon avalanche effect that amplifies stimulated emission in single Super Dots (2017 *Nature*[6]) that starts the new direction of upconversion super-resolution imaging.

And the dots for nanoscale temperature measurement were named Thermal Dots (2018 *Nature Photonics*[7]). In our 2018 *Light: Science & Application*[8] paper, we demonstrated the brightness of single crystal can be tracked by our naked eyes through a microscope, which provides a tool to study the intracellular transport of single molecules.

欢迎了解我们的“dots”专辑。最初我们提出“Super Dots”，即首次实现高掺杂上转换纳米晶，其灵敏度比量子点高3个数量级。2013年，我们在*Nature Nanotechnology*发表文章[3]，研究结果表明我们克服了浓度猝灭限制，极大提升了纳米单晶的亮度。这些在不同时间发光的“Super Dots”，我们将其命名为“Tau-Dots”。在我们发表在*Nature Photonics*上的论文中[4]，通过控制每个“Dot”交替发光，“Tau-Dots”可以促进对多个目标生物细胞、亚细胞成分和病原体DNA分子的高通量同步检测，可以做成时间维度的高级防伪标志，具有广泛的应用。

我们发现通过调整表面活性剂浓度、温度等参数，能够精确控制其大小、形状、表面和掺杂的位置（2016 年发表于 *Nature Communications*[5]），我们将其称之为“Hyper Dots”，未来可以将单个“Dot”构建成一个纳米器件。

2017 年，我们发现这种颗粒在两束光的作用下，会出现非线性光子雪崩现象，放大了单个“Super Dots”的受激发射（2017 年发表于 *Nature*[6]）。我们将这种现象应用到超分辨成像领域，实现了上转换超分辨成像显微镜应用，开启了上转换超分辨成像的新方向。

我们将用于纳米级温度测量的“Dots”命名为“Thermal Dots”（2018年发表于*Nature Photonics*[7]）。

2018年，我们报道了单颗粒可以通过显微镜被我们的肉眼追踪到，为单分子检测和视踪提供了一种新的检测工具和手段，这项工作发表在*Light: Science & Applications*[8]。

Light: Science & Applications cover

*Light: Science & Applications*封面

Most recently this "Super Dots" series has been extended to nanomechanical force measurement in living cells (2021 *Nature Nanotechnology*)[9].

These nanocrystals can all be used for quantitative analysis of biochemical molecules. They can be transported to the point of interest, within a cell, and facilitate measurements of unprecedented sensitivity, down to the single-molecule level. Infrared light can pass through biological tissue to illuminate the dots which then only emit visible and ultraviolet light, which is easily distinguishable from background light. This upconversion of the infrared light enables imaging deep into the body at high resolution and contrast.

Diagnostics in the future can become much faster and more specific using high-throughput simultaneous detection of multiple target cells, subcellular organelles, and pathogen molecules.

最近，“Super Dots” 系列研究已扩展到活体细胞中的纳米机械力测量（2021 年发表于 *Nature Nanotechnology*[9]）。

这些纳米晶体均可用于生化分子的定量分析。它们可以被运送到细胞内的目标点，便于达到前所未有的灵敏度，甚至降至单分子水平。红外光可以穿过生物组织照亮这些“Dots”，然后这些

“Dots”发出可见光和紫外光，很容易与背景光进行区分。红外光上转换能够以高分辨率和高对比度对身体深处进行成像。

通过使用高通量同时检测多个靶细胞和病原体分子，未来的诊断可以变得更快、更精准。

7. To assist our response to the COVID-19 pandemic, your team has developed a rapid COVID-19 test. It only takes 15 minutes to report the result, and the cost of each test is no more than AUD 25. Could you please tell us the principle of this technology? And how soon we could have the products?

7. 为了应对新冠肺炎疫情，您的团队开发了一种新冠病毒快速检测技术。该技术可在15分钟内获得检测结果，且每次检测的成本不超过25澳币。请您介绍一下这项技术的原理和应用前景。

Prof. Jin: This is a very hot topic these days. The current PCR technology used in the market can biochemically amplify the single RNA molecule from the virus. After about 40 cycles, you got a trillion of the copies of oligo molecules, making this technology very sensitive, but it takes too long to have the result. It's a laboratory-based test, not suitable for point of care testing.

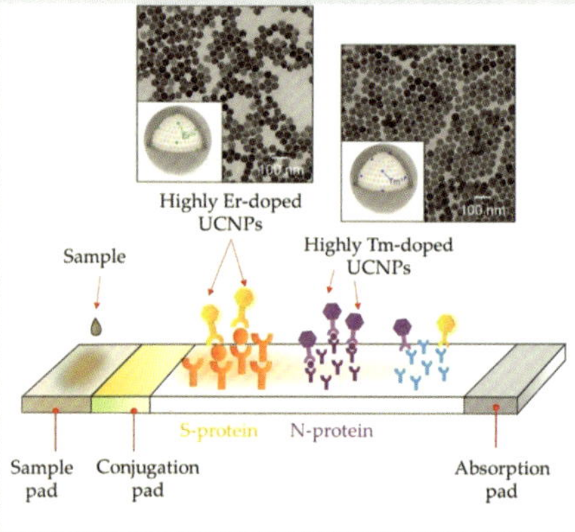

Australian-made COVID-19 iStrip test returns results within 15 minutes. Photo on the left: Super Dot emits intense light in unexpected ways, known as upconversion, that provides ultra-sensitivity by converting infrared into visible light. Photo on the right: The selfie photo of the COVID team, taken at the midnight of 31 July 2020, when the team achieved the first milestone of the project

澳大利亚新冠肺炎病毒测试技术在 15 分钟内获得结果。左图：“Super Dot”发射上转换强光，通过将红外光转换为超强可见光来实现超高灵敏度。右图：团队在 2020 年 7 月 31 日凌晨成功研发这一技术时的自拍照金教授：这是最近非常热门的话题。目前市场上使用的聚合酶链反应技术可以对病毒的单个RNA分子进行生化扩增。在约40个循环后，可获得一万亿个寡聚核苷酸分子，使得这项技术非常灵敏，但需要经过很长时间才能获得结果。这是基于生化实验室的测试，不适用于即时测试。

Our strategy is to target the virus proteins and use Super Dots to optically amplify the signal. After lysing the virus by soap which takes a few seconds, each virus will release a few hundreds of protein fragments, including the spike antigen molecules from the surface. We then take advantage of Super Dots with thousands of emitters to optically amplify each molecule and significantly improve the detection sensitivity. The science is not new, as in our 2018 *Analytical Chemistry*[10] paper, we first applied Super Dots in lateral flow assays and achieved a new LOD of 89 pg/ml for the detection of prostate-specific antigen proteins.

我们的策略是针对病毒蛋白，使用“Super Dots”放大光学信号。在用肥皂裂解病毒后，每个病毒会释放出几百个蛋白质片段，包括表面的刺突抗原分子。然后，我们利用具有数千发光中心的“Super Dots”，通过光放大每个分子，可以显著提高检测灵敏度。我们在2018年发表于*Analytical Chemistry*[10]的论文，阐述了首次将“Super Dots”应用于试纸条检测，并在检测前列腺特异性抗原蛋白方面取得了89 pg/ml的检测限。

Since the pandemic, my team has optimized the same technology for the detection of virus antigen in asymptomatic people. The new test is more than two orders of magnitude more sensitive than the antigen tests now available on the market. The Perth-based Alcolizer Technology has licensed this invention from UTS and branded the strip and detector technologies as iStripTM and VirulizerTM. Hopefully our technology could contribute to the recovery of the pandemic, and to be used in the airport, shops, and nursing homes. As scientists, this makes us very excited, but the commercialization process will depend on the commercial decisions by our industry partner as well as the government regulatory process.

自新冠肺炎疫情爆发以来，我们悉尼科技大学的团队优化了该项技术，用于检测无症状人群的病毒抗原。新的检测方法灵敏度比目前市场上的抗原检测方法要高两个数量级以上。位于珀斯的Alcolizer Technology公司已经从悉尼科技大学获得了这项发明的授权，并将试纸条（iStripTM）和检测技术（VirulizerTM）品牌化。希望我们的技术能够为抗击新冠肺炎疫情做出贡献，并在机场、商店和疗养院等得到广泛应用。作为科学家，这项技术使我们非常兴奋，但是其商业化进程取决于产业合作伙伴的商业决策和政府的监管规定。

8. Since 2012, you have participated in all the series of

Light Conference and Light Young Scientist Forum. In 2018, you started the "Perspective" column for *Light*, and contributed the first Light Online keynote talk in 2020, as well as judging for Light Doctoral Academic League in 2021. As the author, reviewer, editor, and regional manager of *Light: Science & Applications* and *eLight*, you witnessed the growth of our *Light* community. Would you like to comment about your experience with *Light*?

8. 从2012年开始，您每年参加“Light Conference”国际会议和“Light青年科学家论坛”。2018年，您作为Light悉尼办公室负责人，负责“Perspective”专栏工作。2020年，您做了首场“Light在线”公开课主题讲座。2021年，您担任“Light全国光学与光学工程博士生学术联赛”评委。您作为*Light*作者、读者、审稿人、海外办公室负责人，深度参与了*Light*的创刊与发展，一路见证了*Light*的成长与辉煌，不仅为*Light*注入了学术底蕴，

同时为 *Light* 的多元化品牌建设做出了重要贡献。请您谈一谈参与 *Light* 工作的感受和体会以及对 *Light* 未来发展的建议。

Prof. Jin: My experience with *Light* is always pleasant. With the strong supports by Changchun Institute of Optics, Fine Mechanics and Physics (CIOMP), Chinese Academy of Sciences (CAS), as well as Springer Nature, the excellent editorial management team has paved a great foundation for *Light*. The success of *Light* is beyond the profile of being a high impact journal. On each annual "Light Conference" and "Young Scientist Forum", I enjoy the engagement opportunities, and observe the energy, the passion, and the enthusiasm there. The recent engagement channels, through "Light Online", "Light Doctorial Academic League", iCANX Talks, and etc., further take onboard the broader international community and postgraduate students. *Light* sets a great example for publishing business to better engage with the research community with a strong focus on our students. It is a sustainable forum for our young researchers to show their work and to build research connections and networking opportunities.

My roles as the manager in Sydney Office, and the editor for the "Perspective" column gave me the opportunity to stay close with our world-class researchers, and to learn the latest developments at the leading edge of the emerging fields of photonics. I often spend long emails and phone calls, as well as the face to face discussions, with our leading researchers to identify the best Perspective topics. I would like to take this opportunity to encourage our authors to send me emails and arrange time to discuss the emerging directions and the future perspectives of optics and photonics.

金教授：感谢 *Light* 为我提供这个机会，我在 *Light* 的每一次经历都很愉快。在中国科学院长春光学精密机械与物理研究所以及 Springer Nature 出版集团的大力支持下，优秀的编辑管理团队为 *Light* 奠定了良好的基础。*Light* 是以创办国际一流学术期刊为目标，经过近 10 年的努力，大家可以看到，*Light* 的成功不仅仅是作为高影响力期刊。以 *Light* 为平台，在每年举办的“Light Conference”国际会议和“Light 青年科学家论坛”上，我很享受参与这些学术活动的机会和过程，感受 *Light* 系列活动带来的活力、激情和热情。最近，通过“Light 在线”、“Light 全国光学与光学工程博士生学术联赛”、“Light 人物访谈”、iCANX Talks 等渠道，*Light* 已成为多角度的交流平台，远远超过了一家高影响因子的学术期刊，进一步面向更广泛的国际学术社群。*Light* 为新兴科学及新创办的期刊树立了一个非常好的榜样，促进出版业与研究团体紧密合作。这是一个可持续的平台，为广大科技工作者，特别是青年学者展示研究成果、建立联系与合作提供机会。

作为 *Light* 悉尼办公室负责人和 *Light*

"Perspective"专栏编辑，我有机会与国际知名科学家及学者保持密切联系，了解光学及新兴交叉前沿领域的最新发展。我经常与优秀的科研人员进行长时间的电子邮件和电话沟通，以及面对面的交流讨论，以确定最佳的"Perspective"选题。我也想借此机会鼓励*Light*作者与我联系，共同讨论光学和光子学的新兴方向和未来前景。

Opening ceremony of Light Sydney office in 2018
2018年Light悉尼办公室揭牌仪式

9. As the principal supervisor of more than 30 Ph.D. students, including 19 completions to date, could you please tell our future students how you select students

and how to cultivate them to become high-quality researchers?

9. 作为导师，您培养了30多名优秀博士生，其中19名学生已顺利毕业。请您谈一谈选择学生的标准以及培养高水平人才的经验。

Prof. Jin: I'm very proud of my past and current students, and sincerely acknowledge their commitments and contributions to our success as a team. I had 8 Ph.D. students at Macquarie, another 24 students at UTS, and now in the process of recruiting and supervising another 30 or so students at SUSTech and UTS, which is my goal in supervision in the next five years. I would like to take this opportunity to welcome the potential candidates from disciplines, such as photonics, analytical methods, cell biology, data analytics, and device engineering, to join our ever-growing IBMD institute.

金教授：我为我所有已毕业和在读的学生感到非常骄傲，并真诚地感谢他们对我们这个团队的成功所做的贡献。我在麦考瑞大学有8名博士生，在悉尼科技大学有24名学生，现在正在招收和指导南方科技大学和悉尼科技大学联合培养的30余名学生，这是我在未来5年内的指导目标。我也想借此机会欢迎从事光子学、分析方法、细胞生物学、数据分析和科学仪器工程等学科研究的学者加入悉尼科技大学生物医学材料及仪器研究所。

When I select a student, I expect them with the proper research training, being optimistic with the right attitude, and being persistent with a strong desire for science research.

At the beginning of their PhD studies, I encourage our students to challenge the big science questions, and to conduct high-risk and high-return projects. To minimize the risk, I formulate three principles to guide them on how to choose the right research topic:

The student should feel very interested in pursuing the new knowledge around the topic they choose;

The student should have the right skills to start the research, while seeking to learn the new skills;

The topic should be within the scope of IBMD environment, and overlap to a certain degree with their peers' projects, so that they could turn to a peer for discussions whenever they encounter the issues in the lab. It is also good for them to collaborate with each other.

Through the project, I will teach my students to equip themselves the three types of skills:

The professional skills include both the experimental and analytical aspects.

The communication skills include the writing and presentation skills, the collaboration and networking skills and skills to work on the project both independently and as a team. This is most essential to our multidisciplinary research.

I will then show my students how to plan, how to manage the time and resources, and how to develop the strategic thinking skills. Many of my students, after PhD completion, have learned how to do, how to communicate, and how to think and plan.

在选择学生时，我期望他们接受过适当的科研训练，乐观向上，态度端正，坚持不懈，有强烈的科研渴望。

在他们的博士学习阶段之初，我鼓励学生挑战重大科学问题，去开展高风险和高回报的项目。为了将风险降到最低，我制定了三个原则来指导他们

Graduation ceremony
学生毕业典礼

如何选择正确的研究主题：学生应该对他们所选择主题的新知识感兴趣；学生开始研究时应该具备相应的技能，同时寻求学习新技能；研究主题应切合IBMD研究方向，并在一定程度上与同行的项目重叠，以便他们在实验室中遇到问题时可以与同行进行讨论，彼此合作。

通过项目，我将教我的学生掌握3大类技能：专业技能包括实验和分析两个方面；沟通技能包括写作与表达技能；社交技能以及和团队合作完成项目的技能。这些技能对我们开展多学科研究至关重要。

我将告诉我的学生如何计划，如何管理时间和资源以及如何发展战略思维能力。我的许多学生在博士毕业后，已经学会了如何做，如何沟通以及如何思考和计划。

References

参考文献

[1] ZHANGHAO K, LIU W H, LI M Q, et al. High-dimensional super-resolution imaging reveals heterogeneity and dynamics of subcellular lipid membranes. Nature Communications, 2020,11:5890.

[2] ZHOU J J, CHIZHIK A, JIN D Y, et al. Single-particle spectroscopy for functional nanomaterials. Nature,2020,579:41-50.

[3] ZHAO J B, JIN D Y, LU Y Q, et al. Single-nanocrystal sensitivity achieved by enhanced upconversion luminescence. Nature Nanotechnology, 2013,8:729-734.

[4] LU Y Q, ZHANG R, ZHAO J B, et al. Tunable lifetime multiplexing using luminescent nanocrystals. Nature Photonics, 2014,8:32-36.

[5] LIU D M, XU X X, DU Y, et al. Three-dimensional controlled growth of monodisperse sub-50 nm heterogeneous nanocrystals. Nature Communications, 2016,7:10254.

[6] LIU Y J, YANG X S, et al. Amplified stimulated emission in upconversion nanoparticles for super-resolution nanoscopy. Nature,2017,543: 229-233.

[7] ZHOU J J, WEN S H, et al. Activation of the surface dark-layer to enhance upconversion in a thermal field. Nature Photonics, 2018,12:154–158.

[8] WANG F, WEN S H, et al. Microscopic inspection and tracking of single upconversion nanoparticles in living cells. Light: Science & Applications, 2018,7:18007.

[9] SHAN X C, WANG F, et al. Optical tweezers beyond refractive index mismatch using highly doped upconversion nanoparticles. Nature Nanotechnology, 2021,16:531–537.

[10] HE H, LIU B L, et al. Quantitative lateral flow strip sensor using highly doped upconversion nanoparticles. Analytical Chemistry, 2018,90(21).

Professor Jianhua Jiang

编者按

近期，拓扑物理学领域杰出青年科学家、苏州大学蒋建华教授接受了科学编辑张莹的专访。蒋建华教授围绕拓扑光子晶体和声子晶体中的一些基础和前沿问题，进行了深入的分析和解答，展望了拓扑光子晶体和声子晶体领域的发展趋势、应用前景及未来面临的挑战，分享了开展基础前沿研究的经验以及培养学生的心得体会。“Light人物”是*Light: Science & Applications*发起的系列高端人物访谈。本期我们很荣幸邀请到年轻有为、精力充沛、认真严谨、开拓创新的杰出青年科学家——蒋建华。本期采访展现一位深耕在基础研究领域青年才俊的学术世界和科研人生。

Stimulate Innovation to Create a Favorable Basic Research Environment
激发创新活力：营造良好基础研究生态

Science Editor: Ying Zhang 科学编辑 张莹

Editorial:

Recently, Prof. Jianhua Jiang from Soochow University of China accepted an interview from *Light: Science & Applications*. Prof. Jiang works on topological photonics, topological phononics, and nonequilibrium physics. On this issue, he discusses the challenges and opportunities in topological photonics, topological phononics, and other topological synthetic systems. He also shares his experiences in cutting-edge research, the education of graduate students, and other challenges faced by junior researchers. Finally, he gives remarks and suggestions for *Light: Science & Applications*. "Light People" is a featured column of high-end interviews with outstanding scientists. It is our great honor to invite Prof. Jianhua Jiang, an outstanding young scientist, to showcase his research life and the story behind his success.

Light People

Biography: Prof. Jianhua Jiang graduated from the University of Science and Technology of China, where he obtained a bachelor's degree in physics in 2004 and a Ph.D. degree in condensed matter physics in 2010. He later worked at the Weizmann Institute of Science in Israel and the University of Toronto in Canada as a postdoctoral fellow. He joined Soochow University in China in 2015 as a professor of physics. He worked on nonequilibrium physics and material physics for many years. In these research areas, he left his own marks with innovative and influential works that were published in *Nature*, *Nature*

Physics, *Nature Materials*, *Nature Review Physics*, *Physics Reports*, and the *Physical Review* journals. He is a committee member of the National Conference on Statistical Physics and Complex Systems and of the National Conference on Metamaterials. He is also an associate editor of *Science Bulletin* and an editorial member of the *National Science Review*, *Chinese Physics Letter*, *Chinese Physics B*, and *Acta Physica Sinica*.

专家简介：蒋建华教授，中国科学技术大学理学学士（2004 年）、物理学博士（2010 年）。先后在以色列魏茨曼科学研究所和加拿大多伦多大学从事博士后研究。2015 年起任苏州大学物理学院教授，长期从事非平衡统计物理、材料物理等方面的基础科学研究。发表 80 余篇同行评审学术论文（含 *Nature*，*Nature Physics*，*Nature Materials*，*Nature Review Physics*，*Physics Reports*，*Physical Review Letters*，*ACS Nano*，*Science Bulletin* 等）。担任“全国统计物理与复杂系统学术会议”学术委员会委员，“全国超材料大会”理事会理事，*Science Bulletin* 和 *National Science Review* 编委，*Chinese Physics Letter*、*Chinese Physics B*、《物理学报》杂志青年编委等学术兼职。

1. Prof. Jiang, you pursued your graduate study at the University of Science and Technology of China and then performed postdoctoral research at the Weizmann Institute of Science in Israel and the University of Toronto in Canada. After this, you joined Soochow University in China as a professor. We know that you have worked in many different research directions in physics. Would you like to tell us what made you interested in the study of topological physics? How did your postdoctoral experiences affect your current research?

1. 蒋教授，您本硕博就读于中国科学技术大学，之后在以色列魏茨曼科学研究所和加拿大多伦

多大学从事博士后研究，2015年起任苏州大学物理科学与技术学院教授，长期从事拓扑物理、非平衡统计物理等方面的基础科学研究。最初是什么原因让您对拓扑物理等基础研究产生浓厚兴趣？您在国外的两段经历对您回国后的学术研究有哪些影响，对您的科研事业有哪些促进作用?

Prof. Jiang: When I was working at the Weizmann Institute as a postdoctoral fellow, at a certain time, it seemed that everyone was working on topological insulators. In such an environment, I started to learn topological physics and work on topological insulators. In a very short period, I completed several research projects[1][2][3]. One of them became the first work on Weyl semimetals in cold-atom systems[2] and was recognized favorably by the community. However, my postdoctoral advisor, Prof. Yoseph Imry, was negative toward my working on such a popular research area. After carefully considering his opinions, I concluded that it is indeed very difficult to leave indelible marks in such a popular field. With this understanding, I quickly quit the field. Later, I realized that topological physics could be invaluable in photonics, phononics and related fields, and it could even lead to unprecedented applications, and I entered the field of topological physics again. However, this time, I focused on topological photonics and phononics. For this purpose, I went to the University of Toronto for another postdoctoral study with Prof. Sajeev John on photonic crystals and related physics. My stay in Toronto was quite useful for me to learn photonics seriously and eagerly and to think more about how topological physics can be applied to photonics. On the other hand, my collaboration with Prof. Yoseph Imry never ceased. In fact, starting in 2012, we developed a new field called "inelastic thermoelectrics". I like both fields, topological photonics/phononics and inelastic thermoelectrics. Therefore, when I started my group at Soochow University, I worked simultaneously in both of these fields. This collaboration was pleasant and fruitful until Prof. Yoseph Imry passed away in 2018. His influence on me is enormous. Most important were his taste and approaches in doing physics. He liked original and unique research. He was always pursuing originality and uniqueness in our studies. On the other hand, he was also a master of simplifying complicated projects, which was very helpful for me as a young researcher who was easily attracted by complex and "colorful" skills and techniques. Prof. Sajeev John visited the Soochow University every year for our research collaborations. His opinions and ideas have had a great influence on me and my colleagues.

蒋教授：我在以色列魏茨曼科学研究所做博士后的时候，有一段时间似乎每个人都在研究拓扑物理。受到环境的影响，我也开始学习并尝试研究拓扑物理。2011至2012年我在很短的时间内也做了几个工作[1][2][3]，其中一篇成为最早在冷原子系统中研究Weyl半金属相的论文[2]，现在已被引用100多次。但是，我的导师Yoseph Imry教授反对我在这样一个热门的方向开展研究。我经过深入思考之后，觉得要在此方向留下痕迹确实很困难，不可替代的工作太少了。因此，我又以极快的速度退出了这一研究领域，直到后来我觉得拓扑光子和声子系统的研究可能具有巨大的基础研究和应用前景，我才又重新进入这个领域。这次我专注于研究拓扑光子学和声子学。为此，我到多伦多大学专门向光子晶体的创始人之一Sajeev John教授求教，成为他的博士后。在多伦多两年多的时间，我学习了光子晶体和光学材料的很多知识。另一方面，我和Yoseph Imry教授在2010年开展的热电输运研究一直没有中断，我们开拓了一个被称为“非弹性热电效应”的新领域。由于我对这两个领域都很感兴趣，2015年我在苏州大学建立研究组的时候，同时在拓扑超材料和非平衡物理方面开展了研究。Yoseph Imry教授和我的合作一直延续到2018年他去世。他对我的影响是巨大的，最重要的方面是要形成科学研究的原创性和自己的特色。另外，他还是一个化繁为简的大师，这对于像我这样迷信复杂绚丽技术的年轻人是一个很好的教益。Sajeev John教授经常到苏州大学来访问。他对我甚至苏大物理学院的很多老师都产生了非常重要的影响。Sajeev John教授对我们而言最重要的帮助在于他的评价和判断。

2. At the beginning of 2021, you and Prof. Yin Pu from Nanjing University in China made the experimental discovery of Bulk-disclination Correspondence in Topological Crystalline Insulators published in *Nature*[4], which is an important milestone in the study of topological materials. In this work, photonic crystals are used as analogs of topological crystalline insulators to perform the experimental realization and study of disclinations at the macroscopic scale and the induced nontrivial topological effects. This opened a new pathway toward the experimental study of topological physics that was inaccessible before, giving fractional

charges a central role in topological materials. What were the biggest challenges for you when working on this project? What are the opportunities and challenges that you could see for topological photonics in the future?

2. 2021年初，您和南京大学蒲殷副教授合作，在*Nature*上发表了题为“Bulk-disclination Correspondence in Topological Crystalline Insulators”的重要研究成果[4]。利用光子晶体作为拓扑晶体绝缘体的类比，通过构建光子晶体旋错结构实现探测体-旋错对应关系的物理系统。该工作为拓扑物理和材料的研究开辟了新的道路和方向，显示出光子晶体和超材料在基础物理研究中的重要价值。该项工作突破了哪些瓶颈？请您结合该项工作谈一谈拓扑光子晶体的发展趋势、应用前景及未来面临的挑战。

Prof. Jiang: The development of topological photonics and phononics has two driving motives. One is to utilize topological physics to discover new effects and phenomena in photonic and phononic systems or to improve the performance of photonic or phononic devices. The other is to exploit the advantages of photonic and phononic systems to realize and observe topological phenomena that are difficult to realize in condensed matter systems.

The famous work on the experimental observation of the quantum anomalous Hall effect by Prof. Qikun Xue and coworkers is well known in the community. One of the reasons is that it was an extremely difficult and challenging experiment. One challenge is that the bandgap of a quantum anomalous Hall system is very small. Therefore, the experimental system has to be in a clean state at a very low temperature. Otherwise, the disorder effect or the finite-temperature effect may ruin the quantized anomalous Hall conductance. For photonic and phononic systems, because they are not restricted to equilibrium or near-equilibrium conditions, the experiments do not have to be performed at very low temperatures. For instance, even for GHz microwave photons, the photonic energy of which corresponds to 10 mK, the measurements can be done at room temperature because there are many more exciting photons than thermal photons in the experiments. In fact, one can perform photonic pump-probe measurements with a frequency resolution of 1 MHz or lower. Moreover, with the macroscopic realization of topological photonic systems, both the pump and the probe can be designed for various setups, allowing versatile measurements of the bulk and the boundary states.

In our recent papers[4][5], we use topological photonic systems to realize an important principle: the band topology can be probed via defects. This is the long-sought bulk-defect correspondence that goes beyond the bulk-edge correspondence. Although it was proposed in

2009[6] and later[7], such fundamental phenomena were not confirmed until recently. In 2018, we demonstrated the first case of bulk-dislocation correspondence, where a dislocation in a magnetic photonic topological insulator leads to the formation of a robust defect mode[5]. This year, we used a disclination in an all-dielectric photonic topological insulator to verify the bulk-disclination correspondence[4]. The disclination not only leads to topological bound states but also leads to fractional charges. Such fractional charges bound to the disclination are sensitive to the crystalline symmetry, leading to fine experimental discernment of various topological crystalline insulator phases that cannot be distinguished via spectral properties such as bulk-boundary or higher-order bulk-boundary correspondences. Here, utilizing the nonequilibrium nature of photons, we are able to measure the photonic local density of states and hence reconstruct a fractional mode charge that has a one-to-one correspondence to the fractional charge in electronic topological insulators via band filling at zero temperature. I think this is a quite remarkable demonstration of the merits of photonic topological systems.

Currently, topological photonic crystals and other topological metamaterials have become one of the focuses of research on metamaterials. These materials provide new scopes for linear, nonlinear, and quantum optics. For instance, in nonlinear optics, topological lasers have demonstrated their advantages of greater stability and better performance. In addition, topological physics can be exploited to design stable and low-loss photonic crystal fibers. Topological modes bound to defects can be used as robust cavity modes. In the future, we expect more surprises from topological non-Hermitian, nonlinear, and quantum photonic systems.

蒋教授：拓扑光子／声子学的发展一直有两个主要的驱动力。其中一个是通过拓扑物理实现新的光子／声子功能器件或改善原来的光子／声子功能器件。另一个驱动力更基本一些，就是光子或声子系统具有电子系统所没有的一些优势，因此可以实现电子系统中无法或难以实现的一些实验证实。

薛其坤院士的著名工作反常量子霍尔效应之所以蜚声海内外，一个重要的原因是该实验极其困难。其中巨大困难的核心之一起源于电子系统必须处于近平衡状态，由于拓扑带隙对应的能量很小，因此要求电子系统处于一种极低温的平衡态。而对于光子和声子实验系统而言，由于光子和声子不受平衡态分布的限制，相关的困难也荡然无存。例如，尽管光子的拓扑带隙只有几个GHz，对应的温度在100mK这个尺度。但是，在室温下的光子实验中可以按照人们的意愿以1MHz左右的频率精度任意激发和探测微波光子。此外光子／声子系统的优势还包括光子／声子晶体设计、制备及测量上的优势。由于光子／声子晶体通常处于宏观尺度，它们在制备和测量上具有电子系统无法具备的优势。

在2021年的这篇*Nature*论文中，我们通过光子实验验证了一个重要的原理：通过测量拓扑缺陷可以研究和获取材料的能带拓扑性质[4][5]。长期以来，人们一直想找到边界态之外的拓扑物理性质作为识别拓扑材料的特征。虽然在2009年人们已经提出了相关的理论[6][7]，然而在实验上一直无法观测和证实。我们的工作首次在实验上测量和验证了一种拓扑缺陷disclination（中文翻译为“旋错”）导致的分数电荷[5]。该分数电荷仅依赖于光子带隙的拓扑性质。当然，光子系统中的分数电荷是一种类比，其含义是光子带隙以下的光子局域态密度的积分。我认为这个工作最精彩的地方在于，通过非平衡光子实验可以验证平衡电子系统的物理性质[4]。另一方面，该工作首次凸显出拓扑缺陷导致的分数电荷作为一种新的拓扑物理可测量量。该物理量属于体能带的性质，这意味着一种新的可测量拓扑物理量的产生，区别于之前人们普遍关注的拓扑边界态。

如今拓扑光子晶体和其他拓扑超材料已成为人

们最关注的超材料系统之一。这些超材料为光的调控、非线性和量子光学的发展都带来了新的内涵。例如，在非线性光学领域，拓扑激光系统大放异彩，呈现出更稳定和更优越的性能。此外，拓扑物理还可以用于设计稳定、低损耗的光子晶体光纤。拓扑局域态还可以用作频率稳定的光子微腔。在未来，我们期待拓扑光子系统在非厄米、非线性和量子光学领域呈现更多的惊喜和精彩。

3. In 2019, you, Prof. Minghui Lu and Prof. Yanfeng Chen collaborated and achieved important progress on higher-order topological insulators published in *Nature Physics*[8]. What is the main breakthrough in this work and your other works on higher-order topology? What do you expect from the future development of higher-order topological phases?

3. 2019年，您和南京大学卢明辉教授、陈延峰教授课题组合作，在高阶拓扑声子晶体领域取得了重要进展，相关成果以“Second-order Topology and Multidimensional Topological Transitions in Sonic Crystals”为题发表在*Nature Physics*[8]上。该项研究的难点是什么？您对高阶声拓扑绝缘体的未来有怎样的预期？

Prof. Jiang: I remember when we started to work on photonic topological systems with time-reversal symmetry, such as all-dielectric topological photonic crystals[9][10]. My group and other research groups are obsessed with gapless edge states, which are very difficult to realize in time-reversal symmetric systems since there is no Kramers degeneracy in photonics. I recall that in 2015, my students complained about the large edge bandgap in our photonic topological system. After that, I thought about how to make use of the edge gap instead of avoiding it, although the edge gap is commonly believed to be undesirable since it causes backscattering in the edge channels. At some time in

2016, I realized that this edge gap can be exploited to realize corner states via the Jackiw-Rebbi mechanism in bending edge channels. However, at that time, it was almost impossible for me to convince anyone to do the experiments. In 2017 and later, the concept of higher-order topological insulators became a popular idea in the study of topological insulators. I quickly realized that what we had found was in fact the higher-order topological insulator phenomenon. In collaboration with Prof. Minghui Lu and Prof. Yanfeng Chen at Nanjing University, we were able to quickly make important discoveries in higher-order topological insulators. In our 2019 work, we were among the first few teams to realize higher-order topological insulators for acoustic waves (the two other teams are from Nanyang Technological University in Singapore[11] and the City University of New York in the USA[12]). Moreover, in our system, the topological transitions of the 2D bulk states and 1D edge states take place independently by tuning a single geometric parameter. That is, the edge state topological transitions can be triggered independently of the bulk state topological transitions. This feature is unique to our system and has never been observed before. Later, we performed a series of innovative studies on higher-order topological phases[13]—[20]. In particular, we proposed the concept of higher-order Weyl semimetals[19][20] and the symmetry-protected hierarchy of anomalous multipole topological bandgaps[14][17][18]. Because of our contributions to the field of higher-order topological phases, we were invited to write a review paper for *Nature Review Physics* on higher-order topology[21]. In this paper, research on various higher-order topological states was summarized and reviewed, and future perspectives and challenges were discussed. For instance, from an application perspective, corner states due to higher-order topology can be a good candidate for optical microcavity states and propagation modes in photonic crystal fibers. Looking back on all these points,

I think we are truly lucky to have made innovative contributions to this field in the early stage. I believe that this had a lot to do with our difficulties back in 2016 and our determination to explore the puzzles we faced instead of avoiding them.

蒋教授：在我们开展这项研究的时候，很多人（包括我自己的学生）还在执着于无能隙的拓扑边界态的研究[9][10]。从2015年我们开始研究二维光子晶体的拓扑边界态开始，我们就发现时间反演对称的拓扑光子晶体中，边界态往往是有能隙的。有一段时间我一直在思考该如何解决这个问题，因为一般认为这样有能隙的边界态是不好的。2016年的某个时候，我开始意识到这些有能隙的边界态会导致一个一维的衍生Jackiw-Rebbi机制，从而导致角态的产生。然而，那个时候我发现很难说服同事去开展相关的实验研究。2017年人们提出了“高阶拓扑绝缘体”的概念。我们突然意识到我们所发现的拓扑光子／声子系统就是高阶拓扑绝缘体。这时我们正好设计出一种新型的声子晶体，以这种声子晶体为平台，并与南京大学卢明辉教授和陈延峰教授合作，我们很快在实验室看到了高阶拓扑绝缘体的性质：打开能隙的边界态和角态。我们的工作和新加坡南洋理工大学张柏乐教授课题组的工作[11]以及纽约城市大学Khanikaev教授的工作[12]一起成为最早发现声学系统高阶拓扑绝缘体的工作。另外，有趣的是，我们通过调节单个几何参量（声学散射体的旋转角度）就可以实现二维体态和一维边界态的独立拓扑相变。也就是说我们可以引发一个纯粹的边界态拓扑相变，但不伴随体态的拓扑相变。这是之前的工作未曾实现的，也是这个工作的一个特色。此后，我们开展了一系列有特色的关于高阶拓扑态的研究[13]–[20]。特别地，我们提出了高阶Weyl半金属的概念[19][20]，并通过声学实验观测证实了我们的理论预言。我们提出并通过声学实验实现了对称性保护的异常多级子绝缘体[14][17][18]。2021年，由于在高阶拓扑态方面的一系列原创性的工作，我们与南京大学陈延峰教授和卢明辉教授合作在*Nature Review*

*Physics*撰写关于高阶拓扑态方面的邀请综述论文[21]。这篇论文回顾了高阶拓扑研究的历史并展望了未来。高阶拓扑导致的角态可以作为很好的光学微腔态或光子晶体光纤中的一维波导。我相信高阶拓扑还会给光学带来更多的新机制和新应用。回顾这段历史，我觉得我们是很幸运的。这种幸运也许和我们做研究时的困惑以及努力想在没有“框架”的地方做一些探索有关系。

4. Would you please tell us what difficulties and challenges you have ever encountered in your research? How did you deal with and overcome them?

4.您在潜心科研过程中遇到过哪些困难和挑战？面对这些困难和挑战，您是如何应对和攻克难关的?

Prof. Jiang: We, scientists, are trained to solve all kinds of problems and challenges starting in our student lives. We face different challenges in different stages of career development. At the beginning of my career, the main challenge was to find interesting research topics. In the next stage, the main challenge for me was how to define the value of my research on a long timescale. Now, my main challenge is to search for interesting and valuable research directions for my students, while I am keeping a thinking mind for doing valuable research.

Prof. Jianhua Jiang's group (photo taken at the 120-year-old building of Soochow University)

蒋建华教授课题组在苏州大学本部拥有120年历史的林堂前合影

To address this challenge, both a long-term vision and a pragmatic approach are needed. In recent years, I have always considered what the most valuable problems are that I can find and how I can focus energy and resources on them to create irreplaceable value. Although there are various difficulties when concrete ideas and strategies are carried out, the most difficult things are to form these ideas and strategies initially and to re-evaluate them from time to time.

蒋教授：科研人员在研究生阶段受训练要面临各项挑战，解决各种问题。不同的阶段会遇到不同的挑战。我曾经遇到的挑战是跳出框架构建有意思的科研课题，后来遇到的挑战是提炼科研工作的价值和意义。我现在遇到的挑战是如何为我的每个研究生寻找一个有价值的具体研究方向。要解决这个挑战必须要有足够长远的眼光，同时要有务实的方法和策略。最近几年，我一直都在思考什么是我能想到的最有价值的物理问题，以及我如何才能凑齐需要的人力物力来解决这些问题，创造不可替代的价值。当我们有了具体的思想和一些策略，具体的问题就会涌现出来。有了具体的问题之后，只需要找到合适的方法和资源来解决这些问题就好了。在这个过程中遇到具体的问题，我会按照我的经验和思考寻找务实的路径来解决问题。

5. Active young scientists are the assets of our community in both fundamental sciences and applications. The main challenges for them are probably applying for research funding and publishing high-quality papers. Could you please share your valuable experiences as one of the outstanding young scientists in your research field?

5. 青年科技工作者是科研领域中最为活跃的群体，是推动科技发展、实现科技自立自强的一支重要力量。目前，很多青年科技工作者面临着申请基金项目和发表高水平论文的挑战，您作为基础研究

领域杰出的青年科学家之一，请分享一下您的宝贵经验。

Prof. Jiang: Looking back at the decade after receiving my Ph.D. degree, I grew from technical maturity to thought maturity. In the first stage, I underwent various basic training (a continuation of Ph.D. training), including obtaining physics pictures, writing papers, giving talks, and collaborating with others. Then, I could conduct research independently and try to establish a research group and acquire, harness and retain more funding and resources. Just like other young scientists, I have been trying tirelessly to find a way to achieve success. If there is something special about me, it might be that I have high expectations and standards for my studies. That is, I don't want to solve small problems or even those that many others are trying to solve. I keep thinking about what problems deserve to be solved and try hard to keep uniqueness and originality in my research. Of course, I have to combine strategies with practically doable things. I think leaving time to think, e.g., several years, before making a thing doable is important. During these years, another line of achievable research must be carried out. To do great research, one has to have great visions and ideas. This means that your ideas must go far ahead of most others. The formation of great ideas is something very important that has been missing in our daily research life and in the education of our graduate students. Many of our graduate students have narrow vision and little knowledge, but too much routine thinking. To build a strong community, we need to solve these problems. In recent years, in our community, we have probably also underestimated the importance of original research, especially for young scientists. Facing all these challenges, young scientists must form their own strategy and balance many things.

Work-life balance is also very important. I benefit from

the support of a happy family. I have always believed that life is the foundation of work. I have received much support from my family and friends. I am really grateful for that.

蒋教授：回顾博士毕业之后的10年（我认为也是很多青年科技工作者拉开差距的10年），我经历了从“基础扎实”和“技术成熟”到突破思维框架，开启无边界的思考，训练自己物理思想的操练，写论文、作报告、与人交流合作等各种基本训练，到开始独立研究（全面解决所有的问题），再到形成团队，有能力获取、驾驭和掌握更多的资源。我和大多数青年科技工作者一样，一直在不屈不饶、竭尽全力地寻找出路。如果说有什么特别的地方，那就是我的着眼点从来不小。我不想解决小问题，甚至不想解决别人正在试图解决的问题。我一直在想什么样的问题才是不浪费我人生的问题。当然，我也总会把这些问题和我们实际要解决的问题糅合起来。还有一点很重要，就是一定要在思想上走在同行的前面。平时，特别是不在办公室的时候，一定要思考如何才能在思想上超越同行。如果能做到思考深远，务实地布局每年要做的事情，这样每年都会有很好的收获，研究的道路才会越走越

Prof. Jianhua Jiang in his laboratory
蒋建华教授在实验室

宽。我们很多青年研究员的思维视野不够宽广，认知的范围不够大，解决问题的能力不够强，表述问题和提炼价值的能力也需要提高。这些都是特别需

要注意的方面。科学研究成功最后的表现一定是做了一系列有特色的工作，取得了实际的突破，最好是别人没有想到的、开创性的研究。当然，在策略上我们总是要结合热门和冷门。冷门的东西需要长期的思考和酝酿，热门的东西需要战略、资源、速度和深度，这些都是年轻人要思考和解决的问题。我的长处就是以思想深度换时间、以战略和统筹管理争取时间，这样我在热门的领域也能以微小的资源做得还不错。

我还特别得益于和谐幸福的家庭，这也是我们年轻人要注意的地方。我一直相信先有生活后有工作，生活是工作的基础。我比较幸运的是，我的朋友和我的生活给予我很多的教益。我的妻子教会了我很多管理方面的技能，使得我能驾驭更多的事务，始终把精力集中在那些重要的事情上。

6. At the beginning of 2021, you published an important paper about topological photonics in *Nature*[4].

Three of the four co-first authors are from the post-95 generation. Could you please share your experiences with training the students? Additionally, according to your experiences, could you please talk about how to create a good research environment and build a creative atmosphere in the research team?

6. 2021年初，您在*Nature*上发表了拓扑光子学方面的重要研究论文[4]，该论文以苏州大学为第一单位，4位共同第一作者中3位为95后硕士研究生。请您谈一谈在培养学生方面有哪些心得体会？另外，请结合您的科研经历，谈一谈如何营造良好的基础研究科研生态，培育科研团队的创新能力和水平？

Prof. Jiang: Often, at the beginning of Ph.D. training, I set low expectations for my students. However, I gradually increase it. In recent years, I have set my standards for selecting promising students. One of the first things that I consider is the motivation and quality of general education. These are very important qualities that may help graduate students get through the tough period of Ph.D. study. The other important quality I am looking for is the courage to walk outside of the sphere of one's knowledge to do something in unknown territory. This is key to academic success. The students who are willing to try new things will be appreciated and fully supported by me. I will train them to try new things with some guiding principles. Once they get used to such training, they will grow up quickly. I believe that this will greatly benefit their confidence in research and have a long-lasting impact on their understanding of what constitutes scientific research. Education in innovation is invaluable for our research community. A good sign of a promising student is a thinking mind that is fearless and eager to explore the unknown. Once the students are warmed up for innovative research, I will ask them to go out and give talks or to communicate with collaborators. I try not to ignore their training in other aspects outside of research. Communicating, giving talks, writing proposals, and solving problems in the lab are all very important for their academic success.

From my limited experience, I can tell that the young generation has much better prospects than my generation. They are more educated, informative, and creative. They are often more eager to communicate and have a better ability in communication. I expect them to do great things in the future.

蒋教授：我一开始带博士研究生的时候非常照顾他们，后来我又调整自己给他们逐步增加各种挑战。由于苏州大学的研究生在基础方面肯定达不到我的要求，我逐渐开始寻找其他最重要的特质。我发现适合做科研的学生最重要的特质是“无畏的探索精神”。很多学生墨守成规，对新事物无从着手。如果有胆子大的学生能主动开始尝试性的探索，我认为这是最优秀的科学研究品质。所以，我对研究生的培养除了常规的那些方面之外（其实我不太管这些，只是发现具体问题，解决具体问题），最重要的是培养他们处理新事物的能力。通常研究生第一学期我会要求他们在上课之余学几个基本的模型，第二学期我就要求他们开始尝试解决前沿问题。我给的问题不需要太多的基础，最需要的就是大胆试探，并且一边试探一边思考总结，渐渐形成思想上的创新。平时我也鼓励他们表达思想，因为表达思想是思想创新的第一步，能说出“所以然”比简单的试探更进了一步。所以，往往他们中能干的很快就有了好的科研成果。我很少强调扎实的基础和系统性的教育（但是会鼓励他们根据课题的需要学习一些必要的东西），这样对于研究生创新能力的培养也有好处。我喜欢他们给我一些出人意料的结果，不喜欢他们做一些依葫芦画瓢、搬砖的事（甚至偶尔会批评他们这种智力上的惰性和人格上的软弱）。除了在科研上我鼓励他们开拓自己的边界以外，在很多事情上我都锻炼他们独立的能力。有时候我会派一个学生单独去访问我们的合作者，让他代表我全权处理所有问题。例如，今年我搭建了一个声学实验室，基本上我只负责安排，具体处理问题都交给了他们。这些事情很好地锻炼了他们的综合能力，让他们快速成长，也给了他们与日俱增的信心。

Mr. Zhikang Lin from Prof. Jiang's group holds his experimental sample—a kagome acoustic metamaterial that hosts non-Abelian topological semimetal phases of phonons (This work was published in *Nature Physics*[22])

蒋教授课题组学生林志康（4篇*Nature*系列论文的共同第一作者）和他的实验样品（kagome拓扑半金属，最新论文发表在*Nature Physics*上[22]）

从我的这些有限的经验来看，我们可能都低估了学生的真实创造力和创新能力。我们或多或少受限于循规蹈矩，在学生培养上也有一点儿保守。据我的观察，新生代的学生突破框架的能力、表达自我和表达思想的能力都非常强。他们完全有能力很快走到科学创新的前沿。

7. In 2021, as an internationally-renowned journal in optics and photonics, *Light: Science & Applications* received the latest impact factor of 17.782, ranking the top 3 among all optics journals around the world for 7 consecutive years. Meanwhile, this journal won the China Publishing Government Award, which is the highest award in publishing in China. Looking back on nearly ten years of this journal's founding history, 16 regions and overseas offices of *Light: Science & Applications* have been established at home and abroad. Series of brand activities based on *Light: Science & Applications* have been created and being emerging forward, such as

"Light Conference", "Light Young Scientists Forum", "Rising Stars of Light", "Light Online", "Light People", "Light Academic League", "Light Snapshot", etc. We also had the honor to invite you to attend the 2020 "Light Nano-optics Young Scientists Forum" held at Nanjing University in China, and you shared the report on fractional photonic charge in topological defects. Would you please talk about your feelings and experiences on *Light: Science & Applications* and its community activities?

7. 2021年，*Light*获得最新影响因子17.782，连续7年稳居世界光学期刊榜前三，同时荣获了我国新闻出版领域的最高奖——第五届中国出版政府奖期刊奖！回顾*Light*创刊历程，以*Light*为平台，16个*Light*区域和海外办公室先后在国内外成立，衍生出“Light Conference”国际会议、“Light青年科学家论坛”、“Light未来之星评选”、中国光学领域十大社会影响力事件评选（Light 10）、“Light在线

学术活动”、“Light人物访谈”、“Light全国博士生学术联赛”、“Light国际光日系列学术活动”、“Light拾光”等多项*Light*原创品牌IP。我们也有幸邀请您参加了在南京大学举办的“Light 2020 纳米光学青年科学家论坛”，您分享了“拓扑缺陷中的分数光子电荷”精彩报告，反响十分热烈。请您谈一谈对*Light*期刊和*Light*品牌活动的感受和体会。

Prof. Jiang: *Light: Science & Applications* has established a good reputation and its own development strategies. I believe that *Light: Science & Applications* will be a giant tree with prosperous developments one day. I think the development of *Light: Science & Applications* in the future would depend on its ability to build an ecological system around this tree. *Light: Science & Applications* has established its own brand. I believe that its future will be very impressive and it will have a long-lasting influence in the research community of optics and photonics, including basic, applied, and engineering research and applications.

蒋教授：*Light*现在已经建立了很好的声誉，而且也很有发展眼光。我相信*Light*这棵茂盛的树一定会长成参天大树。我在期刊运营方面也没有深入思考，仅仅觉得*Light*未来的发展更强地依赖于创新性、系统性、前瞻性的思维。*Light*已经有了自己成熟的品牌，将会创造出一个前所未有的生态系统，超越一本杂志的范畴，建立更深远和长久的品牌影响力。

Photo with Prof. Yuhong Bai, the director of Light Publishing Group
蒋建华教授与中科院长春光机所Light学术出版中心
主任、白雨虹研究员合影

References

参考文献

[1] JIANG J H, WU S. Spin susceptibility and helical magnetic order at the edges/surfaces of topological insulators due to Fermi surface nesting. Physical Review. B,2011,83(20):205124.

[2] JIANG J H. Tunable topological Weyl semimetal from simple cubic lattices with staggered fluxes. Physical Review. A,2012,85(3).

[3] JIANG J H, et al. Non-Abelian topological superconductors from topological semimetals and related systems under superconducting proximity effect. J. Physics: Condensed. Matter, 2013(25).

[4] LIU Y, JIANG J H, et al. Bulk-disclination correspondence in topological crystalline insulators. Nature, 2021,589:381–385.

[5] LI F F, JIANG J H, et al. Topological light-trapping on a dislocation. Nature Communications, 2018,9:2462.

[6] RAN Y, ZHANG Y, et al. One-dimensional topologically protected modes in topological insulators with lattice dislocations. Nature Physics, 2009,5:298–303.

[7] LI T H, HUGHES T L, et al. Fractional disclination charge in

two–dimensional Cn–symmetric topological crystalline insulators. Physical Review. B,2020,101:115115.

[8] ZHANG X J, JIANG J H, et al. Second–order topology and multi–dimensional topological transitions in sonic crystals. Nature Physics,2019,15:582–588.

[9] XU L. JIANG J H, et al. Accidental degeneracy in photonic bands and topological phase transitions in two–dimensional core–shell dielectric photonic crystals. Optics Expre ss,2016,24(16):18059–18071.

[10] ZHU X, JOHN S, et al. Topological transitions in continuously–deformed photonic crystals. Physical Review. B,2018,97(8).

[11] XUE H, GAO F, et al. Acoustic higher–order topological insulator on a kagome lattice. Nature Materials,2019,18:108–112.

[12] NI X, et al. Observation of higher–order topological acoustic states protected by generalized chiral symmetry. Nature Materials, 2019,18:113–120.

[13] ZHANG X J, et al. Dimensional hierarchy of higher–order topology in three–dimensional sonic crystals. Nature Communications, 2019,10:5331.

[14] ZHANG X J, TIAN Y, et al. Symmetry–protected hierarchy of

anomalous multipole topological band gaps in nonsymmorphic metacrystals. Nature Communications,2020,11:65.

[15] ZHANG L, et al. Higher-order photonic topological states in surface-wave photonic crystals. Advanced Science,2020,7.

[16] CHEN Y, et al. Plasmon-polaritonic quadrupole topological insulators. Physical Review. B,2020,101(4).

[17] ZHOU X X, HOU B, et al. Twisted quadrupole topological photonic crystals. Laser & Photonics Reviews,2020,14.

[18] XIONG Z, JIANG J H, et al. Anomalous quadrupole topological insulators in 2D nonsymmorphic sonic crystals. Physical Review. B,2020.102(3).

[19] JIANG B, JIANG J H, et al. Higher-order Weyl semimetals. Physical Review Letters,2020,125.

[20] LUO Y, JIANG B, et al. Observation of a phononic higher-order Weyl semimetal. Nature Materials,2021,20:794–799.

[21] ZHAN P, JIANG J H, et al. Higher-order band topology. Nature Review Physics,2021,3:520–532.

[22] JIANG B, HOU B, et al. Experimental observation of non-Abelian topological acoustic semimetals and their phase transitions. Nature Physics,2021,17:1239–1246.

特邀嘉宾（按姓氏笔画排列）

于存，中国科学院长春光学精密机械与物理研究所（简称“长春光机所”）国际合作处职员，主要负责中白国际创新中心外联、俄乌白国际合作与交流等工作；在*Light: Science & Applications*、《国际人才交流》杂志上发表多篇文章。中科院科技翻译工作者协会会员。

Cun Yu works at the Department of International Cooperation in the Changchun Institute of Optics, Fine Mechanics and Physics (CIOMP), Chinese Academy of Sciences (CAS). Her main duties cover the Sino-Belarus International Innovation Center, international cooperation projects and exchanges between CIOMP and institutions in Belarus, Ukraine and Russia. She has published multiple articles in the journal *Light: Science & Applications*, *International Talent*, and is a member of CSA's Science & Technology Translations Association.

刘小翼，古斯塔夫埃菲尔大学（ESIEE Paris, ESYCOM Lab, CNRS, Universit é Gustave Eiffel）博士后。他于2018年在中国科学院长春光学精密机械与物理研究所获得博士学位。2019年，他加入Tarik Bourouina教授团队开展博士后研究，先后受到巴黎高等师范学院基金会帕斯卡讲席助理项目（导师：崔天宏教授）以及古斯塔夫-埃菲尔大学I-SITE卓越法国国家倡议计划项目的资助。曾获得国家奖学金，大恒奖学金特别奖，中科院院长奖学金特别奖，北京市&中国科学院大学优秀毕业生，王大珩光学奖，中科院优秀博士论文等多项荣誉。

Xiaoyi Liu is currently a postdoc in ESIEE Paris, ESYCOM Lab, CNRS, Université Gustave Eiffel. He obtained his Ph.D. degree from University of the Chinese Academy of Sciences, Changchun Institute of Optics, Fine Mechanics and Physics in 2018. He joined Prof. Tarik Bourouina's lab and started his postdoc work from 2019, and was supported by the Chair

Blaise Pascal assistant project of École Normale Supérieure Fondation (Supervisor: Prof. Tianhong Cui) and the Future Program of Université Gustave Eiffel in the frame of the I-SITE excellence French national initiative program successively. He once won several honors such as National Scholarship for Postgraduate Students (2015 & 2017), Special Prize of Daheng Optical Scholarship (2017), Special Prize of President Scholarship of Chinese Academy of Sciences (2018), Excellent Graduate Student of Beijing & University of the Chinese Academy of Sciences (2018), Wang Daheng Optical Scholarship for students (2018), Outstanding Doctoral Dissertations of Chinese Academy of Sciences (2019), etc.

顾衡，江苏大学机械工程学院资格教授。2018年毕业于英国曼彻斯特大学，师从英国皇家工程院院士李琳教授，2018年至2020年在英国卡迪夫大学担任欧盟区域发展基金ASTUTE项目组博士后职位，与威尔士当地企业（包括空客、大陆集团等）开展了一系列项目合作。主要从事激光金属沉积、激光焊接、多材料增材制造等激光材料加工领

域的研究，在*International Journal of Heat and Mass Transfer*、*Additive Manufacturing*、*Optics and Laser Technology*等国际刊物发表论文10余篇，并担任多个国际期刊审稿人。

Heng Gu is a qualified professor in the School of Mechanical Engineering, Jiangsu University. He graduated from The University of Manchester, UK, in 2018, under the supervision of Prof. Lin Li. Heng Gu held a postdoctoral position in the ASTUTE project team funded by the European Regional Development Fund at Cardiff University, UK, from 2018 to 2020. He worked with local Welsh companies (including Airbus, Continental, etc.) on a range of projects. His research interests focus on laser material processing such as laser metal deposition, laser welding, and multi-material additive manufacturing. He has published more than 10 papers in journals including the *International Journal of Heat and Mass Transfer*, *Additive Manufacturing*, *Optics and Laser Technology*, and has served as a reviewer for several international journals.

科学编辑（按姓氏笔画排列）

王卉，现任中国科学院长春光学精密机械与物理研究所（长春光机所）国际合作处副处长，主要从事国际交流、科学传播、国际人才合作等工作；曾任长春光机所与自然出版集团合作期刊 *Light: Science & Applications* 的创刊英文编辑，在《编辑学报》、《国际人才交流》、*Light: Science & Applications* 等期刊上发表 20 余篇文章，并应 SPIE 邀请在 *SPIE Women in Optics* 发表文章。她是 Rose in Science 活动的发起人，也是 iCANX Story 栏目的共同发起人兼主播，曾采访多位国际知名科学家，如诺贝尔物理学奖获得者 Donna Strickland，诺贝尔化学奖获得者 Jean-Marie Lehn，德国物理学会第一任女主席 Johanna Stachel，IEEE 光子学协会主席 Carmen Menoni，澳大利亚科学院院长 Chennupati Jagadish，英国皇家工程院院士李琳，埃尼奖首位华人获奖者王中林等。

WANG Hui is the Deputy Director of Department of International Cooperation in the Changchun Institute of Optics, Fine

Mechanics and Physics (CIOMP), Chinese Academy of Sciences (CAS). She currently works on international communication and cooperation for the CIOMP and was a founding member of the journal *Light: Science & Applications*, which is a joint publication of Nature Publishing Group and CIOMP. She has published several articles in *Acta Editologica*, *International Talent*, *Light: Science & Applications*, etc., and was invited to contribute an article to SPIE Women in Optics in 2015. She is the initiator of the Rose in Science event and the co-sponsor and moderator of the iCANX Story. She has interviewed Donna Strickland, Nobel Laureate in Physics; Jean-Marie Lehn, Nobel Laureate in Chemistry; Johanna Stachel, the first female president of the German Physical Society; Carmen Menoni, president of the IEEE Society for Optics; Chennupati Jagadish, president of the Australian Academy of Sciences; Lin Li, Academician of the Royal Academy of Engineering; Zhonglin Wang, the first Chinese to receive the Eni Prize, etc.

孙婷婷，工学博士，现就职于中国科学院长春光学精密机械与物理研究所（简称“长春光机所”）Light学术出版中心，卓越计划领军期刊*Light: Science & Applications*科学编辑，*Light*子刊高起点新刊*eLight*创刊主编助理，中国科学院国际合作局联合培养交流人才，来自科研一线，曾作为项目负责人主持两项科研课题，并参与多项重要科研项目，曾发表多篇SCI、EI学术论文，申请国家发明专利两项。

Tingting Sun is an Assistant Professor of Light Publishing Group at Changchun Institute of Optics, Fine Mechanics and Physics (CIOMP), Chinese Academy of Sciences (CAS). She received Engineering Doctor Degree from University of Chinese Academy of Sciences in 2016. She currently serves as an Academic Editor for an Excellence Program leading journal *Light: Science & Applications*, and is the Editor-in-Chief Assistant of *Light: Science & Applications* subclassification journal *eLight*. She is also a senior talent jointly trained by the International Cooperation Bureau of CAS. She came from the frontline of scientific research and had profound scientific research background. She has presided over two scientific research projects as the project leader, and participated in many major scientific projects. She has published many SCI and EI academic papers and applied for two national invention patents.

张莹，博士，高级工程师，中国科学院长春光机所Light学术出版中心副主任、副总编、《液晶与显示》执行主编、*Light: Science & Applications*编辑，兼任中国物理学会液晶分会秘书长、中国科技期刊编辑学会青委会委员、吉林省科技创新创业研究会常务理事，2017-2018年美国罗切斯特大学访问学者。曾获得中科院自然科学期刊编辑研究会研究课题一等奖和突出贡献奖、中科院建院70周年优秀作品二等奖、吉林省新闻出版优秀集体奖、长春光机所优秀成果奖等奖项和荣誉；作为项目负责人，主持了中科院、中国科协等期刊类课题4项；作为项目核心成员，承担中国科技期刊卓越行动计划、国际影响力提升计划、登峰行动计划等项目10余项，发表SCI、EI收录论文30余篇，发表期刊出版类论文10余篇，受邀作报告30余次，

受邀接受期刊强国等媒体以及中国高校科技期刊研究会、北京万方数据股份有限公司访谈；参与编写中国科协组织的“建设世界一流科技期刊专题研究系列丛书”分册——《科技期刊出版伦理规范》等著作。

Dr. Ying Zhang is the vice director of Light Publishing Group at CIOMP. He has been a visiting scholar at the Institute of Optics, University of Rochester during 2017 – 2018. He currently serves as the executive editor-in-chief of Chinese Journal of *Liquid Crystals and Displays* as well as an academic editor of *Light: Science & Applications*. He won the first prize and outstanding contribution award of project supported by STM Journal Society, CAS. He has hosted and participated in more than 10 provincial and ministerial projects of China. He has published over 40 SCI/EI and management papers. He also has presented over 30 invited talks and has been interviewed by China's mainstream media such as the Xinhua News Agency. He participated in organizing and editing *Handbook of Laser Technology and Applications* (2nd Ed.) published by CRC, Taylor & Francis

Group, as well as collection "Publishing Ethics of STM Periodicals" organized by China Association for Science and Technology.

郭宸孜，现为中国科学院长春光机所员工，任长春光机所Light学术出版中心副总编、卓越计划高起点新刊*eLight*编辑部主任、卓越计划领军期刊*Light: Science & Applications*（*Light*）责任编辑。曾获第三届全国科技期刊青年编辑大赛一等奖、中国科协优秀科技论文处理编辑表彰、中科院科技出版先进个人奖、长春光机所先进个人、中科院长春分院“青年先锋”等重要奖项，主持了卓越计划高起点新刊、中国科技期刊编辑学会基金课题、吉林省科协科普项目多个国家、省部级项目，作为共作者出版译著《光学与光子学：美国不可或缺的关键技术》（科学出版社），在*Nano Today*，*Nanomaterials*，*Science China Materials*，*Applied Optics*，*Applied Sciences*，*Nanotechnology*，*Japan Science and Technology Agency*（日本科技振兴机构），编辑学报等发表文章18篇。曾代表Light出席联合国国际光日筹备委员会，在国际学术会议作邀请报告20余次。

Chenzi Guo is a managing editor of the journal *Light: Science & Applications*, director of the journal *eLight*, and a fellow of the Youth Innovation Promotion Association of the Chinese Academy of Sciences. She is the co-translator of *Optics and Photonics: Essential Technologies for Our Nation* (Science Press), and have authored/co-authored multiple papers which have been published in *Nano Today*, *Nanomaterials*, *Science China Materials*, *Applied Optics*, *Applied Sciences*, *Nanotechnology*, *Japan Science and Technology Agency*. She is the winner of National Campaign for Young Science Journal Editors, 2019 CIOMP Advanced Individual, and 2020 Chinese Academy of Sciences Changchun Branch Young Pioneer. She chairs the Excellent Move of China STM Journals Project - high - profile new journal *eLight*, and two other state/provincial projects.

袁境泽，博士，高级工程师，就职于中国科学院长春光机所 Light 学术出版中心，现任长春光机所 Light 学术出版中心总编助理、卓越计划领军期刊 *Light: Science & Applications* 及姊妹刊 *Light: Advanced Manufacturing* 科学编辑。作为重要成员，参与中国科技期刊卓越行动计划、国际影响力提升计划等多项国家级、省部级项目。

袁境泽博士曾就读于中国科学院大学，于2017年获得博士学位。她的主要研究方向为近红外光谱学，特别是针对人体血液成分的无创检测。

2017年，她加入了*Light: Science & Applications*杂志的编辑部，成为一名学术编辑。自2012年以来，Light杂志在创刊后的短时间内迅速到达了一个里程碑，成为物理学和光学领域中最引人注目的期刊之一。目前，该期刊的影响因子为17.782，在所有光学领域期刊中排名第3。

自2021年年底，袁境泽博士作为一名访问学者访问剑桥大学先进光子学和电子学中心（CAPE）。

Dr. Jingze Yuan, Senior Engineer, the Assistant

Editor-in-Chief of Light Publishing Group, Changchun Institute of Optics and Mechanics, Chinese Academy of Sciences, and the Scientific Editor of *Light: Science & Applications* and its sister journal *Light: Advanced Manufacturing*. As a core member, she has participated in many national and provincial projects such as the Action Plan for Excellence in Chinese Science and Technology Journals and the International Impact Enhancement Program.

Dr. Jingze Yuan studied at University of Chinese Academy of Sciences and got her Ph.D degree in 2017. Her major research interest was near infrared spectroscopy, especially aiming at human blood constituents no-invasive detecting.

In 2017, she joined the editorial office of the journal *Light: Science & Applications* and became an academic editor. Since 2012, the journal of *Light* rapidly reached a milestone as one of the most visible journals in the field of Physics and Optics within a short period after its launch. Currently, the journal ranks as #3 in terms of impact factor (17.782) among all the journals in Optics.

Since the end of 2021, Jingze Yuan became a

scholar visitor at Center for Advanced Photonics and Electronics (CAPE), University of Cambridge.